SO-ACR-050

## Praise for Robert Dawidoff's *Making History Matter*

"Katharine Hepburn, Ben Franklin, Fred Astaire, Thomas Jefferson, Sophie Tucker, George Santayana, Irving Berlin—surely unlikely companions, past or present. Unless they are journeying with Robert Dawidoff, an historian of remarkable range and imagination. *Making History Matter* provokes, startles, and delights. Page after page Dawidoff reminds me what inspired me to become an historian."
—Mary Kelley, Mary Brinsmead Wheelock Professor, Dartmouth College

"Admirers of Robert Dawidoff's work know the elegance and revelation in his readings of the fate of high intellect in our democracy. In his new book, that fate is shown to be enacted through a perpetually astonishing range of encounters of the ordinary with the extraordinary, the low-down with the high-hat, each inviting and liberating the other's responsiveness. Like good philosophy, this work lets you know what you thought you did not know and shows you how to treasure what you thought you need not know."
—Stanley Cavell, Professor of Philosophy, Emeritus, Harvard University

"I would treasure this book for its brilliant essays on music and the lessons against intolerance *alone,* but there is such wisdom to glean from its pages that I will be reading it again and again for years to come."
—Andrea Marcovicci, Singer/Actress

"I know of no book more aptly titled than *Making History Matter.* In these exhilarating essays, Robert Dawidoff manages to make history come wholly alive and he is equally at home with Sophie Tucker and Fred Astaire as with Jefferson, Santayana, and the brothers Henry and William James. Whether writing about the role of needle exchanges in the dissemination of AIDS, or spoofing some of the deficiencies of academic Cultural Studies, Dawidoff is consistently sprightly, engaging, witty, and brilliant. For Dawidoff, the personal really IS the political and vice-versa, and yet his book is never doctrinaire or polemic. Reading *Making History Matter* is pure pleasure—and truly edifying as well."
—Marjorie Perloff, Sadie Dernham Patek Professor of Humanities at Stanford University, and author of *Wittgenstein's Ladder: Poetic Language and the Strangeness of the Ordinary*

"Not many historians are able to write equally convincingly about Thomas Jefferson, Fred Astaire, and the politics of needle exchange. But Robert Dawidoff can. With graceful prose and supple intellect [Dawidoff] roams the map of America's intellectual and cultural terrain, and he does it with bracing confidence. These essays are a pleasure to read, and they serve the best of Jeffersonian ideals very well indeed."

—John D'Emilio, Professor of History,
University of Illinois at Chicago, and author of
*Intimate Matters: A History of Sexuality in America*

"Dawidoff's remarkable book affirms by example as well as argument the value of the essay for bringing history into the culture at large. He also demonstrates the value of historical scholarship in enriching that culture and the debates within it. It is a morally and intellectually courageous book, written in a personal, pungent, and compelling style, making the case for serious culture and talent that is of democracy, not simply in it, and in so doing he imaginatively and importantly refigures notions of center and periphery, majority and minority, dominant and marginalized, thus expanding our understanding of political culture. It is a book sparkling with insight on a wide range of cultural figures and issues, and it is infused with both wisdom and passion. This history does matter."

—Thomas Bender, Professor of History,
New York University, and author of
*New York Intellectuals*

# Making History Matter

# Making History Matter

ROBERT DAWIDOFF

TEMPLE UNIVERSITY PRESS
Philadelphia

Temple University Press, Philadelphia 19122
Copyright © 2000 by Temple University
All rights reserved
Published 2000
Printed in the United States of America

♾ The paper used in this publication meets the requirements of the
American National Standard for Information Sciences—Permanence
of Paper for Printed Library Materials, ANSI Z39.48-1984.

Library of Congress Cataloging-in-Publication Data

Dawidoff, Robert.
    Making history matter / Robert Dawidoff.
       p. cm.
    Includes bibliographical references.
    ISBN: 1-56639-748-0 (cloth : alk. paper). — ISBN 1-56639-749-9
(pbk. : alk. paper)
    1. United States—History—Philosophy.   2. United States—Politics
and government—Philosophy.   3. United States—Intellectual life.
4. Minorities—United States—Intellectual life.   I. Title.
E175.9.D39   2000
973—dc21                                                    99-17037
                                                                CIP

*For Rena Fraden, Michael Roth,*
*and Charles Young*

# Contents

# PART III. DOING SOMETHING ABOUT IT

# Preface

TODAY LOTS OF PEOPLE read history. The public has always read about the past, but now what history they read and what they learn often clashes with what academic historians are socialized to think the public should read and learn. Like many other historians, I worry that in an age of renewed interest in the American past, the triumphalist and bromidic have tended to usurp that audience. My profession has not yet succeeded in making all that we have learned in the last quarter century real and available to American readers.

This is nothing new. Historical scholarship and historical writing are not the same things. Successful popular history has many reasons to simplify, dramatize, and imagine what for academic historians tends to be an inviolable fund of researched information. One reason to lament the disappearance of philosophy of history from the history curriculum is that we are never trained to think through other aspects of the historian's work that interact with the research scholarship we are taught to value above everything. Yet a detailed monographic account of everything will not cohere into a scientific history, let alone a human one. One way to think about this is to consider the way in which scholarly monographs, especially dissertations and first books, squander the historian's birthright of language. Historians possess the treasure of verbs. The literary critic and the philosopher write about subjects for which verbs have specific and restricted use. Historians write about human living and action, which is what verbs exist to express. But how many graduate schools spend any time at all grounding apprentice scholars in expression and language? Surely one reason historians no longer invoke Clio is that we have forgotten how to address her.

The culture wars have popularized what seems to me a perverse view of the knowledge historians have been accruing. We are seen as politically correct, theory driven, identity bamboozled, multiculturally philistine, and unpatriotic. While I find this view unconvincing, it has taken hold while we have been mired in our monographic necessities and a system of university teaching that prizes a small professional audience in preference to a broad democratic one. Nevertheless, many questions are raised by the politicization of scholarship and the reluctance of many university academics to engage in the basic, even remedial, educational work that is most likely to produce broad public enlightenment. A pernicious class bias separates the professor from the teacher, consigning teacher training to education and credentialing programs, while disdaining adult education.[1] There cannot be one kind of historian, one standard of training, one learning. Professionalizing can streamline, regularize, and bring order to an academic disciplinary system, but it cannot be permitted to define the individual possibilities within that system let alone to monopolize the historical.

This book, a collection of essays I have written about subjects in American intellectual and cultural history, is my attempt to demonstrate how varied are the possibilities within history and how a historian might approach writing for the public. I believe that, taken together, these essays reflect the issues I tried to raise in "History ... but," the lead essay.

Specifically, this collection has four principal concerns.[2] The first is an interest in understanding how American intellectuals and political thinkers have developed the guiding ideas of American political culture. I have been especially interested in how the founders imagined a democratic regime, a culture as well as a polity. I hope that I have shown how consequential were their points of difference, their different emphases and degrees of ambivalence about this democratic culture, not least because I believe them to be abiding.

A second common concern of these essays is the status of claims of superiority in an putatively egalitarian culture and how superior talent might be secured for the purposes of a democratic society. In essays about Franklin and Jefferson, Henry Adams, William and Henry James, George Santayana, Fred Astaire, and Katharine Hepburn, I suggest the strategies such naturally superior people forged to negotiate a culture suspicious of and frequently hostile to claims of superiority. I distinguish between two general positions, which I think of as Tocquevillian and Jeffersonian.[3] The Tocquevillian distances itself from democratic culture, viewing it as if from the outside. The Jeffersonian claims to embrace all of the possibilities of democracy, proposing to submit superiority to the service rather than the disparagement of the democratic, although its effort to stand "inside" frequently resembles a stooping as if from above.

These essays also reflect my own attempt to relocate the perspectives of "outsider" groups—whose Americanness was suspect on account of race, sexuality, religion, or ethnicity—to the center of the discussion of the common American civilization. I have been interested to explore how their marginality was the very condition that enabled, and one might say required, them to do the culture's work, building its civilization and creating many of our most useful perspectives on it. This is evident in my essays on Sophie Tucker and Irving Berlin; it is the very aim of "In My Father's House Are Many Closets," a first try at writing *The Glass Closet,* my forthcoming intellectual history about the role of gay men in the formation of American culture.

Finally, these essays reflect my own claiming of the Jeffersonian as opposed to the Tocquevillian stance. Collecting these various pieces, I realized that I have been concerned to examine all of American cultural expression and to resist (a friend and colleague would add "resent") the categories of formal intellectual history and folk or commercial popular culture. I take all of the subjects of these essays equally seriously, and I hope the essays reflect that seriousness. At the same time, I hope I have avoided the tone of condescension that infiltrates discussions of popular culture, but which has also come to characterize discussions of the likes of Jefferson and Santayana. One may not sway with Jefferson as one swings with Fred Astaire, but it does not follow that Fred was not a Jeffersonian or that you have to kill the joy of him by taking him seriously, any more than you should read Franklin or William James with a frown rather than a smile of concentration. These essays all show my attempt to learn to write about what I love and revere and think is funny and right and wrong. Being incurably literal minded, I have always worried that I was not *thinking* because I never assume the Rodin position. These essays perhaps reflect something like the relaxed posture with which I hope I think about the American subjects that interest me.

As I see it, "History … but" expresses a series of concerns involving the damage we ought to beware of inflicting when considering subjects about which we have strong feelings and beliefs not bounded by scholarly methods. The section titled "The Night of the Living Dead White Men" italicizes my own continuing and undiminished enthusiasms for what some may still call the canon, but which to me is the tradition. "Listening to Sophie Tucker" begins with an essay about the habits of American cultural criticism and concludes with an essay about Los Angeles, "From Ohio to the Big Rock Candy Mountain"—a case study and a case for my historical views. "Doing Something about It" collects some of the journalism I have written; "Stalking the Blushing Zebra" introduces that section with the story of what I think I have learned from writing journalism. It makes me feel good to call myself Jeffersonian, but I am helplessly earnest, afflicted with a veneration fetish, the very model of a modern knee-jerk, bleeding-heart white liberal. The journalism reflects my own poor attempts to make good on my views about the way things were.

I have been lucky to live my life in the university, and to have been able to make my living there. One reason I loved my alma mater, Cornell, was its founder's dictum: *I would found an institution where anyone might find learning in any subject.* On the Arts and Sciences quad at Cornell there are two facing statues, Ezra Cornell standing and founding president Andrew Dickson White seated.[4] To me, the real interest of the two figures was their partnership in the democratic view of learning: practical, Franklinian Ezra Cornell paired with the European-oriented, *echt* nineteenth-century American elite scholar Andrew Dickson White. Behind Ezra Cornell the statue features a splendid bronze telegraph machine, the telegraph having been the source of his riches.

Cornell and White shared a significantly secular understanding of education. White's magnum opus concerned the warfare between science and religion. Together these men and their shared concerns and contrasting expertise serve as models of what has made American education great. But the brazen telegraph has also served to keep in my mind the connection between the material and the ideal, in matters great and small. It is a reminder that one must always be keen to calculate one's own interest in a scholarly project or career. Self-disclosure is not only about identity or politics but *interest,* beginning for most professors with tenure, career advancement, salary, and so forth. Learning to recognize and declare one's own material stake is a contemporary version of Emerson's high-minded exhortations and can remind us of our equal membership in *we the people.*

Nowadays the university is under a veritable siege of change, some of it good and some bad. I hope this book reflects at the least one person's rich experience of the American university and its generous and talented scholars and students. We focus too much on the self-serving worm pit of daily business in the university and on the specialized precincts of our own scholarly interests. In part out of a disdain for the old-fashioned, high-minded discourse of democratic education, whose grandiosity and hypocrisy stuck in our younger craws, we habitually forget the abiding things the university has to offer anybody who is eager for more than a license to have a "professional" life. This book is dedicated to three scholars who have reminded me of why the university is still my home. They are but three of many. The essays in this book reflect the ways in which various people have encouraged and guided me. Many of them are not academics, but all of them uphold in their lives and friendships the brazen telegraph of knowledge.

I have been inspired by the work of many scholars. Their writing has kept me company, excited my interest, shaped my aspirations, and made me proud of being an academic, a scholar, a historian, and an American. Mine are the essays of someone who has been in school since 1950. I recall the scene in *The Empire Strikes Back* when Luke Skywalker leaves his teacher Yoda to go in search of his father, his destiny, and the plot. I knew myself when I saw the movie because I could not help shouting at the screen (in West Covina, California), "Stay in school, Luke!" I hope the essays that follow show why I still would rather be Ichabod Crane than a Sleepy Hollow Boy.

# Acknowledgments

THIS BOOK collects work done over two decades and reflects the advice, encouragement, editing, and friendship of many people. I have indicated throughout those who occasioned or edited specific essays and, in "Stalking the Blushing Zebra," those who made my journalism possible and plausible. Here I can only acknowledge some of the many people who have helped me.

*Making History Matter* is dedicated to three friends and colleagues. For years, Rena Fraden has taken time from her own wonderful scholarship and teaching to hear my writing out. I have depended upon her critical acumen and her steadfast encouragement and abiding friendship. Michael Roth gave me the opportunity to write "History ... but," "The Jeffersonian Option," and "In My Father's House Are Many Closets," and his influence is everywhere in this book, even the very fact of it. Like so many others, I have benefited from his boundless generosity and his own matchless intellectual range. Charles Young has been my friend and colleague for a quarter of a century now. I have relied on his integrity, his dedication to teaching and scholarship, and his philosophical cast of mind, as well on his fellow feeling and his charity. He is the real Village Champ.

Helena Wall, Barry Weller, Michael Kammen, Eve Kosofsky Sedgwick, Vicki Ruiz, Elazar Barkan, Christopher Cannon, the late William Delligan, Michael Denneny, David Freeman, Patrick Macey, Dan McCall, Barbara Herman, Mickey Morgan, Marjorie Perloff, Merrill Peterson, Martin Rochlin, Tracey Strong, Nathan Tarcov, and Alan Trachtenberg are just some of the colleagues and friends who helped me think up and rewrite these essays. Jamie Wolf saw me through the last stages of preparing the book by sharing with me her remarkable eye for the beautiful and her steady grasp of the practicable. Michael Ward realized some key figures and relations in these essays in pen and ink. Jane Silver was indispensable in my writing about AIDS, as she is to the fight against it.

Donald Yacovone, William Jones, Charles Mitchell, LeeAnn Meyer, Emilie Stoltzfuss, Alice Hom, and Mathew Lasar are among the many students by whom, as Oscar Hammerstein put it, I have been taught. Research assistants have spent time on what is collected here, including Ken Shafer and Laura Abeyta-Paulus; Lara Bickell and Jill Acree were indispensable in getting the manuscript together. I have relied upon

department secretaries Sandra Campbell and Vivian Taylor and now
Elysabeth Renteria. Elysabeth Renteria has been invaluable in the preparation of this collection from its inception.

This collection was Janet Francendese's idea. Her keen mind, her literary learning and editing skill, and her shrewd understanding of the
author have been sustaining. And we have remained good friends, despite
being natural enemies, editor and author. Margaret Weinstein has proved
invaluable in the final stages of getting this book to press, considerably
beyond the call—and telephone calls—of duty. Elizabeth Johns deserves
the thanks of whoever reads this collection. Her able editing has improved
the clarity and her intelligent mind has improved the substance of this
book. This book would not be in your hands without the dedicated work
of Janet Greenwood and Lynne Frost, the creativity, receptivity, and pro-
fessionalism of Charles Ault, as well as Jennifer French, Ann-Marie
Anderson, Irene Imperio, Gary Kramer, and the rest of the Temple University Press staff.

My parents encouraged my interest in American history. They gave me
the books—and took me to Cooperstown, Charlottesville, and Philadelphia, where I first saw what has remained in my mind's eye. My father,
Theodore Dawidoff, introduced me to those good old songs and to the
Great Durante, Sophie Tucker, and all that jazz; I wish he had lived to
help me write about them. My mother, Rebecca Dawidoff Rolland, has
always lent generous support to my career. I hope she recognizes her
influential presence in "The Jeffersonian Option." My uncle and friend
Milton Davidoff has always urged me to make something more than a
professor's career out of my historical studies. I hope he thinks I have.

I have had many aces in the hole. Nina Feinberg Wass, Eleanor and
Bill Abbot, Jamie and David Wolf, Robb and Charles Dew, Ann W. Cof-
fey, Andrew, Dana, Cassandra and Thad Kull, Emily Hewitt and Eleanor
Acheson, Bia Lowe, Tirrippio Brown, Karen Ishizuka, Carol Kammen,
Andrea Marcovicci, Daniel Reichert and Alice Wolf Reichert, Kitty and
John Lindow, Judith Ginjold and David Freeman, Sonja Bolle and Patrick
Goldstein, Barbara McNair, the late Will Jones, Molly Mason Jones,
James "Chico" Evans, Torie Osborn, Alex and Leslie Gold, Martin Freed-
man, Willie Lee Rose, and many others have steadied me and readied me.

During the years when I wrote what is collected in *Making History Matter,* I had a home, thanks to Robert Cohen and the late Richard Rouilard,
who saw Camille Beauchamp in Charlotte Vale. Ida cannot imagine my
having written much of what I did without the Pierce family. I am especially pleased to acknowledge Bob Cohen, on whose friendship and counsel I depend. Michael Nava has helped me six ways from Sunday with
this and everything else. He is a real friend, a *camerado,* and like me is
crazy about Mary Pickford, Ramón Navarro, and even Mae Murray.

# ✣ History . . . but

*The small survivor has a difficult task*
*Answering the questions great historians ask.*

Edwin Denby, "On the Home Front—1942"

TIME WAS when the voices in historical narrative were standard ones. Now history is open—to workers, to popular culture, to the middle-brow, to the built and natural environment. And this is a good thing. But without questioning the sincerity of history's eager embrace of all manner of phenomena, I do wonder at its capacity to do them justice. And as other disciplines rush to assimilate historical methods, this historian's wonder increases. The historian would speak both for history the discipline and for history the enveloping occurrence. The historian's embrace is inevitably an explanatory one; the place being offered by the historian is a place in history. That is what history has to give, the matter-of-fact security of historicity.

History's current attraction for other disciplines in part reflects their recognition that history makes it possible to replace some of their self-examination with a genetic account of their existence. It is a way around theory at a time when many scholars are tired out with theory. At the same time, one hears from many quarters a certain unease with the resurgence of the historical. Along with the admission of reluctant need, there is a recognition of all that history claims; this recognition is shadowed by an anxious fear of annexation, like that expressed by the King of Siam in *The King and I:* "If allies are strong with power to protect me, might they not protect me out of all I own?" Most of the disciplines are old rivals of history. Parents, siblings, children of history, they have learned to beware their own need for what history does, even as, nowadays, they diagnose in themselves a deficiency requiring a dose of history.

The professional scholarly study of history is not good for all the things that history is good for. It is what you might call prescription history and

"History...but" was presented at a conference sponsored by the Scripps College Humanities Institute in March 1988. It was first published in *New Literary History* 21, no. 2 (Winter 1990), pp. 395–406.

may be best used only on doctor's advice and under controlled circumstances. Over-the-counter history is a less controlled and less specific remedy, a generalized fix. The history cure draws on many sources and sometimes foregoes altogether the compounds of scholarship for the herbal and spiritual, the voodoo and homeopathic remedies that, as with many remedies, work on certain populations because of traditions outside the stream of modern science and because of what those populations need.

If what ails someone is ignorance of the history that scholarship knows about, there are usually over-the-counter popular remedies, information and interpretation, that historical science has developed for common usage. These include textbooks and general histories and the kind of history you can include in biographies and critical studies, history as a decided-upon addition to something. Consulting the historian to find out things need not entail altering one's method in the light of the historian's advice. The recent uses of history by other disciplines have sometimes meant to go beyond this to more serious interventions, intending not so much relief as metabolic or systemic change. These (medicinal) interventions by prescription seem to involve the doing of a kind of history itself, which is not unprecedented, of course, but which often challenges and changes aspects of the patient-discipline's routine and self-understanding.

The history that scholarship can prescribe answers comparatively sophisticated questions and makes many assumptions about who wants to know what, and how much about what, and why. Much of the knowledge and interest of present-day historical scholarship is rarefied. Communities held together by truth do not necessarily rest on truth established according to the standards of scholarly professions. Art, human expressive fabrication, which moves people to share identity or views or to take up a common cause, does not have the same criteria of selectivity as historical scholarship. What scholarly history cures is only sometimes what ails the history deficient. This applies not only to the doctor but to the remedy. Some curative agents, like popular culture, may not be altogether effective in the historian's preparation. What the historian may have to do to turn these into medicine may take the healing power out of them. It is a case of the historian's capacity not only to prescribe for others, but to master the proper effects of the possible remedies.

There are many kinds of history deficiencies, and it is not always clear which ones plague our fellow disciplines: chronic internal deficiencies or tension headaches brought on by theoretical stress. History soothes theoretical stress. Its inclination is to view it as all in the mind of the patient anyway, and the bias of the historical profession is not to take all that seriously what is only in the mind. The historian resembles that up-to-date television general practitioner, Marcus Welby, who can prescribe all the new treatments—he even understands something of Freud—with a soothing Dutch uncle's persona, so that the latest remedies are dispensed with un-blushing counter-transference and aggressive bonhomie. This aspect of the historian's practice yet clings to the profession's self-understanding. And it is soothing to the discipline, troubled by the conflicting claims and apparent dilemmas that often accompany the attempts to reconcile scholarly practice with contemporary theory, to be told essentially that it is all in your mind, that it isn't the real world, that history is more real than theory.

In part this reflects the ease with which history moves through the various levels of schooling and interest. A Civil War buff has more to say to the most sophisticated scholar of the Civil War than, I think, a philosophical autodidact to a philosophy professor, or a voracious reader to a litera-ture professor, especially nowadays. Much of history's work is still about its simplest and most widely shared functions: telling people about their own traditions, the stories of other peoples, and other things they are in-terested in, the once-upon-a-time stories that make up *History*, whatever else historians or history might happen to mean. (This work abides in the face of some historians' understandable desire to remake the discipline in the model of other disciplines, such as science, social science, and the other humanities, to become more like them in the pursuit of history.)

The voice of the modern scholar is by definition distinct and detached from the phenomena studied. The scholar, however, characteristically spends more time and becomes more identified with a subject's work or deeds than the subject did in the first place. It takes longer to study a life than to live it, longer to interpret a work than to create it, longer to under-stand an event than it took to happen. Sometimes, the historian's stake in a subject exceeds, in intensity and force, that of the original participants. J. H. Hexter's shrewd saw about how he spent his historian's day in the Renaissance was a subtle indoctrination, in the no-nonsense historian's tone, into the mysteries of the historian's craft.[1] It proposed that to devote one's day to the mastery of the detail of long-gone societies was a likely way to understand them objectively. That is one way to do it, of course, and Hexter's work exemplifies a remarkable historical method. But it is not clear that all historical things are best understood by those who devote their days to them after the fact, or at a scholar's distance, or with a scholar's intensity or joy. This is especially true with what is called pop-ular culture. How do you write about something that is a challenge to a way of looking at the world in the language of the world it challenges?

I have never seen a rock lyric quoted in scholarship without feeling uneasy. It seems immediately ungainly, because the cadence of the sen-tence is by definition different from the rhythm of the song.[2] Prose influ-enced by the music, hip prose, does not mate easily or well with the prose of selective scholarly knowledge. The kinds of connections and attributions and scholarship necessary to the study sound funny often as not. I do not think there is much wrong with the study. I do it too. But I worry because the scholarly tone sounds pompous, and it often destroys the pleasure of the thing by transforming the pleasure into a concentration, does more than quote with its quotation marks.

The scholar's awkward agenda is not as off-putting as the faux scholarship of so many rock writers, but it seems to engender a generation gap. The historian sounds old, the journalist less old, and the rock music frequently sounds better unhistoricized. Liner notes recount a history of the music itself. But the inclusion of the music into historical narrative tends to be awkward, arch, pointed, condescending, whether it is written by a fan or a non-fan: the fan sounds like a groupie, the non-fan like a groupie's parent. The writing of cultural history from the rock music and what it represents seems, in turn, homemade, uninformed, parochial, and devotional.[3]

The study of popular culture may well offer a cure for what ails the study of expression and society, but its availability to self-conscious examination remains problematic, and its assimilation to cultural history especially so. The adjustment to popular materials by scholarly disciplines inevitably challenges those disciplines. That is part of the point of their inclusion. Cultural history is only one way of approaching popular material. Cultural history's openness to this material, its agenda of inclusion, has a moral. And if the moral has changed so that it is inclusive as well as judgmental, then the sentence-by-sentence writing of history is still judgmental.

At the heart of Hayden White's project of historical criticism[4] is his identification with the perception by novelists that there was something in history that ruined the fun, took the joy and life out of the things it chronicled and the people who chronicled it. The materials I work with show me some of the problem. I recently wrote about American Jewish entertainer Sophie Tucker and French philosophical writer Jean Paul Sartre, in the person of that disgusted provincial historian Roquentin in Sartre's novel *Nausea*, during the fateful encounter of modernism with African American culture in the twentieth century, an elegant if farfetched association.[5] I couldn't help feeling a kind of empathy for Soph, in there with all the brains and swells. By the time I was done with the whole business, I'd employed the insights of social history, African American history, feminist history, the history of popular culture, immigrant history, the history of liberalism, even modern European intellectual history, to historicize the *last of the red hot mommas*. I imagined her imprisoned, looking back out at me reproachfully, as if to say, "This is the thanks I get for all that good singing?" I suppose she might also have been flattered at the company she was keeping. She would surely have laughed at me, both my earnest historicizing and my worry, advised me to relax and enjoy myself and not to worry about her; she'd met royalty, after all, and had played many a tougher joint than the quarterly into which I was booking her. She would have been proud that one of her fans was a professor. She would have reminded me that it doesn't matter what they say about you, so long as they're talking about you.

But there is a loss when you make culture out of expression, and history out of culture, especially with the stuff of non-high culture—when, say, you put a favorite popular song behind the bars of analysis. Context is imprisoning because, by making the subject a part of history, you somehow risk knowing the stuffings out of it, when all you wanted to do was to keep alive forever what in it so beguiled you. In the name of craft, history licenses the passion you feel for a subject without examining the passion, trapping you and what delights you into becoming unconscious actors in the *film noir* of the cultural justice system.

Cultural history has its own agenda. It may be an agenda of inclusion, but it wishes cultural expression to be included in the narrative of attributed meaning and somehow to fit in with what historians know about societies. It requires a certain kind of mind and education, and the history it writes reflects them. There is probably nothing wrong with this. The historian's literary art, transformed by the ever-fresh wonder of history itself, writing about the past so that you remember what you never knew, can work wonders with most material. But the bias of history remains toward event, toward common sense, and toward a kind of old-fashioned good posing as common sense about things. History is not exactly burdened by philosophy, but it has one and has notoriously provided the examples for philosophy and literature. Since it principally concerns what people do, history has a more conservative tendency than were it equally about the things people think or imagine. Intellectual and cultural history were not Clio's firstborn.

Cultural history would balance expressivity with the ballast of history, but a bias persists toward narrative as a kind of control or discipline and toward change and continuity as the essence of life.[6] That is not just Professor Lovejoy's "great chain of being." Historians tend to be skeptical of psyche and emotion and not to do them justice. History is not very good at feeling or ruminative thinking. Narrative and change/continuity are history's schemes of life, but not necessarily life itself, or what it means to people, just one way of looking at it, as if from a distance. The historian has long explored the necessary difference between describing and being Napoleon. If historians of culture mean to continue to expand their narrative beyond traditional high-culture subjects to a broader range of representative phenomena and voices, they will need to adjust their thinking to the cases.

History makes cultures. Professional scholarship legitimizes cultural production. Contemporary historical scholarship is open to a wider range of productions and in some ways is motivated by a more generous and egalitarian attitude. Everybody gets into historical heaven nowadays. But the tone of the legitimacy, what the phenomenon must undergo to get the wings, has not necessarily changed. And something inside the listener, the wonderer-at, the person motivated by insatiable curiosity to study things in the first place, is affronted. What does history do to art, to feelings, to secrets, in making culture out of them?

History retains a confident air, to some extent a confidence built on its apparent closeness to human experience and the ease with which human beings turn memory into narrative. It is a scholarly activity that parents and detectives, novelists and poets, the religious, the musical, the artistic, the criminal, lawyers, and just about everybody ends up doing. Historians gain their confidence from the seeming naturalness of their activity. And the popularity of history right now reflects that interesting confidence, its lowness to the ground of experience. The theory wars have exhausted many scholars, and the widely perceived isolation of the academic has made the commonness of the historical ground attractive. But history's seductive way of working by inclusion is to some extent based on its enfolding momentum. And it is never more dangerous than when it is most blandly inviting, when it is readiest to take the burden of self-consciousness off the shoulders of those who seek its counsel.

I remember the eagerness with which, as a student, a non-religious Jew, I took to Puritanism. I now realize how vibrant and exciting an introduction to the moral world that was to me. Reading Jonathan Edwards for the first time was a revelation, you might say. I had the sort of reaction to Puritanism, and to other subjects I studied in history—of excitement and mastery of details and even possession—that friends had studying philosophy, literature, theater, physics, and so on. The study of intellectual history was the medium for my own investigation of a structure of conscience and piety that was not readily available to me in late-sixties America on terms that suited my own insides. Not surprisingly I took to the writings of Perry Miller.[7]

I remain convinced by Miller's distillation of the Puritans as a moral reproach to liberalism. His delineation of the Augustinian strain of piety, that deeply self-critical, impassioned attempt at self-forgetting, with its moral seriousness fueling the delirious hope of escaping the rational from the top of the intellectual pyramid, rather than from its base, is what I believe about New England civilization. I welcomed his construct of a Puritan mind and bathed in the details, the logic of Petrus Ramus, the economy of salvation, the fragile, complex Edwardsian solutions. I was a pretend student of divinity. I was an after-the-fact convert to Puritanism, avoiding, of course, the advantages of its belief or the disadvantages of its discipline. It resembled my enthusiasm for Bach's Passions and the gospel singing of Mahalia Jackson and the Swan Silvertones. I was a Puritan, if that meant mastery of the details. And I resented, as if a Puritan, the moralistic compromises of the benevolent American successors. I feared Edmund Morgan's remarkable *The Puritan Dilemma* because I could see that he rendered what I believed a non-negotiable agony into a formidably practical solution.[8] My historical judgments were founded on the rock of my own pseudo-salvation. My historian's day was spent with what I craved, away from what unnerved me, on terms that protected me from both and rewarded me with the odd reversal of investment.

I remember the seminars, the outside discussions, the papers we students wrote, the articles and books we read, the deep delving into the details of a long-outworn faith. *The Puritans are dead, long live Puritanism!* I remember, too, the intense immersion in the details that history graduate students had to acquire. History was our obsessive subject and historiography our informal medium of communication. We learned to express our feelings, our gossip, our aspirations, our everything, in the terms of professional scholarly history. That intense maneuvering of the details of someone else's culture, that need, and that intensity feed scholarship, initiating the graduate student into the days one must live, as Hexter says.

Years later, I taught graduate students who were also believing Christians and who explained to me, with admirable patience, that my understanding of the delicate balance of Puritanism could not be correct. It was not Christianity. They knew their faith, and I knew its history, and we disagreed across an unbridgeable chasm. I think I was right. That is not the point. The point is that my delight, following Miller, in the culture of the Puritans was based on my not wanting grace, my not believing in it, my studying American Calvinism in the most intense detail possible but without the faith that motivated and justified it. This picking and choosing freed my intellectual synthesis of the most important element of its creation—not as a fact, this I had mastered—but as a compelling, motivating apprehension, something my accounting for inevitably fell short of. That made an important element in the study of cultural history, one that was never discussed even in our infrequent philosophy of history sessions. Our training prized and trusted our immersion in the detail and indeed regarded it as the baptism one must undergo in the historian's creed. My delight in the detail was also balanced by my own need for the discipline. I was uneasy with what interested me most. I welcomed the discipline of history to control my passion for it. And although I realize that my associates, then and now, would not recognize themselves in this, I must say I recognize them along with myself, at our best and at our blandest.

The question is not whether immersion in details is a necessary or bad thing, but which immersions reflect professional or subjective choices, why some are OK and others not, and what is to be believed and what not. History, as a profession, arrives in any epoch with a certain tone to take toward the materials of history; it allows certain kinds of questions to be asked and sanctions certain kinds of answers. What historians always agree upon is claiming a certain distance from what is studied. This creates particular difficulties in the study of expressive subjects, worth at least a hesitation, a reflexive suspicion of the consequences of inclusion, its dangerous capacity to function as a kind of control.

Writing gay history, for instance, one wonders what to believe and what to write. The narrative of cultural history has survived for years on certain assumptions—that being gay, whatever that may have meant let alone means, should not and therefore did not matter, was not very significant to cultural production. Writing about gay men in American culture, one is reinterpreting the contribution to and part played in that culture by figures like Walt Whitman, Henry James, George Santayana, Horatio Alger, Lorenz Hart, F. 0. Matthiessen, and Thornton Wilder, who have been central to its cultural history and definition, and whose sexual identity it has been a part of that history to suppress.[9] It is a contentious subject, one that makes one question the history itself. More than the history of the group, the secret history and the relation of the group to the majority culture are troubled. What does one believe? Conventional sources will not yield the answers one is looking for because part of the point of conventional sources is not to disclose gay identity or influence. One falls back on the ancient sources of history: recollections, secrets, gossip, intuition, clues, reinterpretation, imagination, fantasy. But the deciphering of subversive and secret places in culture may constitute a great loss.

Part of the job in writing a history of gay men in American culture is to bring out of the closet a treacherously double-edged situation. Gay men were secret about themselves, creating a secret world, and they also gave in tribute to the culture a defining and participatory energy that, stripped of its own interest, could make the culture see itself as it wished to be seen. To do this subject, you need to study the secret and openly secret gay subculture and the selfless and often self-denying work gay men did in the larger culture. To represent the subculture, you listen for the signals, you give the knock, the wink, and you find out about secrets and pleasure and pain. But is the knowing research or joining? Is the telling history or betrayal? And what does the private culture sound like when the coded language you need to gain entry to understand and live within it is translated, when it is made to sound like just one more subset of the historicized normal, when the private cynicism and mockery become a category, reified into neutral jargon, yet another "contribution" to ... I wonder to *what?*

And the perspective of this secret world on the world at large, its special edge and its particular dualities, can be lost when made too easily the subject of historical discourse. You experience a stubbornness when you care about something, be it culture or habits or privacy or perspective, lest it should come too trippingly off the tongue, be too easily placed. And in writing it, do I become like my religious graduate students unable to accept scholarship's Puritans? How will the history I write affect my membership in the cultures I belong and adhere to? Must I sacrifice the special views of the conventional, the tones of a "gay sensibility," by insisting on their place in the narrative of American history? Will I lose my professional identity in my subjective engagement in the scholarship?

Can the loss involved in doing history be balanced by the gain? You tell about the past because it isn't there. So you gain the story in lieu of the thing. But by extending its range, cultural history increases its control and the potential loss felt by its interested readers. There is some vitality and something passionate and idiosyncratic and just unsayable lost in the transformation of expression into cultural production, enshrined in the historicized accounts of it. What does making history of something do to one's experience of it? This is the question posed by any attempt at representation. But, even as it begs a satisfactory answer, it needs asking. The concern it expresses is part of the process of the recovery of the past for delight's or interest's sake.

Troubling as this is with "great" works, to some extent the exchange is fair, because history, like criticism, is a way to make them seen and heard, and the confidence of the classic is that it can survive any contextualization and triumph over any understanding. As Soph says, don't worry what they say about you, so long as they're talking about you. The frailer works, however, may have more trouble. The occasional, the evanescent, the momentary, the sensual have a harder time with the kind of life preserver history offers, perhaps overburdened by the price in significance that must be paid to be joined to the great chain of explanatory historical being. Sometimes the pleasure is weighed down by the ways in which people see them, by how seriously they must be taken, talked about, and regarded, and by how weary they must feel. And sometimes passing pleasure is the essence of historical truth.

The notion that the best history comes from a certain distance is a problem. Who but someone gay would know to rewrite homophobic history to rescue the whispered voices of the closet? Actually some might and have done, but not many. The thought that the assumptions and methods of contemporary history can go unchanged by the inclusion of a new subject matter, one that really does question the assumptions of much of the history that came before, is problematic. The aplomb with which history includes any new subject by, well, including it, is infuriating. History keeps meeting one's objections by confidently, obtusely, agreeing to include them in its narratives, inevitably on its narratives' smothering terms. And then there is the loss you feel as you turn into narrative something you love, secrets you share, ambitions you harbor, passions you have known and identities you feel, history you have lived, something as real as a song and as secret as gay history. Can the narrative redeem your loss? Should it?

Delving into the effect of AIDS on gay male culture, for instance, one encounters a discourse that is meant for certain fundamental purposes: to find things out, to save lives, to mourn, to entertain, to warn; and the means of its expression—protest, the quilt, spiritual writings, anger—do not blend with the standards and the methods of history writing. One's interest in this history is sometimes at odds with professional scholarly history. As you work it into the cadences of the profession, you feel a loss, an anxiety, and those feelings deserve more than a moment's hesitation. They make you think about who reads what we do, why it is written, and what it is for. In the same way that cultural production should challenge the narrative and the easy, historicizing explanations, it should stay for a moment our narrating hands. Does the history have important work to do in the world, for people actually living in it? Do contemporary events require that we rewrite history and not just write them into history, after their moment has passed or even as it passes?

Those moments of hesitation and doubt may amount to nothing other than anxiety, as history, like time, marches on. But this anxiety, this worry about loss, is properly the business of anyone who takes up history as the solution to disciplinary issues and problems. It is ordering, and it makes an interesting way around certain problems, and it does retain the freshness of all good old things. But the resurgence of history requires also a proper caution. History's method is to annex itself to a narrative discourse. The discourse itself supersedes with explanation and context even that which we might, for a moment, wish to observe as if it was actually happening to us. Regarding the historical event or moment for all it might make us feel and think invites the illusion of independence of time and circumstance. This, along with the illusion of originality, is what history properly disdains as illusion. Nevertheless, human expression apparently requires such illusions in order to do what we love having been done. And it may be that history wishes to be believed in as one believes in an illusion. This is not what scholars are trained to consider.

Engaged in writing gay history, wanting to write more about songs, one feels the anxiety of potential loss. I want to read, teach, and write history so the stories will not get lost and the plight will stay clear, to honor and understand and remember, to enthuse, and to change. You say to yourself (or your training says to you) that history writing *is* superior to quilts and pictures, memories, recollections, folk tales and dish, because it is the medium that preserves them—and that it is superior to secrets and private discourse too. And yet, there is something in what historians do that is like good embalming. What a way to keep something alive, to preserve its lineaments in memory!

It is good to tell and hear a story. It makes us more at home in the world to know the narrative of what we are doing. But that once-upon-a-timeness of history presents a problem for those of us whose motive for writing history is not only professionalized or historicizing but also personal: to remember the things in life that most move and express us and to act on them. Formal culture seems to lose less in the translation into cultural history, or maybe it is that most of the formal culture I know is already historicized. The materials I am working on—popular culture, democratic culture, gay lives and culture, their moral and expressive dimensions—seem to resist the very history one wants to write.

On one hand, I am driven to historicize the grace out of the Puritans and the *hotcha* out of Sophie Tucker; on the other, I am moved to protect the secrets and the activist consciousness of gay men from historicizing—and probably from criticism. And the more history I attempt, the more intense the struggle between my training and my passions. Here, of course, I would like to say that this intense conflict leads to vital, productive history writing. I hope it does, but I mistrust that resolution. I am of two minds. And that suggests rhetorical and, perhaps, moral caution.

There is an anxiety felt by historians of culture whom I know when we begin to turn what we love into culture, into history, into sentences that legitimate at the same time that they vitiate the mysterious and inexplicable way the best expressive things feel. I worry that what gets lost in the telling is what made me want to tell in the first place. At the very least, it seems to me, one must keep this awareness alive as a hitch in the process of historicizing, more than simply a moment's hesitation and doubt. So to "History and . . ." I suppose I am presenting "History but . . ." which expresses a historian's anxiety about the loss in the telling.

**PART I**

# THE NIGHT OF THE LIVING DEAD WHITE MEN

# ⚡ The Jeffersonian Option

THOMAS JEFFERSON'S understanding that the talented should be tied to the regime, like W.E.B. Du Bois's vision of the talented tenth advancing the best interests of the race, suggests that it may be a good thing to sanction the ambition of the intellectually gifted. The Jeffersonian natural aristocratic understanding of stewardship requires that the talented individual make a serious peace with what the democracy requires. It is not enough to be smart and to wish to serve. One must undertake to feel one's place morally within the democratic community. The Jeffersonian says the intellectual can only be the conscience of the democracy if the intellectual's own conscience is democratic.

This essay presents a selection of significant figures in American intellectual history from the point of view of the accommodation of their self-conscious individualism to the democratic claim of equality. I conflate Jeffersonianism and liberalism, knowing something of the historical awkwardness of that fit. Candidly, I mean the knee-jerk, bend-over-backwards, embarrassing kind of liberalism, the kind that approaches politics and culture with a conscious air of difference in the hopes of bonding across difference. I lay claim to the remnant of liberalism that no one else seems to want, the ridiculous part that has brought together Pat Buchanan, *Doonesbury*, *The New Republic*, *Commentary*, the academic left, ethnic groups and religions, President whatshisname, just about everyone in a chorus of rejection. My motto is that while it is admirable (and necessary) to walk a mile in someone else's shoes, you had better be prepared to fall down, go slow, get blisters, and look like a damn fool.

The liberal has been too little connected with the human pungency that makes civilizations, and unlike its conservative counterpart, liberalism has no orthodoxy to confirm this uneasiness of style. The American conservative has usually acknowledged with ease the WASP tradition as superior, privileging privilege. The liberal holds views that undermine the legitimacy of such acknowledgment without necessarily addressing its flourishing habit. All the liberal has, when it comes down to it, is a version of the democracy with which to align politically, sentimentally, and culturally.

---

"The Jeffersonian Option" was first published in *Political Theory* 21, no. 3 (August 1993).

That coalition is ever changing, and the liberal tradition is at its noblest in choosing some people over some privilege and at its silliest in trying to master the technicalities of the choice; it is most problematic when it attacks other people's privileges and not the liberal's own.

What I am calling the Jeffersonian liberal tradition has always and justly been accused of hypocrisy. How could Jefferson hold slaves *and* write the Declaration? How can this one or that one articulate the principles of freedom and equality that are the essence of the American regime and yet participate in its compromises and countenance crimes against those principles? Hypocrisy is a crude way of saying something perhaps more subtle, but the liberal is as suspect to the groups with which she would make common cause as to those who oppose the goals of those groups. The liberal bears the blame for the distance between those goals and their realization for all groups and individuals and for the turmoil of change from those who did not want any change. The liberals' challenge has been, through participation in democracy in the name of some of its highest principles, to accept it as the key ground of their own expressive experience and experience democracy not as a falsehood but as a truth.

The Puritans gave, it seems fair to say, the characteristic tone of moral urgency and the allegorical frame of mind that has proved so important to high-minded white Americans. Their dual emphasis on the individual conscience and the communally signifying detail persists. But the Puritan conscience and the community are meant to have a direct relation. Indeed the conscience characteristically mediates the Puritan individual and community. Your conscience is the voice of the community. How this changes in America from the voice of the godly community to a more familiar conscience is in itself a fascinating story, one the image of Mickey Mouse confronted with a moral dilemma distills. Faced with a choice, Mickey finds himself a witness to a heated debate between an angel Mickey on one shoulder urging him to do right and a devil Mickey on the other counseling him to do wrong. He is meant to choose a version of himself. The curious phenomenon of the cricket (or other little critter) as conscience suggests how oddly forged an image of the self the American conscience has been. The characteristic New England conscience evolved from the Puritan sense of what kind of person one must be to the Yankee notion of the kind of person one ought to be seen to be; conscientiousness requires a witness, yourself or somebody else. When the Puritan ceased to be sure about God, that conscientious energy was liberated to become one of the standard features of American liberalism, that endless moralizing with no place to go but the here and now.[1]

To claim Benjamin Franklin for the liberal tradition is, perhaps, idiosyncratic. But there was a lesson to be learned from Ben, consequential for liberals should they learn it or not. Surely one of the most remarkable feats of Franklin's long career was his capacity to attain the heights of individual accomplishment and personality without seeming to depart from an ordinary exercise of given potential. Even today, Franklin is a comfortable figure, a democratic familiar, someone whose remarkable commercial, political, scientific, intellectual, benevolent, diplomatic, and sexual accomplishments add up to a friendly wonder, not a superior being.[2]

Franklin's *Autobiography* echoes through American letters; ask Henry Adams about his models for "self-teaching"; ask James Gatz where he got his Platonic idea of himself as Jay Gatsby.[3] Franklin appears to have understood from the outset what was necessary to pursue one's individuality in a way that did not separate one from the common. It was a constant element in his life and work that Franklin avoided giving the offense of his superiority to the community of equals he claimed to prefer. His emphasis on utility reflected, in part, a consciousness that what one thinks or imagines should be able to cross the bridge from self to others. Such crossings share the essence of utility and practicality. Far from demeaning the speculative, they fantasize its good-natured sharing with the hopeful aim of raising the general level. Poor Richard, Franklin's wonderful persona, is not a deception but a kind of philosophic conceit, someone not Franklin who could be Franklin, an offering by a genius to his context. Franklin lent a helping hand to his fellows in the guise of one of them without—and this is important—doing much more than simplifying his knowledge of the world for public consumption.

In Richard's proverbs one can find the secular preacher's role that Emerson was to elaborate as a response of the philosopher to the common good of an essentially democratic community. The knowledge of the world that Franklin here imparts is tough and even cynical but also clear and forgiving. And if, inside Richard's bluff homilies, the guile of a very superior man indeed measures in what part the more ordinary world can take him, well, that is not necessarily a bad thing, especially since his conclusions and his advice are not false. After all, he was not preaching deception. It *is* easier for a rich man to be good than it is for a poor man. When Billie Holiday said, "You've got to have something to eat and a little love in your life before you can hold still for any damn body's sermon on how to behave," she was agreeing with Poor Richard's proverb "It is hard for an empty sack to stand upright."[4] Franklin's incisive revision of the pie-in-the-sky text about how hard it is for a rich man to enter heaven is dead on the money as an understanding of American reality. He made the choice to express himself in common terms to ordinary people and chose to think about life in terms that connected his own individuality to common experience.

The name-giving titan of any version of American democracy remains Thomas Jefferson. In itself it is interesting to think about how this almost paradigmatically uncommon man has become one of the civilization's sponsors of equality and the potential of the common. Unlike the even more democratic American saint, Abraham Lincoln, Jefferson retains the valuable quality of representing a response to democracy from someone incompletely of it. The common people produced Lincoln as a challenge to history and, in himself, he validated an unambivalent democratic rise. But Jefferson's was not, like Lincoln's or Franklin's, a genius cast in the mold of common clay. Jefferson resonates because he was an individual of superior gifts, place, and attainments, whose seeking out of the democratic is his abiding wonder for us.

John Adams said there would always be an aristocracy of wealth and power, and that it must be restrained by free institutions. For Adams, the equally menacing democracy of the common people must be restrained by a series of private rights. Jefferson seemed to envision the empowerment of both these elements of society and articulated their transformation. He described a natural aristocracy that, educated by the people, would pursue their interests disinterestedly as public servants discharging a special public trust. He also described a people less rude than Adams knew, a pastoralizing vision of the yeoman farmer, self-sufficient, independent, and strong enough to follow the wisdom of the talented few.

The Jeffersonian pastoral of yeoman farmer and natural aristocrat, in which the sweet and useful described a knowledge that exercised just power, struck Adams, as it has many others since, as visionary to the point of unreality. Nevertheless, the Jeffersonian view of society, which the Declaration's claim about natural rights would require, added up to a shrewd map of what must be transformed to make such a society work. The persistence of those qualities, such as he recognized in himself, that make for individual superiority and sway was Jefferson's reason for inventing forms of superiority that a democracy could trust and bind to itself. If Jefferson imagined a relation rather than an identity between such as him and the democracy, it is his ambition for a relation rather than rule that should interest us.

Jefferson was not interested in lowering himself or blunting his individuality, but he did recognize in the equality on which the free political regime was based a serious moral claim on relations within it. Thus he imagined a people from whom he might have sprung and by whom he might have been elevated and to whom he might thereby have been indebted. Jefferson extended Franklin's understanding of self and, in place of humility and caution, established educational, philosophical, pastoral, and political hopes and structures that intended to realize a democratic community that did not replicate the past but might surpass it. Jefferson's critics say that—like his opposing slavery but not being able to advocate its abolition, let alone deprive himself of the pleasures and comforts of ownership—something wishful and discrepant marred his thinking even to the point of hypocrisy. Jefferson was the first American limousine liberal. That means someone whose principles, especially where other people are concerned, do not interfere significantly with his own life; and someone willing to enforce dangerous utopian fantasies in the name of a cherished good but who is not equally impelled or inclined to face his own privilege.[5]

The interesting fragility of the Jeffersonian attempt to bridge the claims of equality and individuality produced the terms both of his veneration and of his availability to criticism. Jefferson's blithe vision of the connection between the American philosopher and the democratic has beguiled American history; its failure haunts it. The Jeffersonian liberal remains specially liable to this charge because the relation of the extraordinary to the ordinary, which underlies its hopeful vision, can so easily overwhelm and lapse into domination. Who, after all, was Jefferson kidding? He wrote of natural rights and equality, but look at him and at his friends and slaves and milieu. The distance between the effusive philosophic truths of the Declaration and the reality of his own life measures not only the "hypocrisy"[6] but the philosophic lightness of his point. Jefferson's thinking does seem to know more about other people than about himself and to make himself a rule to others in a somewhat impetuous and presumptuous way. Most people are not and cannot be Jeffersons. Most people come no closer to him by pretending that they are as good as he, even that they understand him. White liberalism starts with a pretense of being like him that turns the complexity and disappointments of Jefferson's thinking into the blithe hypocrisy of which he is then accused.

Thus the Jeffersonian fictions about *the people,* the construction of the image of the yeoman farmer, the constant living within the contradictions between knowing slavery to be wrong and having slaves, the risking of the inevitable discrepancies when taking a stand with "ought to be" rather than "always has been" constitute the hallmarks of a tradition that suggests itself to the individual in democracy. This is the rule of equality as applied to one's sense of individuality, not the rule of one's sense of individuality extended to a sense of everyone else. This remains the most emphatic of the Jeffersonian awarenesses of democracy: the possibility of the useful and the practical as the visible results of the true and the beautiful. They establish a demystified community where even the common people can recognize and come to nurture the uncommon person. who in turn responds by feeling beholden to that community. Small wonder that Jefferson was the quintessential and founding American class traitor, who in America is the liberal, not the radical. He did not let people see themselves in him as Franklin did, or see himself in them as Whitman came to. But he did find a remarkably daring way of refusing to privatize even the monopoly of truth.

Jefferson and Emerson had more to do with one another than most readings allow. The crucial connection of American democratic history is between those two because they represent the interesting, fertile, and manifestly creative adjustment of the smart to the most. Each had an acknowledged share of his century's intellectual achievement. Each was a noticed and admired participant in a worldwide development, but central to the Enlightenment and Romanticism principally in America and a second-rank figure in the great world. America was still a province of the great worlds, and its European, African, and native inhabitants had not composed the full and flawed relations of their own civilization and empire. Carlyle and Nietzsche read and admired Emerson. But Jefferson and Emerson remained icons of an American civilization. Emerson rivaled Jefferson in effect. Jefferson invented many things, but Emerson first played the role of preacher-turned-philosopher to the America that Jefferson had sketched out. Emerson was bred in the native version of the Jeffersonian vision, the New England preachery. His career explored the creeds and beliefs that might give to his readers and audience, principally middle-class Americans, a sense of themselves and the world that suited their purposes and accorded them individuality. There are as many Emersonian liberals as there are Jeffersonian liberals.

Read Emerson backward from his acceptance by Victorian Americans. Piece his thinking together from the mottoes, the proverbs, and the words carved in stone and wood over arches and mantles in the American institutions of learning. It is an understandable characteristic of the academic studies of Emerson that they have wanted to rescue him from the embrace of Victorian American culture. One reads Emerson to restore his rebelliousness and his challenges, to reanimate his ambivalence, and to emphasize his distance from what was his great and remarkable American audience. The lines of this interpretation made particular sense after the Second World War, when Emerson was so ingrained in midcult that it was hard to tell if it was Emerson or Oscar Hammerstein who wrote "hitch your wagon to a star." Emerson's claim on America's attention, however, cannot be reduced to the various inscriptions of his writings on various American generations and institutions. Read backward from their acceptance by the democracy, Emersonian individualism, idealism, and philosophizing have encouraged a remarkable strain of thinking and work that has populated Jefferson's arena with specifically American natural aristocrats—superior, self-consciously individual people with a sense of their responsibility to a democratic and American context.

The Emersonian characteristically views the self as separate but its fate as joined. The New England conscience, that shared possession of William Lloyd Garrison and Frances Perkins, Olive Chancellor and Isabel Archer, Katharine Hepburn and Eleanor Roosevelt, that characteristic form of American do-gooding and self-discipline, was fed by Emerson, however much scholarship, smart reading, and interpretation tell us that he meant nothing so ironclad and unambiguous. Like the spacious in Jefferson, which can sponsor hypocrisy as well as idealism, the spacious in Emerson is the sky over the deeds of women and men based on a conscience in which the calculation of what the individual owes the many forms the vision of social life. That this vision can turn out to be bossy, patriarchal, matriarchal, controlling, racist, insensitive, foolish, prudish, genteel, and an excuse for minding other people's business does not alter its status as the source of a remarkable reform creed for prosperous Americans. And the New England Emersonian conscience, with its sense of what the individual owes the many because of their natural equality, whatever their unequal circumstances, is the distinctive source of much of American reform.

In its simplest version, it seems to find that a way in which to better the world is what one owes oneself. Equality of souls and a sense of what is due the self, as defined by what is due to me, grounds the conscientious understanding of what is right in the world. It is a missionary, schoolmarmish, reformer's activity. For all the reading of Emerson that would have us mistrust his view of community and reform—and he was notoriously skeptical of action and joining—nevertheless it was a sound reading of Emerson that impelled antislavery and education and women's rights and all the impulses to restrain capitalism with culture and decency. That this restraint so often became genteel, wishing to cure rather than to educate human passion, to purify rather than to settle with human institutions, to control rather than to satisfy human appetites, to give a false neatness and moral to the tumult of human life, could not invalidate its power as a philosophy and as a philosophy with culture-wide adherence and effect.

There is a very difficult moment when the Americanist must with Emerson, as with Jefferson, confront the difference between a vision articulated and the vision shared. If that means the gap between articulation and reality with Jefferson, his apparently unconcerned disappointment of the expectations arising from his ringing declarations, with Emerson that often means the specifying of his rhetorical invocations with particular actions. And the characteristic action is the democratic action on Emersonian grounds of prosperous well-meaning Americans, the authors of Victorian high-minded trickery whose solid self-satisfactions appear to justify repressive and provincial conventions on grounds of the highest flying of the Emersonian spirit. How disappointing to *realize*, as the transcendentalist might put it, how far from the tree those bourgeois acorns fell.

Emerson addressed but never really merged with or saw himself as one of a people. Even his democratic messages or his messages that encourage equality do not approach messages of identity. We are all individuals with these challenges and capabilities, he says, but we are not really the same. In addition, the structures and institutions of the Emersonian, like the Jeffersonian, continue to differentiate the people from the individual. Individuality in some sense remained a differentiation without a corresponding adhesion.

For Walt Whitman, "adhesion" completed the process of individuation and justified it. Whitman saw individuals wherever he looked and where even Emerson appears to have addressed an audience and an audience as yet undifferentiated. Whitman's enumerations, those incantatory listings of things that people do and are, which parallel his lists of feelings and apprehensions and desires, are a naming of the special in the most. And one great Whitman act of joining is the seeing of myself in the other, of me in you and you in us—that restless, generous mirroring that hopes to make a mystical reunion of individuals and the community without the repression and without chaos. The process by which Whitman worked was hearing what people said they wanted and who they were, and by saying that as if about himself.

If the pursuit of happiness made a poetics, it would be, for good and ill, Whitman's. The transforming quality of this poetics was its creation of a world in which the extraordinary sense of one's self (indeed, the preoccupation and obsession with oneself) is saved, or at least proposes a saving, by the willingness to grant to others what one grants in the first place to oneself: to see others as you see yourself. The risks in such an apprehension are just what Tocqueville suggested they might be. The question seems to be whether one is able and willing to imagine someone else as equal but different from oneself. If the democratic imagination can only envision how someone else is like me, then it is indeed a solipsistic, lowering tyranny. Whitman, however, was capable of something beyond that. He imagined a normal that would allow him to thrive but that was not in any sense limited to his own desires and wants.

Despite being a radical, among many unliberal things, Whitman was also a liberal, thanks to the closet. Much of Whitman's expression was homoerotic, and much of his sense of self was what we would now conventionally call gay. Whitman suggests an original instance of the formation of the literary closet. At some point, he realized that his own desires were not merely different but dangerously different from the point of view of a society in which he hoped to thrive. Whitman was an enthusiastic American democrat whose poet's vocation divided him from his times less than his sexual views and orientation might. His realization that there were some kinds of individuality that could not be outspoken, even in the land of the free, did not, as it did later with Santayana or Henry James, inspire him to escape or give him a second sight on the principles of democracy. No, like many others, it gave him a hidden agenda for emphatically stating the conventional democratic.[7]

Whitman's celebration of the democratic and the rights of the individual and adhesion offered both a cover and a chance for his own nature. If Whitman's literal and fevered version of democracy were ever to come to pass, there would be room for the homosexual. But the version he propounded was one in which the intense camaraderie of men and the devotion of the individual to the democracy and the poet's song of democracy must stand for the open possibilities of his own private life and somehow sheath the unconventional with a normalcy that would protect it in disguise. Whitman's emphatic democracy protected him in two ways. By articulating the democratic, he claimed a role, an office that excused his lack of conventional arrangement and gave his own life a function within society. The articulation also protected the possibility of his own preference. In time, the equality of individuality in the adhesive fraternal democratic community will have a place for the likes of Whitman too. For some, the closet was a platform for seeing through and superiority. For Whitman, it was an office of imagination and illumination of a conventional roomy enough to include him.

There is an odd shock in realizing that the kind of person Whitman proposed as the basis for a community was himself. He went beyond the superior offerings of a Jefferson or an Emerson. Whitman in effect said *not only may you find in your self what I find in mine and on that account deserve democracy,* and allowed *I find in myself things I am willing to let you find in yourself, and these are common uncommon things.* Whitman was a common man, except in genius. He was not a patrician like Jefferson or Emerson. He was also aware of his own sexual unconventionality, and striving to free it and driven to protect it, he imagined a democratic community more rooted in identification and love of others than either patrician had ever a need to contemplate. Whitman might plumb the depths of an ordinary life and discover an extraordinary soul, but have to celebrate as much the life as the soul because what was extraordinary turned out not to be safe to keep on saying. The closet in Whitman instigates and necessitates a seeing of the democratic possibility that, for all its awkwardness and exaggeration and other faults, is movingly founded on his personal experience as an individual within democracy seeking to realize its potential, not detach from its limits.

The day before her husband was inaugurated as president in March 1933, Eleanor Roosevelt made use of the quiet shrine that Henry Adams had erected in Rock Creek Cemetery in memory of his wife, a Saint-Gaudens figure on a Stanford White base. It was the public shrine of his private feelings, offered, one might say, as a private gesture and a public slap. For Americans would never understand it, as he wrote in *The Education of Henry Adams:*

> The American mind ... shunned, distrusted, disliked, the dangerous abstraction of ideals, and stood alone in history for its ignorance of the past.
>
> Personal contact brought this American trait close to Adams's notice. His first step, on returning to Washington, took him out to the cemetery known as Rock Creek, to see the bronze figure which St. Gaudens had made for him in his absence. Naturally, every detail interested him; every line; every touch of the artist; every change of light and shade; every point of relation; every possible doubt of St. Gaudens' correctness of taste or feeling; so that, as the spring approached, he was apt to stop there often to see what the figure had to tell him that was new; but, in all that it had to say, he never once thought of questioning what it meant.... As Adams sat there, numbers of people came, for the figure seemed to have become a tourist fashion, and all wanted to know its meaning. Most took it for a portrait-statue, and the remnant were vacant-minded in the absence of a personal guide. None felt what would have been a nursery-instinct to a Hindu baby or a Japanese jinrickshaw-runner. The only exception were the clergy, who taught a lesson even deeper. One after another brought companions there, and apparently fascinated by their own reflection, broke out passionately against the expression they felt in the figure of despair, of atheism, of denial. Like the others the priest saw only what he brought. Like all great artists, St. Gaudens held up the mirror and no more. The American layman has lost sight of ideals; the American priest had lost sight of faith.[8]

This passage hardly contains Adams's furious disappointment that Americans yet again refused to understand the superiority of his private feeling, which he, like other great benefactors of great artists, had offered them as a shrine they might visit and understand as mute participants in the panoply of an ordered society of a hierarchy of place, taste, understanding, and art, with the philosopher Adams at the distant head. Now, of course, many more Americans share Adams's understandings and taste than he ever expected might. The question remains, however, of what that taste inevitably understands about itself. Is there any way between Adams's resolute contempt and the democratic relativist tourist who would see "Grief" as a less compelling stop on the road of monuments, less interesting than

Graceland, for example, just as its creators are less interesting than Elvis and Colonel Parker for most Americans?

Eleanor Roosevelt and her girlfriend Lorena Hickock sat before "Grief" and Eleanor told her friend, "In the old days, when we lived here, I was much younger and not so very wise. Sometimes I'd be very unhappy and sorry for myself. When I was feeling that way, if I could manage it, I'd come out here alone, and sit and look at that woman. And I'd always come away somehow feeling better. And stronger." In her moment of private feeling, facing the sacrifice of her life and tranquillity and her privacy to the most pressing needs of democracy, with her most private life sitting at her side, Eleanor Roosevelt drew from Henry Adams's monument to his wife and to his sensibilities and to the blighted hopes of his superiority what he said any Hindu baby might. She also drew from it what he never did: the strength to feel her fellow feelings with her fellow Americans in an hour of national emergency even greater than the 1890s, when Henry Adams could think so eloquently about the impending collapse of civilization and himself but could not see his reflection in the mirror the democracy held up to him. Eleanor Roosevelt took charge of the mirror like the great artist that she was.

I have a picture of Eleanor Roosevelt with my parents at an American Association for the United Nations meeting in the 1950s. My parents are proud and happy looking, while Mrs. Roosevelt rather towers over them in a white hat and a matching daisy corsage. Her gracious and warm look and those unmistakable eyes make the connection with the occasion. She was our family hero. I have a letter she wrote me answering an invitation to speak before a small group of high school students in 1960:

My dear Robert:

I was very much pleased by your kind invitation and I want to thank you warmly. I wish I could speak for your group but I am sorry to say I have all the engagements I can keep between now and the summer.

With many thanks for your thought of me and my regrets.

Very Sincerely Yours,
Eleanor Roosevelt

I know from the biographies that mine is one of hundreds of thousands of letters she wrote conferring individuality in everyone's encounter with her. There is the famous *New Yorker* cartoon of the miners in the pits saying, "Look, it's Mrs. Roosevelt" or the many song lyrics about her various doings: "It's pleasant at the White House, but I'll tell you how I feel: the food is simply terrible / just sauerkraut and veal. If Mrs. R. would stay at home, I'd get a decent meal / But that's off the record." Or "So Missus R., with all her trimmins' / Can broadcast a bed from Simmons / 'Cause

Franklin knows / *Anything Goes.*" A colleague told a story about how an elderly Mrs. Roosevelt, as a trustee of Brandeis University and tired after a day of meetings, went into the kitchens to thank the staff of cooks and waiters personally, one by one. She knew it was important to them, and showed everyone it was important to her. Even her enemies credited her sincerity.[9]

Eleanor Roosevelt was raised to be a genteel, aristocratic lady, American style. Her unusual family and personal circumstances no doubt contributed, along with her remarkable capabilities, to her unparalleled career as a private American person in public life, having, if you think about it, the career for which Henry Adams longed, a stable companion to statesmen. Bred and wedded to power, without elective office, she held power through her ability and her virtue and her intelligence and diligence. She was, in a sense, the unusual combination of the Tocquevillian and the Jeffersonian. Bred to noblesse oblige and educated by Mlle. Souvestre to public service, Eleanor Roosevelt was meant to serve in the female sphere. Her first move out of that remained class-bound and position-bound; although Henry Adams's gloom depressed her, they shared a social world.

Through her marriage and her experiences as a wife, daughter-in-law, mother, and hostess, Eleanor Roosevelt gained a greater ease with the world and was able to do her very important women's work as an upper-class woman tied to a public figure. She extended this sort of work as far as it could go. She was, however, engaged at arm's length. The people she felt obliged to were, in most important ways, not her own but apart. She was a female Tocquevillian, her uncle's niece, genteel in her prejudices and in her ultimate reticence, and a reformer in ways. She saw the America she agreed with as a place to which one owed duty.

That changed. She came to see herself anew, through the remarkable movement of women in politics. It is fair to say that Eleanor Roosevelt was the greatest public figure produced by the early twentieth-century women's movement. She was very much the product of Victorian genteel female civilization and then of its bluestocking, blue-blooded offshoots. Her long line of influences included, prominently, women involved in suffrage, political organization, reform, labor organizing, feminist and peace causes, and importantly, those who lived as women together. Some disagreement remains about the extent to which Eleanor herself participated, but there is no doubt that her intimate world was one in which lesbian relations formed a core friendship and one common pattern of women's domestic life. The personal stress and crises that led Eleanor to view her life as needing redefinition are interestingly like those of William James and George Santayana. The crisis in her marriage, Franklin's affair with Lucy Mercer and her unwilling recognition that their love was not exactly an exception to the patriarchal rule, her aggrieved perception of her dom-

ination by her mother-in-law and the genteel world of women—all forced
Eleanor Roosevelt to question the purpose and meaning of life itself.[10]
Because she was a woman, her decision has usually been seen personally or as part of the drama of a marriage or of Franklin's remarkable
career. But whatever the sources in private drama, her transformation of
her own life was the making of the great modern liberal who accepted
the possibility of a public life in a democracy by accepting her own personal implication and specification in the experiences of democracy. To
learn from, before trying to teach, the democracy was Eleanor Roosevelt's
life-long quest. And yet she retained the particular Jeffersonian quality,
often ridiculed but crucial to the fate of intellect in a democracy, of refusing to surrender her own intelligence or to disregard the knowledge that
ought to constitute power. She learned and taught what she learned.

The most admirable and ridiculous thing about Eleanor Roosevelt was
her direct action on Jeffersonian lines: she acted as if she were like those
she wanted to help but did not pretend to be one of them. She square-
danced and visited mines and planned seven-and-a-half-cent dinners and,
overcoming her native prejudices, befriended and championed Jews and
blacks. Unlike many on the left or the generations of the sixties, she did
not act out the pastoral of her identification. Eleanor Roosevelt was determined to preserve her own character and advantages, but to use them
ceaselessly to identify with and serve the larger public. She listened to and
learned from ordinary citizens, and that was her great accomplishment
and one, it is clear from the histories, that irritated but proved very useful to Franklin Roosevelt.

There was policy and strategy and thought in her work. She was the
informal head of an informal network of liberal political women and men
that grew out of the progressive period and deliberately pursued its aims
within American politics for most of the century. With all the advantages
and some of the same sense of inheritance and destiny of Henry Adams,
Eleanor Roosevelt fashioned for herself a position a Tocquevillian might
envy as a steward, engaged in the flow of democratic life. One need go far
to discover a more remarkable use of intelligence to represent a people.

More than any other figure, she welcomed democracy as a discipline
and did not allow it, as Huey Long or Al Smith or many others did, to
overwhelm or embarrass her conscience. Her capacity to identify with
other women, and then successively with other groups, to see in the democratic mirror how they shared problems, is the theme of her columns
and her writings and her amazing etiquette book.

Eleanor Roosevelt's wisdom has tended to be ignored and her intellectual accomplishment to be undervalued. Her newspaper columns, her
forays into every aspect of public life, her acute feelings for the public
event, her energetic infusion of ordinary public life with her ideas and her

reformist desires, her parenting, you might say, of the body politic, amounted to a remarkable example of just the sort of natural aristocrat Jefferson
imagined with a great deal more. *You Learn by Living* sums up the education of Eleanor Roosevelt, as ordinary and straightforward and even
casual as *The Education of Henry Adams* is extraordinary, ironic, and
delicately wrought.[11]

Adams's masterpiece insists that life taught him that his education was
a waste because it distinguished him and the world did not reward distinction. Eleanor Roosevelt took a different route. Her experience corrected
her expectations and her class and educational preparations, but unlike
Adams she tended to regard that as a completion rather than as a disappointment. There is a view of life in her writing that is in some ways less
demanding of fate than Adams's but perhaps more demanding of the
human person. Hers was the courage to temper her wisdom by what she
had learned and by the ways she resembled other people rather than was
unlike them.

She wrote her book, she says, in answer to the many questions asked
her that amount to "what have you learned from life that might help solve
this or that difficulty?"

> Of course, no one is equipped with such wisdom. No one is adequate to
> give such blanket answers. No one finds ultimate solutions. But the ques-
> tions are questions we all meet in our lives; they are questions we must all
> answer in some way. Not with finality, for life is too fluid, too *alive* for
> that.... When one attempts to set down in bald words any answers one
> has found to life's problems, there is a great risk of appearing to think that
> one's answer is either the only one or the best one. This, of course, would
> be nonsense. I have no such all-inclusive wisdom to offer, only a few guide-
> posts that have proved helpful to me in the course of a long life. Perhaps
> they may steer someone away from the pitfalls into which I have stumbled
> or help them avoid the mistakes I have made. Or perhaps one can learn
> only by one's own mistakes. The essential thing is to learn.[12]

Like Henry Adams, Eleanor Roosevelt knew of flux and energy. Like
him, she understood the presence of chaos. Like him, she grappled formidably with despair. Her answer was centrally different from his, but it
responded to the same question. Where he thought to draw the line of
his distinction and to record how the common world had disappointed
him, she tried to cross the boundary. Feeling her own individuality rather
too much, as did Adams, she sought to temper it in community rather
than loose it in angry despair. There is a sacrifice of complication in her
answer that, of course, adds greatly to the complication of living and the
burden of responsibility. It is not surprising that the distinction that Henry
Adams confers on his reader as a kind of benediction has grown in appeal

as the kind of individual he described has multiplied in tandem with the growth of education, comfort, "individuality," and experience in America. His solution is probably intellectually more absorbing; it refuses finally and brilliantly any compromise with a world of action. The book secures the privilege that sustains an Adams. Eleanor Roosevelt, on the contrary, saw the isolation of her privilege as its false retreat and decided to sweep it away. Her "Eleanor Roosevelt" carried a message of identity hewn from a distinction great beyond denying. Eleanor Roosevelt took the American democratic point:

> Learning and living. But they are really the same thing, aren't they? There is no experience from which you can't learn something. When you stop learning you stop living in any vital and meaningful sense. And the purpose of life, after all, is to live it, to taste experience to the utmost, to reach out eagerly and without fear for newer and richer experience. . . .
>
> One's philosophy is not best expressed in words; it is expressed in the choices one makes. In stopping to think through the meaning of what I have learned, there is much I believe intensely, much I am unsure of. But this, at least, I believe with all my heart: In the long run, we shape our lives and we shape ourselves. The process never ends until we die. And the choices are ultimately our own responsibility.[13]

Eleanor Roosevelt addressed the very problem that has preoccupied the Tocquevillian: that is, the effect of democracy or convention on the possibilities of individuality. Her answer, although forged from and along with Pragmatism, shows an Emersonian good sense and rhetorical clarity that cannot be reduced to the Henry Adams first-person third-person that aims at restriction but must achieve the Emerson/Whitman first-person third-person of inclusion in a language that anybody might recognize and aspire to. With Adams, of course, one joins an exclusivity by reading. On the contrary, Eleanor Roosevelt enjoined a democratic universality:

> There have been pressures on men to conform. At first, probably, there was pressure to conform to the taboos of a tribe, later to a church or to an autocratic government. But the outer pressures have always been more or less balanced by an innate drive in human beings to find and be themselves, to develop their whole natures, to make their lives an expression of the unique being that each of us is.
>
> Today, the outer pressures are not as drastic as they have been in the past. . . . They are, however, more dangerous in a way because they are more insidious. These are the pressures to live like our neighbors, to think like our community, to reshape ourselves in the image of someone else. The net result of this surrender is the destruction of the individual and the loss of his integrity. But the appeal is attractive, for it is the lure of the group. the promise of belonging.

It is a brave thing to have courage to be an individual; it is also, perhaps, a lonely thing. But it is better than not being an individual, which is
to be nobody at all.
There are two very different kinds of conformity, but they tend, somewhere along the line to blend, unless we are always aware of the difference.
One of them is essential if human beings are to live with one another in a
civilized way. That is social conformity, which is basically only a kind of
good manners, which is, in turn, formalized kindness. The other, the dangerous one, is conformity to alien standards or ideas or values because it is the
easy way, or because we think we can get farther in our job or profession
by not fighting for what we believe in, or because we will be more popular if we surrender our own convictions to fit the community.[14]

Eleanor Roosevelt, like Emerson, understood what Henry Adams, like
Tocqueville, and all of them, like Jefferson and Franklin, understood. The
question remained what to do about the knowledge. And Eleanor Roosevelt
(like William James) suggests the extension of what one sees in oneself,
expressive individuality, to others, not the measuring of the others by
what one sees in oneself. The inner light illuminates you because it illuminates me. Walk a mile in someone else's shoes. You go to your church
and I'll go to mine, but we'll walk along together. She quotes Spinoza but
echoes William James: "The trouble is that not enough people have come
together with the firm determination to live the things which they say they
believe. Spinoza once made a profound comment: 'Men believe a thing
when they behave as though it were true.'"[15]
There is much to admire in her book, but its special interest remains
in its accessible and unapologetic responses to democratic questions. Near
the conclusion, Eleanor Roosevelt addresses the Jeffersonian issue of the
natural aristocrat, or the problem of public service in a democracy: "First
of all, let me say that few people have ever deliberately prepared themselves to become public servants." This is her own answer not only to
Henry Adams and Thomas Jefferson but to Franklin Delano Roosevelt
and to her whole class. She also says you need material security (and the
cooperation of your family) in order to ensure your independence, your
capacity to stand on your principles when necessary:

> Third, the man [!] must have a genuine love of people and a deep desire to
> achieve something which can be accomplished only through public serv-
> ice. . . . The basic success of any politician lies in his ability to make his own
> interests those of his constituents, so that he merges into the community
> which he serves.[16]

She understood the problem, and her answer was as profoundly Jeffersonian as her medium was unashamedly middlebrow. The vanity that might

interfere with the natural aristocrat's best service to her country by keeping her own conscience and joining the nation's community did not trouble Eleanor Roosevelt. And, it must be added, the interest of her writing is not as great as the interest in her living. FDR was always the patrician in a democracy. His superiority was reinforced by his handicap; it fairly burst forth with vitality and courage. His travail released Roosevelt's superiority. But he was always singular and, accessorizing himself with his superiority, was appreciated for it. His wife was something else. She crossed a boundary into identification and appeared willing to lose herself in the crowd, from which her height or hat or accent or awkwardness or shining light of ideals nevertheless kept her visible. She could not go unrecognized because she never tried to hide herself, but she never feared to lose, as Santayana or Adams did, her singularity in a crowd. Like Whitman, she knew there was an identity to be found in the very adhesion she craved.

Indeed, Eleanor Roosevelt appears to have conceived that democracy afforded a relief to feelings of isolation even as it challenged individuality with conformist pressures. No wonder she made so many enemies. She made Jefferson's enemies all over again. She betrayed every fixed identity to which she might be assigned with the claim that the identity of the self is only completed by paying attention to other selves in terms of what they think they want. The genteel tradition, like the more strictly Tocquevillian, appreciates that one must guide but not that one must learn from the democracy.

Eleanor Roosevelt made a point of crossing the lines between people that were not supposed to be crossed. She took on causes of the workers, the women, the Jews, the blacks, the children, the people of the world; she imagined them as history affected them, and she learned from them. If you compare *The King and I,* that somewhat odd reflection on colonialism and self-determination by the great American lyricist, Oscar Hammerstein II, to its original form as *Anna and the King of Siam,* you notice how much Anna in the musical has been influenced by Anna Eleanor Roosevelt. Like Katharine Hepburn's Rosie in *The African Queen,* Hammerstein's Anna reflects the essential point of Mrs. Roosevelt in public life: that the smart in a democracy learn from the best in the most.[17]

The Jeffersonian accepts the need to teach and the need to learn from democracy and is willing to stomach the awkwardness and sacrifices of style that this engenders. Walking a mile in someone else's shoes is necessary to understand them, but it does hurt your feet and does make you look foolish. The comic glory of Eleanor Roosevelt was her willingness to look ridiculous and even compromise her own individuality in matters of style and manner and aesthetics in order to discover the community that democracy might realize. It was and remains a punishing discipline, one less satisfying than the aesthetic that, like Henry Adams, celebrates the distinction of the individual or, like the hip, that creates out of mass culture new forms of distinction.

The Jeffersonian insists on the awkwardness of the differences between you and me as a precondition of useful exchange. The biggest difference is that democracy may not confirm one's sense of being special, more intelligent, or more deserving. Democracy requires that one be prepared to gamble everything all the time and assume that what you value of truth and wisdom will survive each throw of the dice, that is, of life. Henry Adams lived all he could but would not learn by it. The Jeffersonian lives all she can by learning from it.

# ⚡ Franklin and Jefferson: Before "the Democratic Fact"

HUMAN SUPERIORITY has always troubled the democratic. By "superiority" I mean to suggest the person with uncommon native abilities, attributes, and talents, as well as the person whose advantage amounts to a superiority of status. Riches, position, beauty, intelligence, determination, charisma are some of the qualities acknowledged as human superiority. Some superiorities are random and native while others derive from position, privilege, wealth, and so forth. Superiority requires construction as well as discovery. Polities therefore establish some view of individual genius and especially a hierarchy and ideology concerning it. Democracy, like any other regime, ends up constructing, institutionalizing, and privileging certain kinds of superiority, but it is driven by a notion of the superiority of the collective, the ordinary, and the equal. The American founders struggled with the issue of how to allow for the kinds of superiority they valued in a regime committed to the elaboration of individual "superiority" and to the radically different and still-suspect democratic principle.

Scholars have been usefully interested in the shortcomings of the United States as a democratic regime whose mandate is to preserve, protect, and defend individual liberty as the right of all human beings, a right founded in nature and deriving even the extraordinary from the ordinary. A constant discourse respecting the achievement of a fuller democracy is useful, notwithstanding the inconvenient view that American democracy so little resembles its ideal that its democratic character and provenance must be questioned. Still, if the promise of democracy constitutes a perspective from which to judge the regime, it distracts from the degree to which democracy exists, albeit in an imperfect state that institutionalizes systematic harm.[1] However else one may regard Alexis de Tocqueville, it is surely his fundamental decision to grant the United States its democratic character, and the ways in which that decision magnetized his attention and his observations, that have made *Democracy in America* the Americanist classic it remains. Like Ralph Waldo Emerson's, Tocqueville's acute sense of the problems equality presents to individuality gives us access to an issue that mattered as much as democracy did to the founders, and perhaps more: the future for people like them in the nation they were constituting.[2]

Abraham Lincoln's understanding of the nation's founding amounted to a revision of the founders' views of democracy from the point of view of the democratic and the national. Much in his career suggests his preoccupation with the necessity of and danger posed by what I am calling superiority. By now, it should be possible calmly to take into account the difference between the founders' views of the democratic—which they saw as a choice, like any choice of regime, from among potential evils—and those that properly flourish within such a regime. The sources of unease with what I follow Gordon Wood in calling the "democratic fact" were various. Wood's cogent account of the founders' views of democracy includes the observation that "they found it difficult to accept the democratic fact that their fate now rested on the opinions and votes of small-souled and largely unreflective people."[3] The democratic "fact" does not mean the fulfillment of the democratic promise but refers to the democratic character of the regime. The concern, unease, and, perhaps, pain that the prospect of democracy caused in the very men who set it in formal motion is an ambiguous subject for Americanists. Nevertheless, it is a necessary aspect of any careful study of American political thought and intellectual history.

Madison's attempt to render superfluous the virtuous character of a citizenry, upon which it was traditionally thought free regimes must depend, has properly absorbed our attention. His skepticism about human character and his inventive parlay of human selfishness into politically viable self-interest merit all the attention that has been paid them. But Madison's rise to founder of choice reflects a certain preference on the part of scholars for the practical solutions he devised over the serious consideration of the survival in a democratic regime of several kinds of human superiority, including that of virtue, which he hoped to trump. Too, Madison's appeal to generations of political scientists and historians surely has had to do with the character of their own enterprises, and, inescapably, the limitations of their own self-understanding. He believed that the regime might be able to divide and therefore contain the dangers to the new regime of superiorities of rank, wealth, and even political power. Madison anticipated the view that the United States version of capitalist democracy might prove a success in the only way he figured a regime was likely to be, by default. The Bill of Rights served his and Jefferson's purposes by explicitly limiting government power in the spheres of individual liberty. It also served to ground Madison's experiment by preferring individual interest and its shifting combinations to authoritative collective opinions.

Jefferson made the most complete republican synthesis and mastered his fear of democracy to boot. But his mastery was connected to the confidence and abstraction of his focus. The very inconclusiveness of his work has made it possible for subsequent generations to think he understood them. In *The Jefferson Image in the American Mind,* Merrill Peterson has shown how one can read American history through the uses to which Thomas Jefferson has been put.[4]

The Madisonian grasp of what is difficult and unyielding in the world and his tough-minded arrangements for a republican future may satisfy appetites the Jeffersonian vagueness in the middle distance fails to whet. In the United States, Madison's "self-interest" makes more common sense than Jefferson's "happiness." The Jeffersonian vision of a future in which democracy served its own best interests by securing its own best counsel, his attractive pastoral visions of content and self-sufficiency, may pain rather than inspire nowadays. Nevertheless, Jefferson supplied the imaginative grounds of faith in a democratic republic that Madison's own solutions foreswore but that he recognized might ease a future that worried him.

The Jeffersonian political imagination generated notions of freedom of expression, notions with which Jefferson did not always himself keep faith. It emphasized the value of the high-minded practical, the connection between philosophy and the common life, the responsibilities of the highest human types to the activities and purposes of the new republic and its ordinary citizens. The care with which Jefferson invested both the ordinary and the superior person with a role in a free and enlightened future was his companion piece to Madison's apparently harder-headed political thinking. Their different approaches should be considered in tandem, and we are fortunate in having at last an authoritative edition of the Jefferson-Madison correspondence to consult. Jefferson supplied the possible connections between the highest human qualities—those Madison's Federalist essays do not rely on—and the republic that will need more than the metabolic luck of a system of dispersed interests.[5]

The fate of the superior in a democracy is a tricky issue. Democracy remains properly skeptical of any claim to individual superiority, independent of a democratic public, while capitalism rationalized material success as reflecting a kind of superiority that validated John Adams's concerns about the rich as well as the poor being always with us. But no human society can claim immunity from some notions of superiority. This is what Adams was reminding Jefferson about in his responses to the latter's natural aristocracy. Democracy also prefers a model of superiority that suits itself, a plan for which was Tocqueville's chief subject. Jefferson's hope remained, it seems clear, that a notion of intellectual superiority might flourish in a democracy founded on Enlightened principles. Jefferson's idea was that this new regime might institute some understanding of human superiority that would not have to define itself against the democratic. He was not especially concerned to undermine conventional notions of superiority, founded in personal qualities, class, gender, race, riches. He thought that the democracy could compete for the allegiance of the truly superior by attaching their interests to the good of the whole.

The Jeffersonian version shares with the Tocquevillian the attempt to secure for the democracy the talents of the superior. The Tocquevillian is concerned to erect an alternative point of view to the democratic, founded in a principled resistance to its claims, a vision of bulwark and rescue. It is an American tradition of viewing democracy as if from the outside, one Americanists have assumed rather than thought through. The Jeffersonian eschews resistance and rescue for a hopeful and high-minded cooperation. Each view shares a distance from democracy, holds up a mirror that reflects other people, and never examines the Jeffersonian or Tocquevillian's own interests. This does not trouble the Tocquevillian since distance from the democracy is his very object; and the rewards of that perspective are exactly those of feeling as if outside of democracy. The Jeffersonian, however, is founded on a claim of serving the democracy. It is Jefferson's attempt to stabilize his peers' shared mistrust of a democracy they favored into a construction of the democratic uses of the nondemocratic.[6]

Jefferson's own was not a democratic experience. His role as democratic founder has rightly and routinely been contrasted with the way he went about his life and political career. But it was not hypocrisy or frailty so much as dissonance he enacted. Previous examples of American high-mindedness, like that of the Puritans, may have failed integrity's tests but retained the close connection between profession and behavior. The Jeffersonian sundered that connection. The Declaration provides no system for holding oneself accountable. This, as it were, launches the Madisonian machine in which random interest assembles itself into patterns of association and action, regulated but not collectively accountable. The Jeffersonian does not altogether embrace the self-denial of Madison's view that virtue is a wish, not a dependable element in the construction of the regime.

The Jeffersonian version of active virtue translated Enlightened reason into the conviction that the qualities in people the rational requires must be privileged. Jefferson's farthest seeing was his belief in the argument that this kind of superiority might make to a democratic people. He realized how unpredictably talent occurs—although he was always trying to make order of the chaos of inborn ability and to rationalize accruing advantage—and created a reason for a people to acknowledge such superiority by patronizing it. He also (inconveniently, from the late twentieth century's perspective) did not renounce conventionally institutionalized superiority out of hand. He wanted to perfect the talent search in order to populate a hatchery. He wanted to bring the "natural" and the "conventional" into closer approximation. Madison and the others shared Jefferson's hopes that their like might flourish in the new regime. Their striking difference was not about whether some people are really better or smarter than others. They differed—if indeed their differences amounted to a difference—about how the Americans could be persuaded to foster a class of citizens whose natural superiority might be constructed with the society's aims and principles in view, and whether it was prudent to persuade them. This tension between a natural aristocracy that owes its construction and its allegiance to a democracy and one that sees itself as independent of anything but its own counsel is lodged in the heart of American intellectual history. The secondary distinction regards the location of intellectual inspiration, loyalty, and the sources of wisdom. For John Quincy Adams, W.E.B. Dubois, John Dewey, Martin Luther King, and so many others, these were abiding issues: what higher law is higher and whose.

In the famous exchange with John Adams about the natural aristocracy, Jefferson argued that the nation required a system to tie the talents of its best minds to the good of the people. Adams, like Madison, simply did not believe Jefferson's elegant flight of rationalist fancy could work. It would end up, as indeed it has, in creating new sources of the abiding minorities of wealth and power that would always divert and challenge free government. In their different ways Adams and Madison relied on the science of politics to attempt to compensate for what they viewed as the inevitable dangers in any government. Jefferson imagined differently. His natural aristocrats have something of the angel (Madison's conditional "if men were angels" angels) about them, albeit an anticlerical, rational angelic. The democracy had but to assume the responsibilities of education of its most gifted, and they in turn would exercise their talents for the disinterested good of the people. It is important to place this concern with the "best and the brightest" in its proper context of Jefferson's educational vision, which hoped to train the people to seek and profit from expertise and gain their own measure of independence and opportunity.[7]

Jefferson saw things more clearly than many of his critics have realized he did. Among the many rewards of reading Albert Jay Nock's neglected *Memoirs of a Superfluous Man* is his lucid if bitter, resonant, and critical account of Jefferson's centrality.[8] Madison was skeptical about improving the people for a system that would select the talents the nation both needed and feared and bind them to the national interest; Jefferson's vision responded by constructing *disinterest* as an interest. (Nowadays "disinterested" has come curiously or fatefully to mean the same thing as "uninterested.") To Adams's historical pessimism, it suggested the possibility that a class of privileged citizens could be cultivated whose ambitions would be satisfied and their threat to free government avoided. This vision did expect that rationalist disinterestedness, supported by education, would result in a knowledge of what the nation needed; no more did it insist that there were answers about which all reasonable people should agree or that disinterestedness did not result from independence, as understood by English political tradition. Jefferson proposed an improvement upon that independence, by freeing it from a propertied stake of one's own in the instance of the natural aristocrat.

The Jeffersonian confidence in such notions had many sources, but certainly it reflects Jefferson's view of himself and his colleagues. Jefferson did not see himself as the creature of his privileges and advantages, let alone the contingencies of his life. Madison and Adams supposed that their own example could not be built into a human constitution and their self-knowledge was an element in their nation building. Jefferson believed that he was who he was because his pursuit of reason kept him disinterested, and he was always trying to figure out how the United States could hatch all the Jeffersons it might need. This was also a founding moment of American liberalism because it codified the notion that the good of the nation, defined in the Declaration's terms and weighted with a specific commitment to expertise, required the service of the best and brightest. That they could be identified and that they could be trusted to identify their self-interest with the good of the whole is Jefferson's legacy to American education: that reason might trump interest.

Jefferson's natural aristocrat accepts the Declaration's famous universal claims as binding. He also negotiates a relation to the popular that is founded on the Jeffersonian awareness of his own superiority. Superiority in this sense is not that of property, lineage, or character (or, ultimately, race, sex, and class, although that realization is still taking its own sweet time) but that of talent. There is in all of this a guiding assumption that knowledge, pursued along the rational natural philosophic lines congenial to the eighteenth century, is adequate to the tasks of politics. It exalts the independence of the natural aristocrat at the same time it expects that independence to yield to a good the democracy has no need to define. It is like the genteel humanist or professional social science assumptions that good books make good people, a connection between talent and character that remains unproven. But it does describe in rough outline the striking development of the American higher education system.

The arguments for the multiversity familiar from the 1960s were Jeffersonian, and they effected a version of what Jefferson had in mind. However uneasily, American democracy has tried to educate its natural aristocrats and relied on their advice. Jefferson did not anticipate that knowledge might become its own interest, develop its own stake, and commodify the rational in a way that was like rather than independent of the system of interests it was meant to referee. Nor did he think through the consequences of maintaining the independence of the natural aristocrat, not requiring that class to see itself as part of rather than ancillary to the democratic. (Richard Hofstadter's stringent view of the anti-intellectual character of American culture remains essential to any estimation of the Jeffersonian experiment in the identification and cloning of superiority.) Nor, it must be added, did Jefferson really think through Madison's understanding of the ways in which interests might promote civic responsibility and especially the improving effects on citizens of the constant requirement to compromise and thus in some ways understand other people's interests.[9]

None of this is to say that Jefferson failed to grasp how resistant a democratic people might be to its best counsel, or how superiority of the type he valued might inspire democratic resentment rather than love. He did not identify with that view and regarded it as something in need of fixing. He came up with an elegant and resonant blueprint for the required machine. Remember that Rube Goldberg was as much Jefferson's as Benjamin Franklin's inventive progeny, although it is unlikely that Jefferson would have gotten Rube's joke. (Franklin not only would have gotten the joke, he would have recognized it as his own.) To prize what is rare and to believe it ordained by nature, not decision, need not lead one to expect society will follow suit. Jefferson had fewer illusions about the recalcitrance of the real Americans than his pastoral, agrarian writings would suggest. Indeed, the difference between his natural scientific and political scientific views amounts to a lower threshold of hope. He made more than his share of wishful scientific observations, and many passages in the *Notes on the State of Virginia* suggest how his eye for truth might cloud his eye for detail.[10] Jefferson lacked personal experience of what amounted to the democratic fact. He could only project onto a people what he imagined might be possible grounds for re-creating the deference that he enjoyed and knew the worth of; but the deference paid to him was not simply the result of his own natural aristocracy but of the constructed aristocracy that accompanied it.

Haunting Jefferson's notion of the superior was a failure of imagination. He could not really imagine how someone he never was or could be might react to him, yet this knowledge is essential to the effecting of his idea. His projections may have beguiled Americans, but they did not transform the democratic republic in the way he hoped. His own faith in reason was never a simple equation between the scientific and the good, but the faith in reason he recommended to the democracy too often boiled down to just that. The useful was never sufficient for Jefferson, although it has often been for the Jeffersonian. The Jeffersonian saw the fate of democracy as depending on the relation of the superior persons chosen from it to the majority who remained in and of it. Jefferson did not question that superior talent could know what was best for the democracy disinterestedly. He did not question whether the disinterested can comprehend the interested. This affected both the wisdom and its reception. Jeffersonian visions chart democratic hopes better than they navigate American waters.

I am not claiming that Jefferson was wrong, or that his attempts to construct a place within the democratic for the nondemocratic were ineffective. Rather, I am saying that this powerful model of how to reconnect the United States to the very things Madison excluded from the empire of interest was frequently baffled by its failure fully to imagine alternatives to a disinterested class possessing disinterested knowledge (although believing in disinterested knowledge is more plausible than believing in its disinterested use). And the Jeffersonian, like Jefferson, has never learned the American habit of explicitly and *consciously* consulting its own interest, even as part of a calculation that might transform it to "self-interest, rightly understood." That has both ennobled and hobbled the enterprise. Readers of this essay, whatever their politics, are likely to be part of the Jeffersonian class, although unlikely to be from Jefferson's class. The Jeffersonian model of imagining a people receptive to the best wisdom because they sponsor it abides. It also draws on an imagining of democracy as fundamentally other and holds risk for those whose own superiority is a democratic construction and whose disinterestedness is hard to distinguish from the interestedness of others.

Jefferson's strategy for securing a role for the talented after the democratic fact was not the only one: Benjamin Franklin had also thought about this issue. Characteristically, Franklin did not resort to the kind of comprehensive idea Jefferson articulated to Adams. Nobody liked a plan or a scheme more than he, but his manner was decidedly less elaborate than the Virginian's. Perhaps the reason Franklin has had so much less attention from students of American political thought than Jefferson, Madison, Hamilton, Washington, Adams, and so forth was his reluctance to commit his plans to quite their level of explicit articulation. Too, the occasions that prompted his writing were the moment-to-moment events that led toward the great occasion of independence, which called forth such a profusion of systematic political thinking. Franklin had been ceaselessly devising plans for his country for a lifetime, and independence was an event of his maturity, not his youth.

Franklin remains the founder less traveled, and this is unfortunate.[11] Lincoln shared Franklin's unmediated experience of the people from whom the Constitution meant to draw its authoritative We and to construct its defenses against the evils of democracy. Although it is hard to imagine a standard for natural aristocracy that would have excluded Jefferson, Madison, and Adams, and any notion of superiority that would not have included Washington, a scholar-athlete if there ever was one, Ben Franklin owed his superior position to his own superiority. He made his way in the world as only a few people ever do. Franklin was an avatar of the Jeffersonian natural aristocrat. Franklin was so various, so talented, so *useful,* and so realized that he frequently baffles scholars. For all our conscious veneration for the founders, there is a way in which scholarly attention cuts them down to our size. No sensible scholar ever mistook Franklin's size for his own, however. Franklin has continued to outsmart Americans, scholars and gentlemen alike. It is hard to think of knowing more than Ben Franklin about the things he knew about, or understanding better what he understood.

Franklin also resembles Lincoln in that he remains a sustaining element of the nation's folklore. Even today, he remains a comfortable figure, a democratic familiar, one whose remarkable commercial, scientific, political, intellectual, diplomatic, intimate, and moral abilities add up to a friendly wonder, not a superior being, despite the fact that if Franklin was not superior, nobody was. President Kennedy once remarked about the guests at a glittering intellectual and artistic dinner that the White House had never before seen such company, since Thomas Jefferson dined alone. There are no such punch lines about Ben Franklin. Jefferson remains the sum of his superiority. Attempts to humanize him through his domestic arrangements may dent but do not dislodge him from his eminence—in part because, as his contemporaries and biographers attest, he was not a man one knows in the democratic way. He was reserved and presented no character, except what of his own stamped his work in the world. Franklin, on the contrary, was one of America's first great characters, in the sense of the characters around whom the contemporary English novel centered. If he was at least as complicated and hard to know as Jefferson, people seldom experience him in that way. The awareness of his complications amplifies Franklin's human substance.

Robert Lawson's 1951 children's book *Ben and Me: A New and Astonishing Life of Benjamin Franklin, as Written by His Good Mouse Amos, Lately Discovered* is a charming example of Franklin's easy place in the national lore. If you ask folks about Jefferson, they will mention the Declaration, Monticello, the things by which he intended to be remembered, having codified his own fame as well. Ask the same people about Franklin and you will hear about kites, lightning and electricity, stoves, maybe Poor Richard. Nor is this confined to the popular mythic. Franklin's *Autobiography* echoes through American letters. Present in Henry Adams's model for "self-teaching," it was where James Gatz found his "Platonic conception of himself" as Jay Gatsby. The contemporary popular economist Adam Smith expressed the point about one's sense of Franklin: "The I Ching, Jung had said, was like having an old courteous friend— I supposed a Ben Franklin, who would talk to you in axioms. Asked about the Stock Market, the old and courteous friend got vague and could not find his glasses." In *The Cartoon History of the United States*, Franklin is Ben, Jefferson is the sum of his thinking. Franklin has the status of a Disney critter, an ancestral Jiminy Cricket.[12]

Of course, good old Ben crystallizes one aspect of Benjamin Franklin in a telling way. He was a character fashioned by Franklin from his own complex weave for the very purpose of endearing his superiority to a kind of democracy. He made himself up in a way that would secure his position without inciting his fellow citizens to resentment. To do this he gave the impression, most famously in *Poor Richard's Almanack* and his autobiographies, that he was ordinary. He gave rules, suggested methods, advanced a discipline, shared wisdom as if to say that his rise and Richard's nostrums were identical.

This is not the place to expand on the subtle formations of Franklin's self-presentation, which is hardly fresh news. But to juxtapose the shrewdness of Franklin's democratic self-invention to Jefferson's hope for the natural aristocracy is illuminating. Franklin appears always to have understood the necessity in English North America and its successor regimes of pursuing one's uncommon individual superiority in a way that did not irretrievably offend the common. He came by this knowledge the hard way, because unlike Jefferson he was a self-made man, who seen his opportunities and took them, followed the main chance, made his luck, and so on. The example of Franklin validates most of the hoariest clichés about the possibilities of American opportunity. He knew he had to watch his back and that the people from whom he rose would not easily forgive the perception that his rise amounted to distance. His plans for cooperative associations, public improvements, collective endeavors, share a two-fold truth. They are in themselves worthy, and they also prospectively address the possible resentment that people might feel by refusing to be seen as the superior individual everybody knew him to be. Like Washington's incarnation of Cincinnatus, Franklin's humble guise as Poor Richard's Ben went to the heart of what Americans had every reason to fear from even the venerated superior. Of course the Americans had to deify Washington so that he could not tell a lie. Franklin's genius was in part his excellent advice about how and when to lie.

Franklin's emphasis on utility was less abstract than was Jefferson's. It also embraced a significantly expanded universe of what use might be and for whom. John Randolph's taunt that Jefferson designed a plow that delighted French *philosophes* but failed the test of Virginia soil expressed what has been a continuing charge leveled against the Jeffersonian in American life. Even Randolph could not have made this joke about Franklin; his practical credentials were in order. Jefferson was his junior in the international Enlightenment and never gained the immense recognition that Franklin did on account of his scientific work and personal power. Franklin cut a sophisticated figure in Paris, but somehow his exalted position was not the subject of his public character. His emphasis on utility reflected in part a consciousness that such as he ought to be able to translate his understandings to others. Such crossings are the essence of practicality, good-natured sharing and the hope of raising the general level.

Poor Richard was not a deception but a philosophic conceit, someone not Franklin who could convey Franklin's messages on a presumptively equal footing. But the key is not only the educational, scientific, and civic plans for improvement Franklin pioneered and, like the other founders, advocated. Franklin rested his scheme on his shrewd self-fashioning. It is hard to resent the superiority of someone whose scientific genius produces a stove and who tells you about it in the very voice of someone who uses it. Jefferson's ceaseless and admirable observations of everything never resolve into the kind of story of science that Franklin's electrical experiments do, nor did his inventions have much to do with ordinary people. Franklin offered his own persona as an IOU to his fellow citizens, defanging their hostility to the evidence in success of his superior ability by showing himself as someone just like you and me, whose accomplishments were in our power to imitate. Franklin lent a helping hand to his fellows in the guise of one of them without doing much more than simplifying his knowledge of the world for public consumption. One sure ground of his invention was his own life experience and his knowledge of human beings. Franklin had to find and develop an audience and had to learn what that audience would seek and what it would tolerate. Jefferson's audience was differently constructed and seemed to require a system of delivery to a prepared populace rather than a simultaneous translation of wisdom and its source into some democratic vernacular and, equally important, vice-versa.

Our awareness of Franklin's cosmopolitan versatility has tended to make us stumble over Poor Richard's maxims. But it was the character not the advice Franklin invented. Richard's advice does not differ from what Franklin knew about the world. Jefferson's natural aristocrat hesitated to give the almanac of practical advice that Richard's did. Homilies and home truths need not concern the best and brightest. Too, Richard's address was popular, in vivid contrast to the retained counsel of the Jeffersonian. Franklin understood that the rational sources of advice, the province of the educationally privileged and, perhaps, intellectually superior, required packaging. Access to the highest truths and attainment was what Richard and Ben promised. The power of knowledge depended on a keen sense of the climate of reception. Prepared by his own experience of core democratic facts, an experience Jefferson had not had, Franklin presented his superior wisdom as the commonsense advice of a regular fellow on terms of equality.

Poor Richard's proverbs condense a tough, even cynical, knowledge of the world as the context of maxims. They are essays to do well, rather than good, but as usual Franklin reversed the point of his Puritan home culture and codified what they *did,* works not grace, as opposed to what they *said,* grace and works. "Doing good by doing well" may be a better motto than "doing well by doing good." It reverses the Puritan belief and anticipates Madison's thinking, if not his solution. Franklin's counsel is clear and forgiving. If, inside Richard's bluff homilies, the guile of a very superior man indeed measures in what part the more ordinary world can accept him, his conclusions and advice are sound. His deceptive and prophylactic persona is a shrewd simplification, analogous to the advice, which is rendered so that ordinary people can use it. It is counsel with the narrative pungency that makes it possible for a body to think it through independently. But it is not concerned to advance the austere rationalist method itself, as Jefferson was.

Madison hoped to redeploy the classic confrontation between rich and poor in terms of shifting combinations of interest. He despaired of incorporating virtue or wisdom into any viable system, but did have expectations of common good resulting from his scaled-down moral approach. Franklin, however, had already discovered a way in which to render virtue and wisdom in democratic terms. The character of the advice giver was reassuring. The advice itself was tailored to the ordinary circumstances in which people found themselves. If not exactly republican virtue, Richard's maxims give a good account of how Americans might see issues of virtue and wisdom in terms that made sense to them. Franklin's incisive revision of the pie-in-the-sky text of how hard it is for a rich man to enter heaven continues to illuminate. It *is* easier for a rich man to be conventionally "good" than a poor man. "It is hard for an empty sack to stand upright" in Poor Richard's version. This is a powerful statement of an underlying issue of democracy in terms that people can understand and use to think about the broader issues it raises. Billie Holiday echoed Franklin in her autobiography: "You've got to have something to eat and a little love in your life, before you can sit still for anybody's damn sermon on how to behave." And Richard's empty sack is at the core of contemporary social policy debates and should be.

Franklin's motion for prayers in the Constitutional Convention suggests another of the many shadings of Richard's chestnut. "We indeed seem to feel our own want of political Wisdom, since we have been running all about in Search of it."[13] Franklin lightly mocked the ransacking of ancient constitutions and suggested a prayer for guidance. His remarks challenged what amounted to the Jeffersonian method of relying on principled abstractions from which conduct is deduced because of the gap between book learning and people's lives. A key element of the disjunction, however, is not traditionalism but a radical elevation of common sense as an element of sound politics. How do you extract useful democratic wisdom from the uses of reason?

Franklin's speech at the convention's conclusion presents his thinking: "I have experienced many instances of being obliged to change my opinions even on important subjects, which I once thought right, but found to be otherwise. It is therefore that the older I grow, the more I am apt to doubt my own judgement of others."[14] Jefferson would not have failed to take Franklin's point, but perhaps not its clue to what his own idea of the natural aristocrat missed. There was no provision in that scheme or fantasy for translating the best advice into common sense, for consulting the experience of ordinary people, for presenting the advice on terms that respected the given of equality. The vision of the best was one democracy required lest its excesses subvert its purposes. Sometimes, however, there is a faint echo of a parent telling the child being spanked, "this hurts me more than it does you." Connected to guiding principles but not to the climate within which they were supposed to flourish, the Jeffersonian landed less well than it took off.

Franklin saw that wise counsel required substantive and stylistic transformation in order to be received, as well as produced. Whether Franklin did doubt his own judgment is not the question. (The question is one that mattered to John Dewey.) Experience may have been the founders' only guide, but whose experience, of what, and how understood? Elsewhere Franklin shows that he understood Madison's plan as well. His praise of vanity in the *Autobiography* gives a vivid picture of the calculations of interest that might prove virtue's back door to the Madisonian house. "Most People dislike Vanity in others whatever Share they have of it themselves, but I give it fair Quarter wherever I meet with it, being persuaded that it is often productive of Good to the Possessor & to others that are within his Sphere of Action."[15] Indeed, Franklin's method of moral self-improvement provides an excellent foundation for the calculation of self-interest, which was what the Madisonian citizen was meant to do. It incorporated a sound awareness of the interests and feelings of others. But Franklin revised virtue rather than excluding it. His awareness of the ways in which accepting one's democratic context, seeing one's self in equality's mirror, creating a democratic character for the superior individual and for the best wisdom, was an inescapable part of the common project of securing a democratic future against its own tendencies. It also underscores Franklin's special interest to students of political thinking.

Was Franklin a Jeffersonian aristocrat? Yes. But, like Lincoln and Whitman and so many others, he was schooled in what one can call the democracy of the common life. The point is not to divide Jefferson from Franklin, but to suggest how what Franklin knew was something the Jeffersonian would fail to learn at its peril. Nothing forced Jefferson to question his notion of the superior, or the convenient fit between his own privileges and his views of where the nation ought to turn for counsel. But Poor Richard was always having to do just that because he depended on pleasing his readers. It may take a Franklin to find a way to use this democratic fact to think about nondemocratic knowledge. Franklin's notions located the problem of the superior in the push and pull of the common life. Franklin was just as keen as Jefferson and the rest to establish institutions that would create the best kind of enlightened citizenry. He did not prefer the school of hard knocks to the academy but understood the hard knocks democracy had in store for anybody who took its deference for granted. Franklin understood, as well as anyone ever has, the ways in which democracy would receive exactly the counsel Jefferson envisioned. He perfected the tactic that has been an ambiguous but lasting means by which the consciously superior self might take democratic resentment and resistance into account. For Jefferson democratic facts were data; for Franklin democratic facts were facts of life.

# ⚡ "Tails in the Air": Henry Adams and the American History of the European Middle Ages

HENRY ADAMS was no fool. He spent the last years of his life pursuing interdisciplinary medieval studies. Miss Aileen Tone, his secretary and companion, sang to Adams from a book of old French songs, given to her by Kurt Schindler of the Schola Cantorum. Some of them turned out to be from the thirteenth century, songs with whose medieval qualities Adams was quick to sympathize and to recognize as poems to which he had devoted a chapter in *Mont-Saint-Michel and Chartres*. Adams apparently had not connected poems such as those of Chatelaine De Coucy and Thibault De Campagne with scored manuscripts.

From the footnotes in Aileen Tone's collection, Adams obtained catalogue numbers of the original manuscripts in the Bibliothèque Nationale and the Arsenal Library in Paris. They were, of course, not folk songs but the sophisticated *trouveres* and troubadour songs, written by the best poets and sung to some of the best music of the age. The *chansons* became his final aesthetic and scholarly passion. Adams and Tone went to Paris, where he had already arranged for the thorough search of the great Parisian libraries for twelfth- and thirteenth-century songs. He employed two specialists, Henri Expert and Amédée Gastoué, to direct the search. They uncovered manuscripts that had been undisturbed for six hundred years.

Adams was thrilled: "I wish Walter Scott were alive to share them with me, but he is my only companion in these fields, and I fear that even he never heard a note of music for Rebecca or Ivanhoe, or knew that it existed. He would have enjoyed the fun of Coeur De Lion and Blondel quite fresh from the crusades, as good as the west front of Chartres." His aim was aesthetic and his means scholarly. Adams concerned himself with performance practice—how should these old songs be sung? He decided

---

*For Bradford Blaine, Professor Emeritus of Medieval History at Scripps College*

This chapter was first presented at a medieval studies conference on "Narrative, Song and Saga" in Claremont, California, in 1989. I thank Nancy Van Duesen of the Claremont Graduate University music faculty for her invitation to say my little piece.

to follow the literary meter of the poems and encouraged Tone to sing with greater freedom of rhythm. This ruffled Gastoue: "But this is a vast study. We know too little about the rhythmic notation, and there are too many conflicting theories. Perhaps in thirty years we may approach this subject." Adams's rejoinder is revealing: "But we're singing for pleasure, and we're singing as artists. Besides, I can't wait thirty years!" Adams loved the chansons: "they end," he said, "with their tails in the air."[1]

For Adams, what we now call the interdisciplinary was the sensible satisfaction through scholarship of curiosity; its aim was knowledge. He had at last given over the notion, so dear to his earlier career, that knowledge might lead to power, particularly his own knowledge to his own power. He had settled for the pleasures of understanding and the satisfactions of exclusivity: "They are fascinating," he wrote of the songs, "and like the glass-windows, their contemporaries, all our own for no one else will ever want to hear them." Adams's medievalism, like that of his American contemporaries, was elitist and taken up as a way of coping with modern America. He sought the pleasure of the past, a refined and exclusive pleasure, a pleasure that might set him off from the encroaching crowds of modern mass society and give him a language in which to converse and by which to distinguish the chosen few.

Henry Adams, it should be remembered, was also a powerful observer of the modern. He could not look at the modern, however, without keeping the medieval in his mind's eye—as contrast, as measure. He was not a nostalgist. Rather, he was a sublime fantasist who knew that to have the modern meant more than having the new. One had to know what had been new and once been known, what the future had once seemed, what had once beguiled, in order to keep human energies up to snuff. He may himself have come to prefer the medieval to the modern, but his preference was buttressed with scholarship. Somehow the medieval might make the modern bearable and comprehensible.

Henry Adams was by no means the only memorable American beguiled with the medieval. Walt Disney put a stamp on the American fantasy with his unforgettable image of fantasyland. Sleeping Beauty's castle enshrines what peeks out at us from the mock crenellations, moats, and towers of a thousand mansions, apartment houses, universities, libraries, franchised eateries, in the medieval themes of American programmatic architecture, cutting across the lines of public and domestic, institutional and personal, relevant and inappropriate, sturdy and flimsy, jailhouse or pleasure dome. Would you play miniature golf on a course that lacked a medieval castle and moat?

What I am getting at is that the medieval is a key element of American culture. The American history of the medieval, as you probably know, is an odd one. It forms part of Romanticism's influential history. Adams's felt kinship with Walter Scott, his connections with French medievalists remind us of that story. The American democratic aspect of the story is curious since it occurred and occurs in the absence of the medieval. The European medieval replaced the ancient native civilizations and histories that abounded in North America. How much better to trace American liberties from Anglo-Saxon forests than from the wholesale destruction of native peoples and civilizations. The founding premise of American medievalism is connected to the founding premise of the United States. American liberty, at least since Tocqueville, has been regarded as significant in that the Revolution had no medieval feudal remnant to wipe out. And American medievalism is almost always taken up in some way to supplement the conditions of American civil society—to supply the missing feudal remnant, again not incidentally displacing the remnant of real North American civilizations.

Indeed, to be a medievalist in America is to be part of an interesting and conflicted tradition. Henry James lamented in famous comments about Nathaniel Hawthorne the absence of the shadowy ancient things that make a literature. Hawthorne kept trying to write medieval allegorical fables about the Puritans; they gave good allegory but poor Gothic. Charles Brockden Brown and Edgar Allen Poe borrowed from English Gothic writers and pioneered the location of American fantasies (not to mention paranoias) in the medieval world. Where would American politics have been without the abidingly medieval settings of papist conspiracies? What does it take to make a classic horror movie? Have some nice young Americans wander into Transylvania, that culture-wide metaphor for the medieval, there to encounter horrors, ancient feuds and rituals, things that kill but will not die.

It is a commonplace that the medieval stands for what is missing in the modern. Erecting mock medieval buildings, for instance, suggests stability of lineage and class to a society that shocks the traditional sensibility and undermines traditional notions of hierarchy and wisdom. To enclose learning or worship in a Gothic space is to create a place apart, a token of the old that summons the eternal. Compare such neo-Gothic architecture to Thomas Jefferson's Palladian "Academical Village" at the University of Virginia. American public taste in the nineteenth century became as medieval as its founding taste had been neoclassical. The classical advanced an idea of virtue that was political. The medieval in American society concerned itself with other things, the innards of communal life, the passion for intrigue, the feelings of subservience, the desires for dominance, and the unrational, the not practical, the not purposeful. These traditionally public things the American Constitution and Bill of Rights had rendered private. Prudent self-interest may make a politics but it won't make a culture. Prospering Protestant America wanted the rituals and delights of a more complicated Christianity. The slave-holding South could not content itself with classical allusions and, as the antebellum period drew to a close, the medieval became a favored metaphor for that system, better feudalism than wage slavery. The odd juxtaposition of this with the persistent American anti-Catholic prejudice is resonant with dissonance.

American taste has always proposed itself as an antidote to American reality. Much of it was racialist reactions to the industrialized and the mass produced, Anglophile and Eurocentric strategies of control, a wrinkle in the modern brow. But what is it you get from hamburgers at the White Tower, and how about "a man's home is his castle"? Democracy's association with the ancient and the modern was insufficient to furnish a democratic culture, which contained so many longings for the spiritual, the hierarchical, for the certainties and obligations, for the particular sorts of rationalities and uncertainties that characterized the medieval. It is curious to consider the taste for Dante, be it Charles Eliot Norton's or the one Ruth Draper sends up in "The Italian Lesson," the hopeful, odd need to decorate the spacious with the cloistered, to tell the tale of modern terror as if in a figured Gothic way. These express a true connection to what modern democracy misses. Like the taste for the ancient, the oriental, the African, they exemplify in a wonderfully clear way the amazing American habit of appropriation.

I do not mean to describe the extraordinary scholarship of medieval studies in a parochial way. But it strikes me, as an American cultural historian, how very American is medieval studies and how wonderfully "relevant" its concerns. The American university fulfills a part of the monastic dream of a system to preserve and extend old-fashioned skills and knowledge.[2] I must confess to enjoying the medieval as one flavor of the modern, rather than as a wholesale alternative to it. I am Yankee Doodle enough to realize that I would not have been accorded the privileges of medieval culture whose remnants delight me. Machaut did not write for me; medieval Europe was plenty dangerous for a Jew. I like the modern recreations of medieval performance, its collections of medieval art and artifact, the many modern goofs on medieval art and architecture. But I know that one cannot have the medievalism I enjoy without the medievalism scholars pursue with such ingenuity and dedication. My own "reading" of this medieval studies conference is that it continues Henry Adams's insights that the modern cannot be seen except in constant contrast, that such contrast may be a system of control of what unnerves one, that historical study perforce challenges contemporary disciplinary proprieties, that the medieval has particular qualities we moderns—not to mention postmoderns—miss.

I also know that Henry Adams's chief experience of the medieval was pleasure; the *chanson*, the cult of the virgin, the cathedral enthralled him, but not exactly as they were meant to, which was to hold a person in purposeful thrall. American culture licenses and encourages our pleasures outside of their historical habitats and often out of any semblance to historical reality. One happy result of democratic culture and our university system is the numbers of people who get to know about the subjects and experience the pleasures that were so restricted once upon a time, even if their pleasures strike too many of the most knowledgeable and sophisticated as vulgar, anachronistic, and pointless. I was fortunate to study medieval history in college with Professor Brian Tierney, who inspired me with an interest in the medieval that I have never pursued as a scholar but that has given me continuing pleasure as a person.

I know that the thrills I get from Sleeping Beauty's castle, from T. H. White and *Camelot*, from college architecture, from the Gothic Voices (the English early-music performance group), from my peeks at books of hours are no patch on the more intense devotions of scholars. Nevertheless, I believe that the thriving of the medieval in our culture, as an available taste or passion or occupation or decoration, is one of its success stories. The American history of the medieval began in dissatisfaction but has, I believe, grown into a cultural possibility. All the more reason to resist the pressure to dismantle the medievalist scholarly enterprise, which forms a part of the marginalization of the past that strikes me as the hidden agenda of humanities politics in our day. Our cultural institutions must try very hard to keep up with the energy of our culture's appropriations; even though they frequently try to spoil the joke of it all, they are the only means by which we can grasp the fun of it all.

# ∦ Willie's and Harry's Excellent Adventure

WHAT FLOURISHES in this correspondence is the intimate, fraternal exchange of two remarkably gifted American writers, fascinating for its view of their lives, compelling for its taste of how civilized and alert people shared their impressions and experiences. The letters afford a glimpse of family life in a time when the family as extended kindred clan made more sense than any other affinity. There are also glimpses of what a bygone world seemed like to two brothers on whom nothing was lost. Finally, we have in this volume their last burst of correspondence, a sustained encounter with age and how it does or does not change the aging.

Our interest in the brothers is different from theirs in each other. Reading this correspondence, one is struck by how much they did not have to say to each other, and, often, how little they had to say, how much went without saying, and how much simply did not get said at all. Family was the atmosphere of their letters: homely, intimate, and private. The much-chronicled, fabled James family shared with other unhappy and happy families the round of human relations and domestic events. The William and Henry letters retail their own fascination with each other, their family, and friends, while their achievements, circles of acquaintance, and their articulate, voluble, distinct expression turn our attention to other aspects of their lives.

The things that interest their readers most in William and Henry James make fleeting appearances in their correspondence during these most nobly productive of their years. Around the time of Henry's epochal return visit to the United States in 1904, the brothers seem to have engaged each other more fully and on a broader range of subjects than hitherto, and it is the way in which books, events, old friends, disagreements, combativeness, and their different but incomparable intellectual vigor animate these letters

This was written as an introduction to *The Correspondence of William James*, volume 3, *William and Henry 1897–1910*, edited by Ignas Skrupskelis and Elizabeth M. Berkeley (Charlottesville: University Press of Virginia, 1994) and is reprinted with the permission of the University Press of Virginia. I am especially indebted to Elizabeth Berkeley for her patient and helpful editing and John J. McDermott for his candor and encouragement and for the example of his own work.

that make them remarkable and unusual reading. William James, writing *The Varieties of Religious Experience,* corresponded faithfully with Henry James without telling him much except that he was working on the Gifford lectures, finishing them, delivering them, publishing them: "The absurd Gifford lectures are a bad element. I ought to have done them up brown in six months but, trailing as they do now, I begin to sicken of the subject, and am tired as a man might tire of holding out a weight forever, without being allowed either to actively raise it any higher, or to set it down" (1 January 1901). Henry James writing all the late masterpieces might mention finishing a book—"I finished my book, at last, only last night, with an unutterable 'ouf!'" (22 May 1902)—yet he found no occasion to speak of the subject of his books to his brother. Of course, the reader of these letters comes to them having already met, as it were, the brothers in their works and in books about them.

Their correspondence was not conducted equally with respect to posterity. Henry burned much of his correspondence. William's claim that Henry's letters "are almost all kept for the future historian!" (14 August 1900) probably reflected his expectations for his own. Henry's conscious control of his productions made him glad to suppress his letters just as he was eager to rewrite his books. His eye on posterity was controlling and selective. William, perhaps, contemplated future readers of his letters with equanimity. The brothers acknowledged each other's letters with gratitude and made excuses for their own lapses: "As before, 'details when we meet'; for I am not as good an epistolarian as you, whose pages of effusion to us, considering the market value of every thousand of your words, can only be considered among the marvels of human devotion" (William to Henry, 14 August 1900). Exchanges between the brothers have little in common with the letters to friends and colleagues that form so permanent a part of our literary and intellectual heritage.

Sometimes Henry did rise to his Jamesian epistolary self, especially when making up for an arrears in letters and often when addressing both William and Alice Gibbens James: "How much I feel in arrears with you let this gross machinery testify—which I shamelessly use to help to haul myself into line," he wrote, to explain his typed letter (24 May 1903). William's concerns sometimes spilled over in his letters to Henry; the anti-imperialist diatribe surfaces like flotsam from another cargo: "If war comes, what *shall* we do with Cuba, no one knows. At any rate, it commits us more and more to the hideous old international ornière of the European countries, based on hatred and rapacity" (10 April 1898). Henry characteristically implies agreement with his brother's political views and responds with what the outside world suggests to his always sovereign inner side: "I see nothing but the madness, the passion, the hideous clumsiness of rage, of mechanical reverberation; and I echo with all my heart your denouncement of the foul criminality of the screeching newspapers. They have long since become, for me, the danger that overtops all others" (20 April 1898). But they were not audience one for the other, nor sounding board, nor in the formal sense "correspondents." In this sense, then, the brothers' correspondence must disappoint the modern reader: Art does not speak to Philosophy nor Literature to Psychology here. They were brothers, and these letters have the poignant interest of the last years of their fraternity.

Their joint biography is well rehearsed in the previous introductions to this correspondence. Our story begins in 1897. William's fifty-fifth year was one in which his lifelong vocational search was either resolved or launched in a new path. He made his move from psychology, which had been his way of reconciling medical, moral, and philosophical interests, into philosophy. His professorship was changed from one in psychology to one in philosophy, and he relinquished responsibility for the psychology laboratory at Harvard. More important, he began to think of himself principally as a writer on philosophical subjects. Pragmatism, his radical empiricism, his concern with epistemology took shape in this period. The rest of his professional life followed from this decision—he became a philosopher. When his health began to fail in 1899, he sought to leave teaching but was persuaded to continue. Later, he addressed himself in the public forums available to the modern moral philosopher: international lectureships, public occasions for reflection, and his writing.

Notwithstanding the justifiable importance placed by subsequent readers on James's development of pragmatism, James's forging of his radical empiricism is the key to his philosophical thinking in this period. As John J. McDermott has commented: "To underplay the importance of radical empiricism in any understanding of James is to risk missing him altogether." McDermott isolates the two elements of his thinking: "First, his claim that matter and mind are but functional distinctions; and second, his metaphysical version of the position previously taken in the *Principles,* in which he held we have feelings of the relations which exist between objects of our experience." These concerns emerged as "the central preoccupations of his entire speculative life."[1] In *Pragmatism* James states: "In our cognitive as well as in our active life we are creative. We *add,* both to the subject and to the predicate part of reality. The world stands really malleable, waiting to receive its final touches at our hands. Like the kingdom of heaven, it suffers violence willingly. Man *engenders* truths upon it."[2] The Jamesian thrust resulted from his own battles with nihilism and its engendered despair, his belief in a universe at once in need of and responsive to human action and intelligible to human understanding and, perhaps most influentially, his understanding that both nature in general and the human in particular share the reality of process, however finite they may at any moment seem. His letters to Henry do not explicitly concern these views, but they do record the energy and concentration that went into his thinking and writing and the ambition that went into his presenting of these views. The William James of these letters is, among other things, restless—restless to express and convince and to be believed.

The books and essays that James published in those years tell the story of his accomplishment and his ambition, while his letters provide a record of his travels. He traveled to Europe several times, the Gifford lectures at Edinburgh and the Hibbert lectures at Oxford highlighting what became journeys in search of a cure for his worsening health. He crisscrossed the United States as well. His publications during this period included *The Will to Believe, and Other Essays in Popular Philosophy* (1897), *Human Immortality: Two Supposed Objections to the Doctrine* (1898), *Talks to Teachers on Psychology and to Students on Some of Life's Ideals* (1899), *The Varieties of Religious Experience: A Study in Human Nature* (1902), "Does 'Consciousness' Exist?" and "A World of Pure Experience" (1904), "How Two Minds Can Know One Thing" (1905), *Pragmatism: A New Name for Some Old Ways of Thinking* (1907), *A Pluralistic Universe: Hibbert Lectures at Manchester College on the Present Situation in Philosophy*, and *The Meaning of Truth: A Sequel to "Pragmatism"* (1909), and *Some Problems in Philosophy* (published posthumously in 1911).

Pragmatism and radical empiricism were his contributions to philosophy. He wrote to a friend in 1903: "I am convinced that the desire to formulate truths is a virulent disease. It has contracted an alliance lately in me with a feverish personal ambition, which I never had before, and which I recognize as an unholy thing in such a connection. I actually dread to die until I have settled the Universe's hash in one more book."[3] The William James of these letters may strike the reader as a less collected and self-knowing person than the persona of his public writings.

For Henry James 1897 was a benchmark year. He had survived the commercial disappointments of a fiction-writing career that had begun with the international success of *Daisy Miller* in 1878 and had lodged in the estimable rather than the lucrative. More importantly, he had survived the public disaster of his attempt to find fame and profit as a dramatist. The public humiliation of the premiere of *Guy Domville* in London in 1895, where the audience greeted him with a quarter hour of catcalls, had shaken him to the core, but he emerged from this debacle with his artistic purpose if anything stronger and his memorably personal late style born of himself and responsive to his own ideas of art. The year 1897 also marked his settling in Lamb House in Rye, first with a long-term lease and two years later with a purchase. At fifty-four Henry James had a permanent home, if not a family of his own, and he remained the center of a remarkable group of friends and acquaintances, a sought-after and valued companion. It also appears that James had come to some sort of understanding of his own homosexuality, a recognition of his feelings for a series of young men, principally the sculptor Hendrik Andersen, but including Morton Fullerton, Joceleyn Perse, Percy Lubbock, Hugh Walpole, and others. The late writing, which reflects his deep possession of his own many-faceted soul, was, despite the many disappointments, the work of a supremely self-confident artist.

From 1897 until he stopped writing after William's death in 1910, Henry James wrote "The Turn of the Screw" (1898), *The Awkward Age* (1899), *The Wings of the Dove* (1902), *The Ambassadors* (1903), *The Golden Bowl* (1904), "The Jolly Corner" and *The American Scene* (1907), and the revisions and prefaces for the New York edition of his writings (1907–9). In addition his many stories of this period—"The Beast in the Jungle" (1903), for instance, and his critical and autobiographical writings—form an extraordinary body of work. However controversial their style and limited their immediate commercial appeal, these books established Henry James as a master of English and American literature. These were years also of strain and worry and then, if not quite all of a sudden, of physical decline.

The Henry James who showed his face to his brother in this correspondence, however, was not the elaborate, impenetrable, conscious, and controlling creature of his own life. Henry was always the sweeter of the two brothers. Perhaps at times the more selfish, but certainly the sweeter. He lavished care, for instance, on their sister, Alice, where William did his duty. One senses in this correspondence the subtle, self-effacing participation that Henry had learned as a bachelor who engaged in other people's lives. His letters reveal an immense and fond interest and sympathy in other people's doings that were surely reciprocated by his brother's, but perhaps Henry was more sensitive and more delicate in his empathy and in his second-hand enjoyments. As he aged, Henry's habits became more settled, he traveled less, and, if he had ever really been, was peripatetic no more.

In his last years, William traveled extensively, put his views forward energetically, wrote constantly, and raised the stakes not only of his philosophical positions but of his career as public philosopher and pundit. He plunged into the marketplace of ideas with publications and fulminations. William accepted the responsibility of intellectuals for changing public opinion. Writing to Henry in 1908, he sounded the Jeffersonian note: "Stroke upon stroke, from pens of genius, the competitive regime, so idolized 75 year ago, seems to be getting wounded to death. What will follow will be something better, but I never saw so clearly the slow effect of accumulation of the influence of successive individuals in changing prevalent ideals" (19 December 1908, p. 372). The significance of this move appears in part a willingness to risk the high-mindedness of those two early examples, Ralph Waldo Emerson and Henry James, Sr.

Like Emerson, James took the public podium. His bitter disagreement with the drift of United States public policy and public culture, and his occasionally expressed dislike of Americans and their habits that come through in his letters to Henry, reflect William's unresolved attachment to his role of the intellectual in a democracy made up of those who were not his equals. It produced in him a version of the dilemma it produced in others of his generation, but he was unable to resolve it in the candid elitism of his brother or of Henry Adams, or in the disciplined service to a democracy with the noblesse oblige of Oliver Wendell Holmes, Jr. Putting together his public writings and his letters to his brother reveals a William James caught in the dilemma of American democracy and its abrasions on the vanity and ego of the superior intellect. This sense of his dilemma intensifies the contradiction between his public calls to the ideal and his private discomfort with some aspects of American life and his distaste for many of his fellow Americans. The exchange of letters with Henry in response to the planning of Henry's American trip reveals this interesting situation and is especially valuable as a commentary on William's public positions and Henry's *American Scene.*

William's original comments, from his letter of 3 May 1903, are interesting in themselves for his view of national life, as well as for his projections onto the presumably equally fastidious Henry: "One thing, for example, which would reconcile *me* most easily to abandoning my native country forever would be the certainty of immunity, when travelling, from the sight of my fellow beings at hotels and dining-cars having their boiled eggs bro't to them, broken by a negro, two in a cup, and eaten with butter . . . The *vocalization* of our countrymen is really, and not conventionally, so ignobly awful that the process of hardening oneself thereto is very slow, and would in your case be impossible. It is simply *incredibly* loathsome." The next year William wrote: "The thing is to make good nature & human tolerance your mission, remembering that God made these people and Christ died for them, and that the business-ideals, and ideas of personal comfort which animate them are also part of His plan, as much as your ideals are!" (8 February 1904). As he wrote in another letter about himself, "Between no-scruples & over scruples the path is hard for such as me" (12 July 1905).

Henry and William had great differences. William was a liberal; Henry was not. William liked variety and democracy and had general sympathies, for all his inbred snobbery and ceaseless judging. Concerning the reform movements in New York William could write: "The problems are focussed and dramatized in a superior way. Altogether all this hideous house-cleaning that the American people is going thru, appear to me full of excellent democratic promise" (8 September 1907). William sounded the note of the Jeffersonian democrat in the twentieth century. Henry, although more sympathetic in his dealings with people, was essentially antidemocratic and conservative, less implicated in their modern fallacies and often less likely to view them as intrusive. But his choice of England over America and his aristocratic and literary sympathies made him less and less the American child of New England reform. He appreciated William's commitments but seems not really to have shared them. What aroused Henry to civic action was the world war that made him change his citizenship to English and essentially to take sides among empires. For William, the possibility of the republic, the American republic, a simpler and more respectable time, existed as a lever on present-day politics. He chose a republic over an empire and virtue over commerce, not between empires as Henry did.

In 1897 William gave the oration at the dedication of the Augustus Saint-Gaudens monument to Robert Gould Shaw and the legendary Massachusetts Fifty-fourth Regiment of black soldiers. As someone who had avoided serving in the Civil War, James might have seemed an odd choice. He approached the occasion with the customary mixed feelings, but "now that it is over, I am very glad to have been associated with an occurrence so purely ideal in all respects. It makes me feel more solid, civically, than I have ever felt before" (5 July 1897). It is interesting to speculate on the civic solidity he felt and its connection to his increasing public outspokenness.

William was taking his memorably strong public positions on American imperialism and militarism, and gave a full measure of devotion to ideals that most in his own generation had come to abandon. His letters to Henry reveal how furious with his country's foreign adventurism he was. This social concern made him an intense Dreyfusard and one of those white Americans who recognized the dimension and shame of American racism. In 1903 he sent Henry a copy of W. E. B. Du Bois's *Souls of Black Folk,* urging it upon his brother as "a decidedly moving book" (6 June 1903) and useful reading for his American trip.

Henry, it must be said, did not share his brother's racially progressive views. His letters reflect his backsliding, along with that of most of his generation, from the advanced racial views of the New England abolition and union circles of his youth. This attitude is reflected in his casually insensitive language when he decries a rumor of his engagement to a Miss

Grigsby, calling it as "fantastic & gratuitous a folly" as would be a report of William's daughter Peggy's engagement to Booker Washington, or "that Aleck is engaged to Grace Norton" (6 May 1904). Similarly, during his American trip, he commented on Charleston, South Carolina: "I find poor shabby, niggery blighted Charleston quite *really* southern & balmy & *coloured*—otherwise than niggerishly; with blooming magnolias & throbbing palmettos & flowering camellias—great clumps—& a blue, blue sea" (10 February 1905). Henry's attitude toward race was essentially conventional. Nor was the private William entirely free of prejudice. What strikes one about William was his relative unconventionality on just those issues that had moved his father's career and generation, and equally the strange combination of arrogant self-assertion and genuine principle that stirred him.

"Emerson is exquisite!" wrote William in the spring of 1903:

> The reading of the divine Emerson, volume after volume, has done me a lot of good, and, strange to say has thrown a strong practical light on my own path. The incorruptible way in which he followed his own vocation, of seeing such truths as the Universal Soul vouchsafed to him from day to day and month to month, and reporting them in the right literary form, and thereafter kept his limits absolutely, refusing to be entangled with irrelevancies however urging and tempting, knowing both his strength and its limits . . . seems to me a moral lesson to all men who have any genius, however small, to foster. . . . You too have been leading an Emersonian life— though the environment differs to suit the needs of the different psychophysical organism which you present. (3 May 1903)

Noting a newspaper mention of the Emerson commemoration at which William was to speak, Henry wrote: "Would to God I could sit there entranced by your accents—side by side, I suppose, with the genial Bob! May you be floated grandly over your cataract—by which I don't mean have any manner of *fall*, but only be a Niagara of eloquence, all continuously, whether above or below the rapids. . . . It affects me much even at this distance and in this so grossly alien air—this overt dedication of dear old E. to his immortality. I hope all the attendant circumstances will be graceful and beautiful (and *not* with either Ellen or Edward for the centre of the fire-wheel)" (24 May 1903). This pretty much sums up how the brothers differed over their shared inheritance, William making good, Henry making gentle fun, each in his highly special way devoted.

If Emerson was one magnetic pole of William's vocational life, his father was another, and William's later life brought him closer to the concerns of his father's life, if not to his father's habits or opinions. William stuck by the lights of his father's generation; they were his inheritance and his birthright. His richly productive final years reflect his attention to the problems of the true and the natural, the supernatural and the ideal in the world, and, indeed, the language of truth and the status of the divine in the modern pluralist context that Emerson and Henry Sr. had in their ways explored.

For both brothers work was a key issue. William, complimenting Henry's edition of his work, marvels at "what a colossal worker you are," and not much liking the labor, he again salutes the laborer: "But what astounds me is your power of steady *work*! " (4 February 1908). One wonders if the Jamesian vocational search has not been too much seen in terms of substance and not enough in terms of dedication. Perhaps William and Henry discovered what their father did not, the power and importance of work tied to necessity. And a public. For that was the other discovery of William's later years, the importance of the public. Like Henry—albeit complaining—William sought a reading public; he also relished an audience for his lectures. He had become tired of the classroom, probably because temperamentally he was not much for patient correction but rather one for having his say.

The subject of disease and death, a preoccupation of the James family, became pressingly part of reality for William James. The correspondence with Henry is frequently troubled by William's health problems and his intermittent nervous disorders. Doctors, episodes of angina, the ups and downs of the chronically ill balance his vivid accounts of people, places, seasons, and his activities. His wife and children populate William's letters, and his tone of earnest parenting and amused and critical observation about his children's characters keep him from the morbid gloom that his increasing invalidism might be expected to have highlighted.

But the unhappy facts of his health remained, and his mortality engrossed more of his correspondence and perhaps accounts for the increasing intimacy and openness of his letters to Henry after 1904. It is also worth noting that James's ill health may not always have coincided with his complaints of ill health. He remained what he had always been, someone whose energy and high spirits competed with indisposition and depression. Whatever one's conclusion about the nature of the complaints and the complainer, this correspondence offers the reader an excellent opportunity to take the measure of William James's experience of his own body and spirit. His severe grippe, vertigo, insomnia, and doubts about his decision to keep writing in a popular style surrounded his composing in 1908 of the Hibbert lectures, later published as *A Pluralistic Universe*. How much did illness deter him, how much enable him, and how much were his complaints the necessary exhaust of the engine of his creation? The letters hold no certain answer, of course, but they suggest connections between illness and creativity that might have interested a William James less sunk in his own version.

William's letters reveal that bluff tone of his, candid, direct, unheeding of the feelings of his correspondent, though always repentant when apprised of having hurt somebody's feelings. To Henry he was the least insensitive. Some of his letters to his sister, Alice, make painful reading, although she was quite capable of responding to her big brother, as witnessed in their exchange of July 1891, several months before her death but in the midst of her contemplating it. On 6 July William wrote an extraordinary, self-revealing letter:

> I know you've never cared for life, and to me now at the age of nearly fifty life and death seem singularly close together in all of us—and life a mere farce of frustration in all, so far as the realization of the innermost ideals go to which we are made respectively capable of feeling an affinity and responding. Your frustrations are only rather more flagrant than the rule; and you've been saved many forms of self-dissatisfaction and misery which appertain to such a multiplication of responsible relations to different people as I, for instance, have got into. [He goes on to talk about the new science that will understand "nervous weakness" and his own interest in the psychopathic and spiritual phenomena.] Father would find in me today a much more receptive listener—all that philosophy has got to be brought in. . . . It may seem odd for me to talk to you in this cool way about your end; but, my dear little sister, if one has things present to one's mind, and I know they are present enough to *your* mind, why not speak them out? I am sure you appreciate that best.—How many times I have thought, in the past year, when my days were so full of strong and varied impressions and activities, of the long unchanging hours in bed which those days stood for with you, and wondered how you bore the slow-paced monotony at all, as you did! You can't tell how I've pitied you. But you *shall* come to your rights erelong. Meanwhile take things gently—look for the little good in each day as if life were to last a hundred years. Above all things save yourself from bodily pain, if it can be done: You've had too much of that. Take all the morphia (or other forms of opium if that disagrees) you want, and don't be afraid of becoming an opium-drunkard.[4]

Alice's reply included the following, for she too knew that her brother's tonal limitations did not include deafness to the James family registers: "So when I am gone, pray don't think of me simply as a creature who might have been something else, had neurotic science been born. Notwithstanding the poverty of my outside experience I have always had a significance for myself, & every chance to stumble along my straight & narrow little path, & to worship at the feet of my Deity, & what more can a human soul ask for?"[5]

Like Alice, Henry could give as good as he got, and their letters reduced William to the confines of that extraordinary hothouse arena of their upbringing. It is fascinating to observe how the brothers both were and were not stuck in the patterns of that upbringing. William continued to live the peripatetic life in search of truth that his father had lived and educated the children to live. Unlike William, Henry, having seen his opportunity, took it, and settled in his proper home.

The letters also show how lasting and real the fraternal connection remained. William could make Henry bristle as nobody else could, to wit their exchanges about the financing of Lamb House or Henry's travel plans. William retained the elder brother's capacity to put the younger on the defensive. This was surely compounded by the very different life and very different personal arrangements of each. When William threw cold water on Henry's travel plans, he elicited a remarkably energetic and plaintive response: "You have travelled and gone to and fro—always comparatively!—so often and so much. I have practically never travelled at all—having never been economically able to; I've only gone, for short periods, a few times—so much fewer than I've wanted—to Italy: never anywhere else that I've seen everyone about me here (who *is,* or was, anyone) perpetually making for" (24 May 1903). He goes on at surprising and angry length. But the great reserve of resentment and feeling of deprivation of his due is one to which William James had special if unintentional access.

Writing in the wake of the death of their old friend Francis Boott, about whom he had been critical and from whom they each received a legacy, William had this to say:

> I wish he were back for an hour—that we might congratulate him on the will and hear his laugh over our appreciation. In fact I wish he were back for several hours of more tender and sympathetic communion than life yielded although life yielded plenty that was intimate enough. But the sense of shortcomings seems an inevitable companion of death and makes me resolve that you and I shall hereafter abound and super-abound in every form of flattery and affectionate demonstration, blind to evil, seeing nothing but good, giving credit for ten times more than we see and laying aside that grudging, carping and critical attitude which Alice says is the moral keynote of the James family, [I never did! A.] in spite of other merits which she acknowledges. [adores! A-]. (14 March 1904)

Precipitous, rushing William making resolutions for both of them, annexed Henry without heed into his own sense of what it meant to be a James; but perhaps he was making a real resolution, for the letters do increase in warmth and intimacy, and if the world still gets its lumps, the brothers seem kinder to each other. For Henry, intimacy with William held few of its earlier discomforts, and the letters reflect it. For if William seems the stronger for being forward, Henry's apparent passivity hid recesses of strength. His following had become finally an assent.

Henry's letters sometimes show him experiencing William's blunt views as interfering and judgmental, as they likely were. In response to Henry's plans to visit America, William advised him not to come: "When one is once adapted to an environment the thing is to stay there and not revolutionize one's insides. Where one *is* ought to remain one's Absolute, and one's motto should be 'dwell deep.' One can't do that in more than one country, so *stay* where you are. More than ever do I feel now that the crudity of America, once left behind, would do nothing but shock you" (21 September 1901).

Henry had his ways of coping with William's interference and his judgmental pronouncements. Henry was clearly William's equal and he as well as William acknowledged this. When he received an angry response from Henry, the repentant William replied:

> I hasten to retract all my dampening remarks, now that I understand the motives fully. The only ones I had imagined, blindling that I am, were fraternal piety and patriotic duty. Against those I thought I ought to proffer the thought of "eggs" and other shocks, so that when they came I might be able to say that you went not unwarned. But the moment it appears that what you crave is millions of just such shocks & that a new lease of artistic life, with the lamp of genius fed by the oil of twentieth century American life is to be the end and aim of the voyage, all my stingy doubts wither, and are replaced by enthusiasm that you are still so young-feeling, receptive, and hungry for more raw material and experience. It cheers me immensely, and makes me feel more so myself. (6 June 1903)

In their writing they aimed differently. Where William had high standards, he also saw himself in the tradition of plain and exacting discourse aimed at a vigorous reading public. Voltaire's reading public might have suited him, also Franklin's and Emerson's. He never understood Henry's chosen company of writers, like Flaubert or Turgenev, for whom the immediate public was a possible but not decisive stand-in for posterity. William aimed at particular audiences, his peers and his public, and surely hoped that his works would last; but he was impatient and iconoclastic. He had ideas and wanted them to be believed.

Henry's relation to the reader was more complicated and in some ways much less yielding. His late style seems bent on imposing not convincing. But he was also a writer unto himself who kept more and more to his own train of thinking and writing, where William still expected that his writing would be judged by the clarity with which it conveyed its ideas. It seems paradoxical perhaps, but for all the exchanges of letters where William's fondness cannot hide his impatience and his peremptory issuing of his judgments, the steel of Henry's artist's voice shows through his surface warmth in a way that William's never could. One cannot imagine Henry saying as William did: "*Writing* is the genuine way for me to work off my energy" (22 October 1905).

One aspect of Henry's life and one that must affect our reading of their letters was his sexual orientation. There appears little doubt that Henry James was what was just beginning to be called homosexual and that were he living in our more open age, he might well have ventured his orientation in an open way. In addressing such subjects, one risks anachronism and the violation of Henry James's own deepest understandings. To call someone of his generation and his extreme reticence *gay* is to make a point about him that has more importance for us than it may have had for him. Historical outing serves many purposes, but to elide the private, the reticent, the closeted, and the ambiguous into a categorical identity, as contemporary discourse almost forces one to do, is not necessarily the best way to understand Henry James. Nevertheless, James's sexuality, and the largely homophobic speculation about it, has been a significant element in biographical discussions of him and critical discussions of his work. James's indirect albeit interested writing about sexuality and James's own sexuality have been confused. In this context the concerns of contemporary clarity or anachronism may reinvigorate our capacity to understand James in terms unlikely to have been agreeable to him.

There is no need to think Henry James unsexual or sexually dysfunctional. He was, as most would have been in his situation, sexually discouraged and perhaps sufficiently so as to be unwilling to act sexually. He was surely not comfortable with his minority orientation, not really willing to discuss it, and not convinced that it was a moral possibility for him. The evidence of his life and writings suggests that he became more comfortable with his feelings as he got older. His circle included homosexual men (like Howard Sturgis's Queen's Acre menage), and whatever he did about it, Henry James indulged his feelings for some younger men by attaching them. His most recent reliable biographer, Fred Kaplan, concludes that he was not prepared to take his feelings into the physical.[6] But by the time of the correspondence in this volume, Henry James was not unaware of his love for men and perhaps had become selective about hiding an orientation he was not really prepared to enact.

In this regard certain letters between the brothers are poignant and significant. William was hardly the person to help his brother "come out." William's bluntness and his judgmental side must only have wounded Henry's confidences, should the younger brother have been tempted to venture them, which is unlikely. In such a time, one could, after all, come out only into the closet of the discreet same-sex life of women and men with the same orientation—newly diagnosed as *homosexual*. By this time in his life, Henry may have come out into this closet, which allowed, at the very least, for some sentimental friendship, some passionate yearning, and some good companions.

Henry was not about to reveal his inner struggles to his loving but morally often conventional brother, a brother who, after all, concluded that his son William didn't bring home his Parisian artwork because of all the nudity. William and Henry may have shared the same view of homosexuality as an openly led way of life. They were also both gentlemen and discreet in the old-fashioned way, and for all their closeness, indeed because of it, attentive to what we would call boundaries. William was more likely to violate Henry's boundaries in border raids of bossiness. Henry's care about such crossings gives us clues to his own determination not to be violated, especially in an area such as his sexuality.

Two letters appear to concern Henry's situation. William's of New Year's Day 1901 mentions that "your friend H. C. Andersen called the other day. Alice saw him and fell in love. I haven't seen her so pleased with anyone for a long time." Is this William's way of acknowledging Henry's special friend, the man he was in love with? Then there is Henry's extraordinary letter of 6 May 1904, disclaiming any engagement to Miss Grigsby, who is, "I believe, a Catholic, a millionaire & a Kentuckian, & gives out that she is the original of the 'Milly' of my fiction *The Wings of the Dove,* published before I had ever heard of her apparently extremely silly existence." Not content with dismissing the rumor, Henry insists that any engagement is as likely as miscegenation (Peggy's engagement to Booker Washington). That is revealing. He concludes his letter "always your hopelessly celibate even though sexagenarian Henry." Who is to say how celibate? But clearly it mattered to Henry that William saw him as single and celibate, even as he indicated in some confused way that his engagements of the heart would bear resemblance to another case of forbidden love that law and society named unnatural along with the kind he would have preferred.

Although it is hard to think of Henry James speaking directly to anyone *about* the feelings, what one knows from his letters to Andersen and others was his capacity to express his feelings with directness and warmth. The whole matter of James's late style can be seen in some ways as his response to what he had come to know about himself. Ralph Touchett in *The Portrait of a Lady* and Olive Chancellor in *The Bostonians* could be written in a relatively straightforward manner because, although they may read gay to us, they would not have been taken that way in a world where one simply did not take people that way, because, and the evidence of his developing self-consciousness supports this, Henry James did not yet take himself this way.

The late style is coincident with Henry's unmistakable discovery in himself of the something he had at once to venture and to hide, a kind of self-knowledge that had to be hedged about elaborately lest what it was really exploring and venturing be revealed. Remember too that it was Alfred Douglas's letters to Oscar Wilde that convicted Wilde; even today much of the evidence for prosecutions of homosexuals is in writing. William's aggressiveness about Henry's late style might be seen as his knocking on the door of his brother's closet, but I don't think so. William understood as much of Henry's situation as Henry was prepared to let him. He sympathized with Henry's being alone and supported him in his attempt to make a stable domestic life. For all William's concerns about finances, he recognized how important Lamb House was for Henry and supported his need to have his own place, the center of his own life. He willingly shared his own children with his brother and knew two things about that sharing: that he was doing his children a favor and that he was giving his brother what his brother hadn't got, a family of his own to care about and nurture.

The letters reveal that what concerned Henry about William was William's health and the health and doings of his family, their family and friends, and the chunks of world they shared and had known together. What concerned William about Henry was his health, his financial security, and his career. The brothers and sister-in-law—for Alice Gibbens James was very much included by Henry in his letters to William—concentrated on exchanges about their daily lives, commotions, and movements: endless details and arrangements, who is to be where, when, and on what errands, large and small. There is no sustained literary or philosophical discussion here, slight narratives rather, and seldom much more than remarks about people and events. It is the correspondence of two surviving siblings; their brother Robertson existed only as ill-met, worry-making Bob.

Bob led an alcoholic's unhappy life (1846–1910) that shadowed the happier ones of his older brothers. Like his companion in family resentment, Wilky (Garth Wilkinson), and, in her own way, sister Alice, Bob suffered from the uneven shares of love, luck, and attention in their famous family. Bob's alcoholism received little of the sustaining sympathetic interest that his elder brothers lavished on their own and each other's complaints. One of the delights of this correspondence is the brothers' mutual chewing over of Fletcherism. The American nutritionist Horace Fletcher's system of chewing all one's food into liquid pulp to ensure bodily and especially digestive health was William's gift to Henry.

I am sending you a book by Horace Fletcher, with certain passages marked for you to read. Every word is true about it. You are in a very favorable situation for learning his art of chewing, which he says it takes a good three months for a man to acquire automatically. It may make a great revolution in your whole economy, however, and I advise you to give it your most respectful attention. I am quite sure that it meets my case to a T, and I am going to try to become a muncher, as he is. He is a very charming man, has made a fortune at business, and owns a palazzo on the Grand Canal in Venice, where he keeps his family. (1 January 1904)

Henry took to it and his letters (and telegrams!) about his pursuit of Fletcherist regularity, his reading of the man's words, his encounters with Fletcher are a charming subplot of the larger theme of systemic disorder. Bob's own Fletcherizing was more interesting to his brothers than his depression, let alone his alcoholism. William in particular, although he shouldered the responsibility of Bob, tended to be judgmental and even harsh. Henry's sweeter nature did not necessarily indicate much understanding. They never got beyond the notion that Bob's drinking was something to be moralized over.

Robertson James was a sometime subject of his brothers' correspondence, toward the end particularly. In ways that suggest his fundamental alliance with William, despite his more emotional expression, Henry responded to some happier news of their brother: "Also I've been overjoyed at your reports & at Alice's, of your happy impression of Bob. It brings tears to my eyes to think of him at last in quiet waters—if they *be* waters unadulterated. Heaven grant he be truly a spent volcano" (17 October 1907). The next year William wrote of dining with Bob and his wife, Mary: "Bob's hair is quite white, & he's grown a white beard, clipt short. Also lost flesh, in consequence of fletcherizing, since a most violent attack of indigestion which he had a month ago. He was very grave and not very genial. Mary more at ease than usual, plump, & looking like a rosebud. She escorted us to the Edward Emerson's, and told me on the way that Bob had occasional sprees in Boston, but they didn't outlast one day; she says his life is absolutely monotonous, his only recreation being reading. He looked more normal than for many a year" (15 November 1908).

A year later, Henry reported his first word from Bob in some years, "which I immediately & rejoicingly answered." The communication was "humorous & fairly friendly, but queer & latently vicious or invidious—all, however, in a harmless & sad & imaginable way (as out of the bitter depths of a consciousness of comparative failure & obscurity—comparative to you & me, with our 'literary talent' &c!) which moves me to nothing but tender & unexpressible (not quite *in*expressible!) compassion for the image of narrowed-down savourless life that he presents. Little has he too reduced himself to having either to give or to take!" (31 October 1909). It is troubling how easily the older brothers managed to continue the family pattern of dismissing their younger brother. Bob was surely a trial to them, to himself, and to his own family, but there is something less toughloving than selfish that he seemed to bring out in his brothers. Indeed the sense that there was not enough love to go around, not enough attention for more than two brothers, if for them, persists. The James family notoriously noticed its sick children more than its healthy ones, and the correspondence between Henry and William retains suggestions that their earliest patterns persisted into their last days and that Bob suffered for this.

The eager love Henry gave to his nephews and niece is fully acknowledged in these letters. On 17 October 1907, he wrote William: "But it's into the status of your children that I throw myself most, & into all that it must say to you & to Alice to have them so interesting & so valuable. It says indeed almost as much to *me* as it can to you both! What you speak of as to Bill as you find him on his return is most truly felt: he strikes me as essentially & intensely *entire*. And it's all right to be entire if it doesn't mean you're prematurely concluded. He has visibly great power of growth. Harry is a blessing to me 'all the time'—of Harry I can't trust myself to speak. And will you tell Aleck that I am hovering on the very brink of answering a Delicious Letter I've just had from *him*? I owe one, as I have said, to Peg as well, but hers shall go straight to Bryn Mawr. *She* sounds most handsome & precious."

It is a remarkable and happy thing to think of how generous was William's sharing of his own family with his bachelor brother. The letters show how Alice and William and Henry shared a parenting interest in the boys and Peggy. If there is anything happy about Henry's death in 1916, it is the knowledge that his last years were comforted by the filial attentions of William's children and that, as William wished, Alice Gibbens James attended him in his final illness.

If the brothers shared a private language, it was surely the language of sickness. It is a commonplace that the James family viewed ill health as a currency; indisposition gave a child purchase and at least momentary attention and pride of place. Their youthful invalidism was long past, and William and Henry led active, vigorous lives. But as they aged, real ill health triggered the old family discourse of digestion, dyspepsia, disease, and degeneration. The ills and their cures engross these letters, and, despite the real claims of William's heart troubles and Henry's digestive unhappiness, they fall into talk of sickness as if into an old familiar tune. Many, many letters allude politely to some indisposition of the other's and, although they only sometimes respond to each other's work in detail, ill health invariably elicits answer, suggestion, commiseration, comparison, and too many registers of response to name here.

Of course the correspondence in this volume is, as were their lives, shadowed by William's declining health. It was real enough, but it also partook of his lifelong emotional troubles. The point is that the real response by either James as to how they were was a self-conscious discourse on their systems as much as their feelings, thoughts, and doings. For them, their insides, their inner selves, and their indwelling genius were all of an organic piece.

"But my nerves have all gone to pot," wrote William from Italy on New Year's Day 1901, "& I really feel 'kind o' OLD,' as the Adirondack guides say when they wake up in the morning after a night of tending the campfire. My *intellectual* vitality seems for the first time to have given out. . . . The fact is that my nervous system is utter trash, and always was so. It has been a hard burden to bear all these years, the more so as I have seemed to others perfectly well; and now it is on top and 'I' am under. However, I shall win through after a fashion, and in six months, under home conditions, I shall doubtless become very different." William's nerves have proved a subject in themselves, and these letters sadly trace the displacement of his nerves by his deteriorating heart. His comments on spas, doctors, and cures are wonderfully alert, keenly critical, and, best of all, full of that very suspension of disbelief he urged upon the world in some of his greatest writings. Writing to Henry in the familiar language of sickness and health must have been a relief for William, who seemed so well to so many.

For his part, Henry was plagued by digestive disorders and complained of them regularly and in surprising detail. He welcomed William's commiseration and suggestion, although he was quick to resent any attribution on his brother's part of his indisposition to nervous illness. Writing in 1901 he paid tribute to shared invalidism and their shared nurse, William's Alice: "I marvel at your courage in being able to think of such heroics without the support of Alice—while I, who have no right to her, whine for her like a babe." He looked forward to being together again: "It will do me unutterable good to see you & have you with me—& every benefit I can lavish upon you I will lavish to the *comble*." Then, in reply to William's diagnosis, he went on in a testier vein:

My illness had no more to do with a "nervous breakdown" than with Halley's comet: I *had* no nervous break-down whatever—& no reason to have one. It came from the rebellion of my intensely enfeebled & perverted stomach under the shock of the antidote that had become vitally imperative in the way of the resumption of normal mastication &c again—& which, the vitiation having the deep-seatedness of so many years, has had to be mortally slow to ebb. It had, & needed, no other genesis whatever. I *became* agitatedly nervous (like our poor Alice of other years, a little!) under the depression & discouragement of relapses & sufferings. . . . I am your poor clinging old Brother always Henry James. (15 March 1910)

Their symptoms were their productions, and the brothers displayed their different aesthetics and boundary consciousness in this most intimate commerce as in all their others. Description cannot do justice, however, to these exchanges and their significance, as the fraternal narrative begun in childhood ended only with the shock of William's death. Part of the interest of the brothers' exchanges about cures and doctors is their reminder of how grounded the James family was in the historical experience of what one might call the First New Age, that period of investigation of eastern philosophy, domestic and nutritional reform, and all manner of experimentation that accompanied the antebellum reform movements.

Their roots were in that time of self-discovery and far-flung enthusiasm. William stayed there and parapsychology continued to be part of his work. Henry, despite the satirical undertones of *The Bostonians,* was also prone to enthusiasm of this sort. The brothers' exchange of letters in the wake of a spiritual happening to Alice Gibbens James is curious. As William wrote: "The episode of the message so exactly hitting your mental conditions is very queer. There is *something* back there that shows that minds communicate even those of the dead with those of the living, but the costume, so to speak, and accessories of fact, are all symbolic and due to the medium's stock of automatisms—what it all means I dont know but it means at any rate that the world that our 'normal' consciousness makes us of is only a fraction of the whole world in which we have our being" (6 April 1906).

The correspondence takes many curious turns: travel, seasonal observation, remarks about people, writers, the great and the not so great. The San Francisco earthquake found William and Alice on the spot and Henry frantic about them, and the ensuing exchange of letters of April and May of 1906 makes exciting reading. William's letter introducing George Santayana to Henry's notice in 1897, his acute estimate of Charles Eliot Norton (24 January 1909), and Henry's comments on almost anybody are worth savoring. As they aged, however, the sense one has is of a tighter grip on the America of their youth, and their shared regrets about "progress." America's progress was easier on Henry James, for whom America was a subject now, not a home. For William, American history was almost cruel, but nothing could sink his buoyancy once he was engaged in a subject.

The letters have much to reveal about that vexing question of how the brothers regarded each other's work. The evidence is here for the reader's delight. By way of introduction it is best to suggest that the excerpts that have so prominent a place in the critical and biographical writing are best seen in their proper context. Henry could write: "You surely make philosophy more interesting & living than any one has *ever* made it before, & by a real creative & undemolishable making; whereby all you write plays into *my* poor 'creative' consciousness & artistic vision & pretension with the most extraordinary suggestiveness & force of application & inspiration. Thank the powers—that is thank *yours!*—for a relevant & assimilable & *referable* philosophy, which is related to the rest of one's intellectual life otherwise & more conveniently than a fowl is related to a fish" (31 October 1909; see also 18 July 1909).

It is remarkable how Henry pronounces what so many of his brother's readers still feel for his philosophical writings. One does not doubt the sincerity surrounding the acuteness by noting how little relevant to Henry's own thinking William's actually was. One can take Henry's comments about pragmatism two ways and both serve admirably: "I was lost in the wonder of the extent to which all my life I have . . . unconsciously pragmatised" (17 October 1907). How different from William's reading of Henry this is, after all, is not so certain, although the means of expression is as different as they were.

William's reading of Henry is more widely known, perhaps because his reading represents that large body of readers who would like to like Henry's books and keep thinking they used to be better when they were written more straightforwardly. Reading *Roderick Hudson* in the New York edition in 1908, William wrote: "My brain could hardly understand anything, much *less* enjoy, but it bro't back the old charm. What a colossal worker you are, to have gone all over it verbally again! I am not sure either, that in *that* case at all events, it was not labor lost, or that the simpler and more naive phrasing of the original edition doesn't keep a better harmony. But what astounds me is your power of *steady* work!" (4 February 1908). The preface to *The Wings of the Dove,* William wrote, "throws much psychologic light on your creative processes," but he is reading Plutarch, "one of the modernest of books" (31 May 1909). "In spite of my denunciations of your later works," the proud William wrote in 1907, "I find them admired on every side, and often by prosy people from whom I should least have expected it" (8 September).

The famous exchange in 1905 about *The Golden Bowl* may strike the reader of this correspondence as more good-humored and testing than truly rivalrous, and surely as less hostile than when it is excerpted or anthologized. Writing that he had read *The Golden Bowl* "a month or more ago," William confessed that

> it put me, as most of your recent long stories have put me, in a very puzzled state of mind. I don't enjoy the kind of "problem," especially when as in this case it is treated as problematic (viz. the adulterous relations betw. Ch. & the P), and the method of narration by interminable elaboration of suggestive reference (I dont know what to call it, but you know what I mean) goes agin the grain of all my own impulses in writing; and yet in

spite of it all, there is a brilliancy and cleanness of effect, and in this book especially a high toned social atmosphere that are unique and extraordinary. Your methods & my ideals seem the reverse, the one of the other—and yet I have to admit your extreme success in this book. But why won't you, just to please Brother, sit down and write a new book, with no twilight or mustiness in the plot, with great vigor and decisiveness in the action, no fencing in the dialogue, no psychological commentaries, and absolute straightness in the style? Publish it in my name, I will acknowledge it, and give you half the proceeds. Seriously, I wish you *would*, for you; and I should think it would tempt you, to embark on a "fourth manner." You of course know these feelings of mine without my writing them down but I'm "nothing if not" outspoken. (22 October 1905)

Henry's rejoinder: "I mean . . . to try to produce some uncanny form of thing, in fiction, that will gratify you, as Brother—but let me say, dear William, that I shall greatly be humiliated if you *do* like it, & thereby lump it, in your affection, with things, of the current age, that I have heard you express admiration for & that I would sooner descend to a dishonoured grave than have written" (23 November 1905).

The Master was able to enjoy playing at younger brother and the elder had certainly recognized in his Harry the genius he claimed, however much he wished the boy would say it straight out! Their final allegiance was most deeply personal. As William wrote in 1899: "We live and learn; and even I live as if a slave to family affections! Local affections I have too, and patriotic ones, though the latter now-a-days have bitter bread to eat" (21 June 1899).

Speculation about the brothers' relationship has become a staple of critical and biographical discussion. Probably almost everything that has been surmised is true. Theirs was a kaleidoscopic relation, in which all the colors and shapes of life and feeling were refigured. If it is possible to judge from these letters, William was disclosing if not especially revealing, while Henry was really neither. William appears to say what he thinks and feels, content to be sorry after having wounded or overstepped. Henry had ready a lifetime of caution and strategy. So they stayed elder and younger to the end. What is unmistakable in these letters, however, was shared devotion, loyalty, interest, and love. Their last years found them sharing affection, many observations, and, all in all, a complacent and proud mutual regard. But it is the particular mystery of this epistolary narrative for the reader to piece out who these men were, what their relationship was, how they really felt about each other. The evidence is here for the many conclusions to be drawn, and of course one may draw them, safe in the knowledge that our answers occurred to William and to Henry James at one time or another.

Their correspondence ended, alas, before the story did. In August 1910, William, Alice, and Henry returned to William's New Hampshire retreat in Chocorua. William knew he was dying and asked Alice, who tended to him herself resolutely, to "go to Henry when his time comes." Son Harry was off on a "much needed" shooting and hunting holiday and had to be called home, too late to see his father alive. The night of 26 August, according to Alice, "William died just before 2:30 in my arms. I was coming in with milk and saw the change. No pain at the last and no consciousness. He had [had] morphine. Since Wednesday at 6:30 without intermission. Two weeks ago we sailed for home. Poor Henry, poor children." Gay Wilson Allen's biography of William continues the story: "She had lifted William's head from the pillow and was supporting him when the end came. Next day she was too sad and exhausted to make any entry in her diary, but on Sunday wrote: 'Wonderful beauty of the dear face!' Billy photographed it, and then made a plaster mask. Dr. George Shedd performed an autopsy, and Alice summarized the results in her diary: 'Acute enlargement of the heart. He had worn himself out.'"[7]

It is hard to imagine a more fulfilled and fulfilling life than William's in his later years. His was not ripe old age, but he had realized many of his ambitions and his hopes. The world paid attention as he spoke his extraordinary mind. He cut a grand public figure and a canny one as well, forming himself as he formed his prose into something the professional and middle classes as well as scholars might enjoy and attend to. What makes William James so compelling as one reads his letters to Henry is his candor, his directness, and his range. He took little refuge in style, although he was often funny and wonder-struck, loving and angry, merry, shrewd, and incensed. He took in a universe of inflections without surrendering his vigorous directness—that rushing forward to meet the day that Henry had observed long ago, lagging behind him when they were boys, never catching up.

The boy in the man in the husband in the father in the philosopher in the son in the brother is William James complete and perhaps never more so than in his late letters to Henry. For all their lack of sustained argument, they catch the play of his mind in the quality of his observations, in the vigor and, yes, the beauty of his prose. For nobody brought out the beauty in William James like the company and the challenge of his beauty-loving younger brother Henry. They could be artists together. They could rehearse together the universal individuality of their unformed youth in their father's hopeful eye. Even William's universal genius fell short of that man's imaginings for his dear boys. And together at the last, as these letters show, William found in Henry that warming early hopeful glow.

Henry's last letter to William had to be written to someone else, their dear old friend Grace Norton, as it happened. He had begun it feeling weak "at the prospect of losing my wonderful beloved brother out of the world in which, from as far back in dimmest childhood, I have so yearningly always counted on him, I feel nothing but the abject weakness of grief and even terror" and added this postscript: "I open my letter of three hours since to add that William passed unconsciously away an hour ago— without apparent pain or struggle. Think of us, dear Grace—think of us!"[8] We still do.

# ⚡ Fish Out of Water: George Santayana

GEORGE SANTAYANA made himself anything but plain in his writings. Even when be was memorably, aphoristically direct, he toyed with the contrary, the piquing, the enigmatic, the confounding, and got into the habit of regarding even his own obscurity as an emblem of his integrity, as his boast. He meant it to be impossible to lay a glove on him. Santayana is better remembered for some of what he had to say than for anything particular about him or his long life (1863–1952). He was born in Spain to Spanish parents, who were also steeped in the middle echelons of Spanish imperial life in the Philippines. Santayana's mother was the widow of a Boston scion of the Anglo–New England merchant-prince Sturgis connetion who left the five-year-old George with his father in Spain and returned to Boston to raise her three Sturgis children, George's half-siblings. At nine, George joined her in America, where he was educated in the best Boston manner and experienced what was to be his lifelong position as an insider outsider, welcome by virtue of his birth and his talents within the precincts of societies to which he could never feel that he belonged by right.

Santayana's salad days came as an undergraduate at Harvard, where he drew, wrote poetry, discovered the study of philosophy, made warm friendships, and settled on the tone he was to take throughout his life. He stayed on to study with William James, Josiah Royce, and others in that golden age of American academic philosophizing. He distinguished himself in his studies—and, in his attitude toward them, from his teachers. He began to sound a characteristic note of joyous disdain for ordinary philosophical practice early on. He rose to the rank of professor, and acquired a following of his own.

The confidential report of Harvard's redoubtable, modernizing President Eliot concerning Santayana's promotion to assistant professor in 1897

---

This essay is based on a review that first appeared in the *London Review of Books* of *The Works of George Santayana*, vol. 1, *Persons and Places*, ed. William Holzberger and Herman Saatkamp (Cambridge, Mass.: MIT Press, 1987) and *George Santayana: A Biography* by John McCormick (New York: Knopf, 1987).

suggests the problem he posed to his conventional fellows, a problem he himself understood as a challenge:

> The withdrawn, contemplative man who takes no part in the everyday work of the institution, or of the world, seems to me a person of very uncertain value. He does not dig ditches, or lay bricks, or write school-books, his product is not of the ordinary, useful, though humble kind. What will it be? It may be something of the highest utility; but, on the other hand, it may be something futile, or even harmful because unnatural and untimely.[1]

Harvard came to value him, but his career was marked by those key terms "unnatural and untimely." At forty-eight, having come into an inheritance, Santayana resigned his professorship and left America, spending the second half of his life wandering in Europe, where he ended up living in his famous refuge with the Blue Nuns in Rome.

Santayana wrote poetry up to the point when, as he said, his muse deserted him (one senses that it was his candor that deserted his muse). He wrote several philosophical inquiries, works of literary criticism, and books on the history of philosophy. He developed and, in his view, perfected a philosophical system in several big books, written over many years. He was also, memorably, an essayist, whose observations about America (*Character and Opinion in the United States* and *The Genteel Tradition in American Philosophy*), Germany (*Egotism in German Philosophy*), and England (*Soliloquies in England*) are classics of their kind. He even had an American literary success in the late 1930s with his novel *The Last Puritan,* and finally became, with *Persons and Places,* one of the century's most interesting autobiographers. All his books bear the unmistakable stamp of his stylish, witty, rather formal English prose and abound with original and provocative remarks, keenly observed and gracefully phrased, memorable gleanings from whatever the subject at hand brought to his extraordinary mind.

In his own day, Santayana had many admirers and readers, although the assurance and insolence with which he sought his own way irritated his more earnest philosophical fellows. His contempt for their science, their systems, their colleges and their schools, their politics, their logic, their pretensions, caused him to be at best uneasily regarded by the run of his colleagues, and he took care to ensure that no one ever mistook him for one of them. Having decided that difference was his natural lot, Santayana turned it to his advantage. He claimed to consider every topic, including the topics of philosophy, from outside the prevailing conventions. At the very moment when philosophy was questioning its own sources of power and generalization, everywhere asking, What do we mean when we say this? Santayana seized with maddening confidence the very ground his fellows were scrupulously deserting. He restored the delightful to philosophy at a time when philosophy had ceased to be something someone might want to do in the regular course of a civilized life, on a sunny day, in a beautiful place, in good company, with a light heart, confident of being the better for the pleasure of it.

Santayana preferred to live on his own, associating with friends, attractive men, talented, cultivated, curious, wealthy people, predominantly expatriate Americans, migrating rather than nesting. His understanding of the philosophical life borrowed from the peripatetic and the gentlemanly. He divided his time, as he did his mild allegiances, between the Latin and northern countries. He lived most happily in Spain and Italy, but was most absorbed by America and England, absorbed and attracted, rebuffed and rebuffing.

His old and New English sojourns and acculturation gave him an unnatural perspective on his *patria*. In turn, the perspective his *patria* gave him on the lands of his adoption was critically important. He really did see things about America, and perhaps also about England, in a way that few others have done.[2] He came to America and England, to modern life, from a medieval setting in Avila, where his best chance of getting on would have been to join a Spanish establishment, against the received Enlightenment wisdom of his father. Santayana saw through his father's dogmatic liberalism, while also being prevented by his emigration and his nature from taking up the conventional Spanish life in automatic Oedipal reaction. He was thrown from his mother's narrow perch into the commercial and cultural capital of a new imperium, without being able to make its cause his own: America, after all, won its imperial spurs from Spain while Santayana was in early middle age. He was himself an unconvinced Roman Catholic and found himself in a situation where his Spanish nativity and his identity as a Catholic were always more defining to others than either ever was to him. Within the life of the Sturgis clan, he was a secondary relation of poor relations. To be on the fringe, even of the center, was his fate.

Santayana spent his formative intellectual years as a foreign student in a New England that was branching out and dying out. The old New England fierceness that had made so much of American commerce and culture was being supplanted by the large energies, capitalist rather than commercial, democratic rather than genteel, which the world has come to know so well. Santayana was so placed, almost uniquely, as to regret ancient traditions without sentimentalizing them, to criticize modern conditions without refusing to live in them. His loyalties were diluted as well as divided, and he was alienated in one way or another from them all. He came early to a powerfully defensive insight into whatever might lay claim to him. In his clear-eyed way he refused to substitute one allegiance for another, refused to fantasize, as Henry Adams did or Walter Pater, the substitution for the present of some past. He was as detached from what he cherished as from what he criticized. Neither the present nor the past struck Santayana as susceptible of improvement. The laughter in his books is seldom compromised by huffiness or sentimentality—nor, it must be owned, by passion.

Santayana's upbringing holds a clue to his distinctive attitudes. *Persons and Places* recounts the origins of his cosmopolitan detachment in his odd childhood. He was alienated within his family, finding early a stubborn sense of his natural individuality as a condition of separation, isolation, and difference. Santayana's tone about his family is of a piece with his other writing. The more intimate the subject, the cooler his depiction. The portraits of his father and mother and his sister Susanna are remarkable for their chilly appraisal and their rendering of mixed emotion. No doubt Santayana detached himself from the control and potential stunting of his family circumstances, but he retained what must have been an impressive set of childhood defenses against the incursions of his crowding, indifferent family. The burning resentments abated but remained. As in his writings about America and philosophy, one senses in *Persons and Places* the anger that fuels the detachment, energizes the achievement, protects the child, distinguishes the man.

Reading Santayana, one has little sense of change or development. He was an old youngster and a young ancient. As a young man, his writings sometimes have the feeling of premature wisdom, beyond precocity: how could anyone so young have known what he knew? As an old man, he retained a freshness of response that survived his failing physical powers and kept him to the end interested in whatever there was that was new to him, which he also knew was not new under the sun. That his detachment was his protection was something he understood. That it was founded in his childhood he knew too. That it harbored his resentments, that it nurtured his hurts, that it replaced participation and avenged him on the world, he would not allow, for Santayana claimed that the world did not touch him, that it did not matter to him.

In accounting for his peculiar perspective, Santayana did not address his homosexuality. His autobiography is not coy about his attraction to men. His biographer, John McCormick, concludes that he was homosexual but was, for sound social and personal reasons, unwilling to risk what was in his day at best a precarious preference. To that repression McCormick attributes the distant tone of Santayana's writing, especially his poetry:

One conclusion about his early experience of sexual passion, whether consummated or not, is that he became frightened of the power of sexuality, and that Spanish canniness, and the classical invocation to "Know thyself" led him away from sexual luxury. By the time he composed his paragraphs on "Rational Authority" in *Dominations and Powers,* he could refer to sexual inversion ... as a custom perhaps suited to human nature because it had "not yet proved fatal to all who adopted it." His slow, steady, Epicurean withdrawal from America between roughly 1893 to 1912 ... may indicate not coldness or distaste, but the reverse: warmth, the will to involvement which society and inner wisdom both discouraged. How else relate the worldliness, the humanity, and the sympathy of the informal Santayana to the courtly, formal, almost chilly Santayana of most of the published work?[3]

McCormick handles this subject with a restraint that matches Santayana's own and endorses his renunciation. But *Persons and Places* makes clear that the matter was not so simple. Friendship, Santayana's with the men in his life, is a theme that runs throughout the book. He stopped writing poetry because of what he dared not reveal. *The Last Puritan* comes alive in the clearly sexual excitement of the relationship between Oliver Alden and his father's ship captain, Lord Jim. This relationship moves through a range of feeling from sexual captivation to the disappointments of an unacknowledged and unconsummated love affair to an ambivalent, sentimental friendship. Santayana himself had such a relationship with the second Earl Russell, the great passion of his adult life, a story guardedly told in the autobiography. Santayana's tone toward Howard Sturgis and the gay ménage and milieu at Queen's Acre reveals even more directly the ambivalence of his attitude to homosexuality. And his several explanations for not being married and for leaving America, indeed for his whole emotionally detached life, require this element to make their sad and interesting sense.

For Santayana lived in a closet, and *Persons and Places* is a fascinating book in part for the elaborate way he reconstructs for us the glass house in which he must have lived. The narrowing of emotional response, the insistent detachment in his personal relations, and the persistent animus Santayana felt toward the worlds he inhabited and the people he met suggest that he was not so calm in his renunciation of his sexual nature after all. It is not to say that he should have chosen differently to say that reading *Persons and Places* makes one understand all too clearly why people nowadays come out of their closets. And the evidence that the world suspected something "unnatural" in Santayana, as President Eliot did, suggests the tense interplay between his desires and a world from which he had to protect himself. The cost to Santayana of this suppression of his own nature is reflected in his writing, so critically gripping but, when raised to the level of a positive system, so cloudy and hard to grasp. One is never sure what he is arguing for, surely not belief, surely not unbelief, surely not passion, surely not the absence of passion.

What one sees in him is the genius of the closet, a life dedicated to perceiving everything outside himself clearly in order to protect what he was quite right in thinking would have exposed him to persecution and to enforced, as opposed to chosen, marginality. Much of the insight one prizes in his writings comes from what must have been a defensive awareness of the hypocrisy of the conventional world and of everything that would have posed special obstacles to him. He saw through things while not meaning to disturb them and made a career out of keeping them at arm's length. The perspective on the conventional he affords remains one of the chief benefits of reading Santayana. But he paid a price for this distance, and one encounters it in his affecting not to care what the world thought, his touchiness, his refusal to trust himself to anyone but himself, to trust the world—his "host," as he liked to say, but not, apparently, his home.

What he liked about America were the athletes and the college life. He was drawn to the lives of young men, before business and family life and age compromised what he loved in them and removed them from the particular power he might have over them, from their availability to him for the perhaps sexless, although in feeling certainly sexual, friendships he had with some of them.

One senses in his fascinating descriptions of American and English men a personal attraction founded on an attraction to and revulsion from the civilizations themselves. He left Harvard and America in part because of the impossibility of sharing with the students he taught the camaraderie he had enjoyed with his friends when he was a student. He also left because he could neither win nor accept acceptance on the terms available to him. In a like manner, he would not settle in England. And surely he chose right. America and England must have pained him. Although they seemed to welcome him, what he desired in those places was denied to him. They must always be at cross-purposes with him. And his writings about both civilizations reflect his appreciative desire and his keenly felt exclusion, exclusion on the score of a difference less assimilable than foreign nationality or religion or even temperament. His detachment allowed him to transcend what he had to renounce, to mend his broken heart by means of dispassionate, superior judgment. Observing well was his best revenge.

Surely this suggests an explanation for Santayana's anti-Semitism. He criticized the ancient Hebrew traditions, but blamed the cosmopolitan Jew for abandoning or compromising them. He resented with snobbish fury the pretensions of anyone who thought they could master the tone of the ruling elite or the dominant culture. And he enlisted all his own knowledge of that culture in denying such people the possibility of successful assimilation. His difficult relationship with Bernard Berenson is a case in point. Toward so upwardly assimilating a Jew, Santayana could act out the condescending upper-class prejudice and its snide exclusivity. In this mean if genteel prejudice, he could experience a feeling of belonging founded on an obsessive feeling that the Jews should not be allowed to get away with what he, so much better entitled to belonging, had had to renounce. Surely they were what was wrong with the modern world. He saw himself as refusing assimilation and pretended to be in the same boat as those who attempted it. There was double reverse snobbery in all this, displaced identification and, alas, recognizable homophobia as well.

In discussing his own uprootedness, he writes: "a *deracine,* a man who has been torn up by the roots, cannot be replanted and should never propagate his kind." This explains why the likes of him should never marry. "But," he continued, "I have been involuntarily uprooted. I accept the intellectual advantages of that position, with its social and moral disqualifications. And I refuse to be annexed, to be abolished, or to be grafted onto any plant of a different species." On the one hand, Santayana accepted his situation and made the best and the most of it, indeed was inspired by it. But his uprootedness was not susceptible to the kind of regrafting available to others because it went to the core of his nature. His noble refusal to betray it and understandable decision never fully to venture it made him resentful of those who had the opportunities denied to him. If his anti-Semitism was a natural expression of his class and time and circles, it was also the unnatural consequence of his closet.

At thirty-five, Santayana experienced what he called his *metanoia,* his life crisis, the narrative of which, in the chapter "A Change of Heart," movingly skirts the precipice of his dilemma. In writing of what, in effect, returned him to his early sense of what he must give up in order to live, he achieves a brilliant feat of self-understanding. The almost spoken almost gets said in his concluding remarks about love. "A perfect love is founded on despair," he says, quoting from his own sonnets:

> This paradox is condensed and rhetorical: to get at the truth in it we must expand it a little and ward off certain misunderstandings. It is not love simply, but only *perfect* love, that includes despair. Love in itself includes hope, or at least the desire to preserve the object of it, to enshrine and defend it. And in regard to the object even *perfect* love retains this solicitude. It is only in regard to the lover, as a poor human being, that hope must be cut off, plucked up by the roots, if love is ever to become pure, happy and immortal. The *perfect* lover must renounce pursuit and the hope of possession. His person and life must, in his own eyes, fall altogether out of the picture.

Santayana's closet required simultaneously his absolute independence, his refusal to be regrafted, and his equally absolute need to "fall altogether out of the picture."

Santayana's place is literary rather than philosophical. His influence among philosophers is slight. He wanted readers, not students, and he got them. William James, John Dewey, Bertrand Russell, among others, paid him a wary attention. He himself was always an issue in considering his system. Indeed, he anticipated a personalizing of his philosophy on the part of his critics by insisting upon it himself. The theory of essences that capped his system is difficult to summarize. It is less a philosophical working-through of subjects than an adumbration of attitudes. Santayana identified most strongly with the Greeks and with Spinoza. But his allegiance even to his most admired predecessors was qualified.

Santayana's independence was astonishing and arrogant and attractive. Reading him, one feels that it is possible to fashion from the philosophical traditions of the West an individual philosophical apprehension of life itself. It is in the definition of terms that he does his little trick or performs his little miracle, depending on your point of view. Founded in his insights, his system took flight in the glory of his style. On the other hand, his own system has nothing like the power that there is in his criticisms. He was too aware, perhaps, of too many worlds to believe in the usefulness of abstracting from a single world, as Russell did, or of plunging into it, as James did. What Santayana seemed to know about the world was how difficult a place it is, capable of yielding pleasure but not susceptible of improvement.

Much that gave most human beings pleasure and pain Santayana denied himself. At twenty-four, he wrote to his friend Henry Ward Abbot, taking up a remark of Abbot's about living life "from the point of view of the grave": "The point of view of the grave is not to be attained by you or me every time we happen not to want anything in particular. It is not gained except by renunciation. Pleasure must first cease to attract and pain to repel, and this, you will confess, is no easy matter. But, meantime, I beg of you, let us remember that the joke of things is one at our expense. It is very funny, but it is exceedingly unpleasant."[4]

He not only refused to make a religion of religion, he refused to make one of art, philosophy, human relations, family love, nation state, pleasure. What he refused was any thoroughgoing passion or perspective, outside his narrow denunciatory one. What he retained was an intense and beguiling responsiveness, but one stripped of transforming or utopian partisanship. He had his prejudices and his tastes, his anti-Semitism, his flirtations with fascism, his selfishness and desire for comfort, and the pervasive and insistent and personal anti-democratic bias, which, with his theory of essences, was the principle around which his thinking was organized.

One consequence of Santayana's individuality was that his thoughts seldom sound right except in his own words. He exemplified individuality but was competitive with that of others. *Persons and Places* thrills with his elegant fault-finding. It is as if even the people he loved in his life were fish. He separated their flesh from their bones with delicate precision, and much of the time we really do see the fish in the skeleton. But the understanding this gives is not of the fish swimming in the water. Similarly, his praise of philosophical objects is less memorable than his sharp separation of the skeleton of human error from the appealing flesh of belief and commitment.

Neither the editors of this excellent new edition of *Persons and Places* nor Santayana's protective and fair-minded biographer would accept this view. His own example, and his sense that modern society itself was what the inspired individual must resist, in large measure explains his appeal to so many of the best minds and imaginations of his times, including Ezra Pound, Wallace Stevens, Robert Lowell, Van Wyck Brooks, Edmund Wilson, and Lionel Trilling. Santayana was important because he really did understand the modern age; he was no stick-in-the-mud traditionalist. He read Freud and Faulkner and Lowell with zest and perception. He was a philosopher whose work and whose life made a place for the ancient vocations of philosophy and poetry in the unwelcoming modern world.

The incursions of democracy, rather than the philosophy of essences, seem to be at stake here. One does not mind McCormick's embarrassed, apologetic account of Santayana's anti-Semitism or his admiration for fascism because what the biographer is really saying is that you need not share those views to read and admire Santayana. The question remains, however, of how to read Santayana without sharing his anti-democratic bias. And what is the effect of an individuality founded on a detachment so narrowing of human choice and community? It is worth noting that Santayana got his full measure of experience. He understood Whitman as well as Dante. But he refused participation in life for his own special reasons, and we should be cautious in accepting his renunciation without considering its human sources, along with its philosophical justifications.[5]

Santayana thought of himself as detached in some Greek philosophical sense from the ordinary claims of life, thus uniquely able to comment upon them, unbounded by the horizons ordinary attachments create. We may be persuaded that he was detached. But we may note with what unceasing animus his detachment proceeded and remark that the energy of his detachment is every bit as interesting as the calm he claimed for it.

# ⚡ In My Father's House Are Many Closets

THE AMERICAN CLOSET probably began when Walt Whitman had second thoughts about what he had written. The closet has its origins in the individual's perception of society's intolerance of same-sex love. The tendency in contemporary discourse to treat the closet as something an individual comes out of is politically wholesome. But it risks reducing a historical phenomenon in an unintended way. The previous long period of history was unlike our own in that to avow one's homosexuality to self— let alone to others—was to enter the closet. The big difference between then and now is that to come out in the nineteenth and most of the twentieth century meant to come out *into* a closet. Now, one comes *out* of a closet.

The personal closets, the keeping of the gay secret about oneself, and the cultural closets, keeping gays secret, work together. But they are not the same. The personal closet has often been the ground of a fulfilled and creative if difficult life. The cultural closet and its enforcement by writers, critics, scholars, and editors have always been what they remain today, agencies of suppression willing to commit oppression to achieve their goal. This rough distinction between the personal and the cultural helps to keep in perspective the historical vitality of gay and lesbian writing and living in America.

The closet did not keep Henry James or Willa Cather from writing about their feelings and perceptions, although it certainly affected their expression. Nor was the closet a place where the simple truth was shame and feelings of sexual privation and self-hate. The closet was not a monochromatic

This chapter was originally presented at a conference at Scripps College in 1989. Michael Roth and Norton Batkin of the Scripps Humanities Institute made the conference and this essay possible. My debts to those who helped me are noted in the Acknowledgments, but Eve Kosofsky Sedgwick deserves extra mention because of her encouragement, conversation, forbearance, and friendship. Michael Denneny arranged for its publication in *Christopher Street*. Really reading Judy Grahn, *Another Mother Tongue* (Boston, 1984), Arthur Evans, *Witchcraft and the Gay Counteculture* (Boston, 1978) and *The God of Ecstasy: Sex Roles and the Madness of Dionysos* (New York, 1988), and my friend Mark Thompson's collection *Gay Spirit: Myth and Meaning* (New York, 1987) was crucial to my thinking about these issues.

place to write from or to be in. It was a secret space and an oppressed one. But it was also a specially creative one, whose hardships make those who saw from it and wrote from it all the more interesting and the more worthy of our respect.

If one theme of closeted writing ventures feeling and sexuality in the codes and quiets of literary strategy, another propounds the simultaneous view of the society on which the closet afforded a powerful perspective. This was, on one hand, subversive of social conventions and, on the other, curiously conceiving of the conventional whole. Whitman, not coincidentally, imagined a democratic America that was inspiring and verged on the defining; this also seemed to accompany the suppression of same-sex love in his public writings. The bargain the gay imagination strikes with the culture is the subject of this article.

I will be discussing several white, privileged, all but one Protestant, gay men. Their relation to the dominant American culture was privileged and their closets had to do with their valuing that privilege. I believe that their position near to the ruling elites of their society characterizes the position of gay and lesbian closeted elites in any society—the office is structurally similar—so that George Washington Carver, Bayard Rustin, or James Baldwin, Alberta Hunter or Lorraine Hansberry, M. Carey Thomas or May Sarton (and figures from other American ethnic cultures whose names I do not know yet) may be in relation to their cultural and political elites as my figures are to their own.[1] Their positions do not engross the meaning of the closet, let alone typify the experience of oppression. I say *gay* very often when I am thinking *lesbians and gay men,* but have tried to restrain my reference. I mean to suggest correspondences but not to preempt either similarities or differences.

What are closets for? We have learned from African American and women's history to ask what the society gets out of the oppression. We need to learn to think about what the closet does for the culture as well as to its gay victims. So what are closets for? In a personal sense, the closet is the part of a person that internalizes feelings about being gay that bear the burden of the social hatred directed at the sexual minority. The personal closet is a storehouse of information about the culture from the viewpoint of someone who has reason to view it at a distance, a distance skeptical or longing, but a distance born inside the person. It is necessary for the gay to imagine the society in relation to the self. To be gay and to have the closet in you is to have to know more about society than society knows about itself, since one thing the culture does not want to know about itself is how very much it needs and depends on you.

American civilization has depended upon its lesbians and gay men. The interpretive closet works to keep this fact hidden, unsaid, unacknowledged, unadmitted. If the interpretive closet door is opened, the culture will not stay the same. It is high time to venture interpretive disobedience. Because the culture made it almost impossible to live openly, homosexuals were required to learn American as an alien language, a second language. Coded and secret, like African-American English, it was not culturally separate in the same way. It had less of its own to give away and less to return to, with little independent ethnicity, no family culture—not even a necessary owning of identity—and with only unpredictable sharing of what there was, beyond individual identity, to be shared. The homosexual had to discover that one's native language was not one's own. It could not be trusted as an instrument of desire or assertion or self-definition.

What an interesting discovery. What terror and what richness! One had to understand instinctively the often treacherous meaning behind the culture's simplest norms and pervasive rituals. One had to rely on interpretation and tone; for gay people, inflection was required. The translation of the felt language of love and custom was something homosexuals understood by doing without. The possibility that it was all lies, as it felt to him, enters early into the gay soul.

The closet fostered interpretive skills because it necessitated using an alien language to express, to hide, to act out, to resist, to protect, to revile one's feelings. Being a human being in the closet is like being a human being in the water. One can sink, tread water, float, swim, swim very well and very far, better than anyone else, drown, come to prefer water to land—but water is not the native element. The best you can do is to survive an alien current with an artificial motion. This creates an almost instant doubleness in one's awareness.

The closet was the scene of that doubleness, sometimes of its discarding, sometimes of its being forged into a keen, edgy perspective on the conventional life. It was the very language of American culture that the homosexual had to understand—deeply, doubly—to survive. To get what they wanted or to learn to live safely without, gay men had to speak it convincingly. Expressive activity might reward homosexual survival skills, and the arenas of culture, art, and scholarship might offer the homosexual a haven.

From the culture's side, the bargain was excellent. The culture might, by denying the existence of homosexuality and anathematizing it, appropriate the skills and understanding of gay people. It is gay identity more than homosexual acts that society resists. Acts of definition are necessary to cultures. Intensity of definition more often than not comes from some feeling of distance that has to be overcome with a compensating exactness and passion. The result is therefore all the more useful. Every kind of American feeling might be intensified by being expressed in lieu of the forbidden feelings of gay people, doubled by that distance, fueled by that deprivation, enforced by that culture's menacing.

The interpretive closet may be genteel, but the cultural closet is not, not when a sissy is bullied into a false view of manhood in adolescence, when a writer is warned off gay subject matter, when the price of popularity and fame is to write it straight. The culture has ways of making its point, and one of them is to accuse the gay man of being unnatural. Just say the word "homosexual" or hint it, through most of our history, and the closet door is shut—from the inside. Terror sustains the closet. And what the closet affords in exchange can be considerable, barring the one central thing. A gay can have a secret life, can participate in the culture often as an arbiter, a definer, with an immense role. Male—and the illusion of heterosexual—privilege can belong to the gay who is not otherwise debarred, say by race or class. The culture allows the closeted gay figure much freedom and a kind of privileged abnormality. The absence of equal individuality leads to a situation of cultural privilege in some instances, a certain license, considerable freedom, and, in a way, protection.

At the start, then, there is something in the relation of the homosexual imagination that cannot know itself and know the world as if these were continuous. The closet begins with the suppression of self in the awareness of how others view the self. The closet begins with an act of internalization and interpretation and continues with the fantasizing of the ordinary, the fabrication of the normal. Its assumption is a comment on American civilizations and a value judgment on self in relation to them. The closet knows the normal to be merely conventional and also craves it. In that ambivalent value judgment, as in the judgment for white over black by black, for male over female by female, we see the closet constructed. It is a place where the articulation of one set of values, based on one kind of self, takes precedence over another. This false articulation leads to the many moods we know to characterize the closet, and to the damage for which homosexuals test positive, as do other oppressed people, the habit of shame and self-hatred. Thinking twice about things you aren't supposed to have to think about at all will make anybody a little crazy.

What the culture gets out of this is, in a sense, simple. Society needs extra people to affirm its teachings. Within the family and in the culture at large, the presentations of self and value need teachers, ministers to the normal, people whose job in life is to articulate and train. The daring of the American democratic project made its need for assistants in all forms more desperate. When you read American cultural history, you encounter the anxiety repeatedly voiced during the nineteenth century that there was no normal, that free people could not be relied upon to lead normatively ordered lives. Much of our cultural history has been the attempt to devise and promulgate a culture-wide manual of belief and moral behavior in the absence of established church and hierarchical continuities. This, as George Santayana saw, is why Americans need books with moral and happy endings.

American gays seem always to have been on the cutting edge of American self-definition. Together, marginal groups created the possibilities of the American normal. Horatio Alger could imagine capitalism at its storybook level and also in terms of the world of male relationships that must characterize it. The hidden energies of the American project needed a class of storyteller who would tell some but not all, enough but not too much. The gay in American history will come to be seen as having performed much of the work of the elaboration of culture and empire that characterized its last century and a half. Key to the differentiation of the male and female sphere of that society, active in both, adviser to the family, teacher of the young, icon of art and sport, sophistication and feeling, the closeted gay has given his special intensity and awareness of hidden feelings over to the culture for its own purposes.

The gay in the closet had access to the dominant American culture because much of the American public world was a closed male society that needed gay men for homosocial purposes and as male envoys to the women's sphere. This required the gay man to feel or mime feelings he did not feel, to imagine what was true for others, to fantasize the appropriate. The classic closet imagining is a fictitious act of feeling and translation. It entails imagining the conventions of society with manufactured, endorsing sincerity from the outside in, and with a corresponding inner feeling that conventions are both inauthentic and necessary.

This habit of mind leads to cynicism and to sentimental affirmation, to any trick of tone or heightened feeling that might make the conventional believable. It leads to the brilliant subversions and the sentimental affirmations that seem to mark the gay sensibility. It leads also to a fantasy of control, to the office of interpretation, to a feeling for one's relation to the dominant culture as necessary and important, to collaborate in keeping the secret not so bad, ransoming the secret with altruistic custody of the cultural closet, with the stipulation that one's self, the gay self, needs no acknowledgment. "We'll keep the secret for you."

This is the closet queen as stage manager, the arbiter of the conventional and the true and the good, punctilious and didactic, the culture's expert and priest and defender and, for all his control, its victim. The closet may sometimes lead to subversive, avant garde acts of cultural interaction—the Harlem Renaissance was facilitated by white and black gays and lesbians. The closet may lead to timeless imaginations and feats of intellectual clarity. The closet is an encompassing reality and creative ground.

The gay office in culture is definitional. The culture depends upon classes of people whose imaginations are fired up by denial. Think of how her own oppression readies Mammy to give Miss Scarlett not only service but socializing affirmation. Women embody the values men need in their lives but may not feel like embodying themselves. The gay may do something like that by being the person who understands the conventions, needing to master them although and because they do not apply.

This is a more common situation than the culture's rhetoric supposes. The gay matters to the culture because it is, it turns out, a hard job to follow its rules of love and life. People need more lessons in living than pandas do, who only have to be shown how. The heterosexual normal "family," with all its attendant customs, its social and personal corollaries, requires an enormous amount of training and hard work. The apparent gay mastery of its rules, reflected in the work of the closet, is useful. You can't have the culture without the gay, but you also can't have the gay in it. And that is the closet; it is a pound of flesh.

The interpretive closet has a hard time admitting gay identity precisely because of the uses the culture makes of gay creativity. It makes it possible to prize Henry James's insights and style or share Santayana's views, or even to like Liberace's musical and personal stylings, without risking identification with the gay man who thought them up. By taking the sexuality away from the gay figure and keeping the person in the closet, the tradition and the culture get from that figure a redoubled, italicizing, selfless reflection of itself and its conventions, specially, if not uniquely available to the gay and affirming to everyone else.

How the gay happens to know what he knows is no more a part of that knowledge than how the Afro-American slave understands and comforts his master so well. The closet is about ignoring the gay person's part in any transaction. It is an agreement, still in force, that there are certain things you know but do not speak about. It often, in the case of the privileged figures I am discussing, fosters, protects, and cushions a life. The closet marginalizes the gay person because it recruits what the gay person knows. The gay is not marginal, but central to the culture and to its definition and interpretation.

A note on truth-telling. The most important distinction in cultural as in personal history is when it becomes safe to be open about one's sexual identity. To tell the truth about one's sexuality need not mean to be "out" in the 1920s as one can be today, any more than one is able to be out at fourteen with the same security that one can be in adulthood. Before the Second World War, it is almost necessary to regard the closet, personal and cultural, as a scene of truth telling; the writers in that closet told the truth about their feelings and experiences even when they disguised them or when their truth was the truth of the closet told from within it. Today, except in travesty, it seems we no longer can tell the truth even about it from within it.

Henry James wrote from the closet. James has been used, as so many homosexual writers have been used, to symbolize certain aspects of the cultural enterprise. James can stand for the extreme case of literary style, of cultivation, or expatriation, of the marginality of the traditional cultural project in the democratic world and a subtle, wide-ranging critique of American middle-class life and hopes. But in order to make James symbolic of its own agenda, the interpretive tradition must elide his homosexuality and pass over its prominence in his writings. But homosexuality is a consistent theme in his fiction, a key source of his knowing what he knows. *The Bostonians* and *Portrait of a Lady,* as well as *The Beast in the Jungle, The Ambassadors,* and *The Golden Bowl* explore what James knew as a gay man in his life; they map his closet. The interpretive closet is the tradition that keeps the centrality of his gay feelings and gay characters and plots from his readers.

Harvard's modernizing president, Charles Eliot, said this about philosophy instructor George Santayana, in a private comment on his career at the college: "He does not dig ditches, or lay bricks, or write school-books, his product is not of the ordinary, useful, though humble kind. What will it be? It may be something of the highest utility; but, on the other hand, it may be something futile or even harmful because unnatural and untimely."[2] Santayana was a genius of the closet because he saw through conventions and built his critique on that seeing through, a gay seeing through in considerable part. And his understanding of American civilization pictured it as kryptonite to art and philosophy and hospitable to the moral middle class, to the combination of art and Puritanism that America offered the artist. Santayana recognized this as the demand that the true and the beautiful stay within the confines of the conventionally moral and that the interpretative machinery of American intellectual life would be devoted to that effort at false reconciliation.

Santayana's insights and his writings have been appropriated without their source, in what America regarded as his unnaturalness, being acknowledged. Santayana's views—views that attracted literary Americans from Wallace Stevens to Robert Lowell, from Lionel Trilling to Edmund Wilson, from Van Wyck Brooks and Perry Miller to Gore Vidal—are accepted. You cannot have classic American Studies without them. But their relation to his gay isolation is ignored. He repudiated active sexuality, but retained the perspective his preference gained him. He anticipated an aesthetically and philosophically aggressive, if politically conservative, critique of American conventionality and democracy that had its roots in his own experience of the American closet.

Cole Porter and Lorenz Hart were but two of the many gays in the great age of American popular culture whose contributions had to do with what they knew as gay men and whom the culture kept in the closet for its own purposes, loving the gay art but denying the gay artist.

Cole Porter's extraordinary songs are unrivaled in sophistication, wit, and their pungent moods of romantic sexual obsession.[3] The combination of obsessive love and sophisticated reference is the unmistakable hallmark of the Porter song. His work made the world safe for a variety of erotic feelings and arcane references, and the songs are rich with gay innuendo and filled with room for gay enjoyment. His view of love, so dear to the sophisticated among the American bourgeoisie, is surely part of what he knew as a gay blade who was eager in his private pursuit of pleasure but, of course, barred from anything other than private indulgence. He could not be open, but depended on a certain hard-edged, gilt-edged café society to nurture and protect the sophistication and freedom from convention that would protect him in his desires.

He saw through the conventional, although he had sentimental moments about it. But his songs sing of obsession, of love as something you cannot do anything about, in ways that none of the other great songwriters approach. His knowing lyrics know everything, fight vainly *the old ennui,* and the only thing that surprises him is love, his own desire, when he suddenly turns and sees *your fabulous face* ("I Get a Kick out of You"). His message to his lovers: *taunt me, hurt me, deceive me, desert me* ("So In Love") or *get out of town, before it's too late my love* ("Get Out Of Town"). His sense of love as something forced on a conscientiously reluctant victim, urged on one from the inside jungle that is beyond naming with its insistent beat beat beat . . . is funny and helpless to boot ("Night and Day"). Love is inevitably *too hot not to cool down* ("Just One of Those Things"). Love is obsessive and won't settle down. *What is this thing called love?* The knowing Porter made up the singer of *Love for Sale.* And the self-knowing Porter gave way to his feelings in "I Concentrate on You."

Porter titillated Americans and teased them with what his songs knew about him and everyone else. To see the poet of American sophistication and pleasure as gay would have meant that America had to see something about itself that it instead had Porter see for it. As Porter wrote, *You're not wild enough, you're not gay enough, you don't let me lead you astray enough* ("I've Got You on My Mind"). The point with Porter is that the cultural closet keeps certain feelings hidden, feelings the culture enjoys but does not wish to acknowledge receiving from its gay specialists in love.

Another classic American gay songwriter, lyricist Lorenz Hart, offers an even more poignant instance of the closet.[4] Porter had a cultural license to be sophisticated; no troubadour of ordinary life, he wrote about much of his world in his songs. Hart's lyrics are beloved for their emotional directness and vulnerability. Their sophistication inspires the emotionally central. Nobody wrote so straightforwardly about love and longing and the feelings about self and other that amount to romantic love. "Bewitched, Bothered and Bewildered," "If They Asked Me, I Could Write a Book," "Thou Swell," "There's a Small Hotel," "My Funny Valentine," "I Wish I Were in Love Again," "It Never Entered My Mind"—Hart's songs define what America means by love. And the gay lyricist who wrote of love knew about love from the distance of someone who was gay in a homophobic society that institutionalized the closet.

Hart's lyric evocation of the "normal" transforms the conventional with the deep feeling of his own isolation into a more passionately real normal than the conventional ever yields. It is a norm yearned for, expressed in the yearnings for love of his lyrics. And it would be interesting if people thought, when they heard "My Funny Valentine" or "Blue Moon," of what the songs must have meant to their gay writer. Hart's being Jewish also has inflected his closet and his art. The simple point, however, and it really cannot be too bluntly put, is that the songwriter whose lyrics define what America means by romantic love was a homosexual. His closet is in the songs, in the distance in the love he celebrates. Hart's closet was the distance from which he must have seen, and his genius the bridge of feeling he had to cross to expression.

The best work from the closet knows something felt and true about the culture; its own position is hidden from sight, but not from the trained eye. The conventional comes alive in the closet's wishful fictions, just as it shows its artificiality in the mockery of camp. As with James and Santayana and Porter, there is more in Hart to be enjoyed and learned from him as the closet door is opened.

The opened door forces us to ask how Hart came to know what he knew. It gives new meaning to his irreplacable expression of how it feels to be in love. Say the lyric to yourself—remembering that the song sets Hart's words to Richard Rodgers' beautiful melody. As you recount all those moon/June things your romance doesn't need, you may discover what Hart knew lay behind those foolish conventional things. As you sound the lyrics in your inner ear, as "My Romance" becomes your romance, you may sense what Hart sacrificed to his closet and what you have gained. The song lends us a moment of clarity, "wide awake" to how we ourselves make our "most fantastic dreams come true." Lovers dwell in that uncertain, hopeful, helpless space between our fantasies and their occasion, between me and some you. But sanctioned heterosexual love can sing this song to get in the mood. Hart was imprisoned in his closet, condemned to fantasy without conventional hope.

The closet teaches a curious double lesson: to feel oneself apart and to imagine oneself connected. Those two strands may fuel a *seeing through* or a *seeing as*—or register on a scale in between. The culture gets from its closeted gays a powerful perception of its most intimate and most important matters since its politics and its literature are so often public ways of talking about its private concerns. And what the gay sees from the closet, the culture can use for free because the closet keeps the gay from owning his own insight, from creating the character who says *I know that because of who I am,* from making the pronoun in the song same-sex. It is free labor. The universality of so much closet-seeing reminds us of how specific a human experience the universal inevitably is.

The homophobia that drives the culture pollutes the closet. It is part of the point of the closet that gays learn to be as homophobic as possible; the culture is less concerned to eliminate than to control. F. O. Matthiessen and Newton Arvin, two of the century's preeminent scholars of American literature, come to mind. It is hard to imagine the study of nineteenth-century American literature and such writers as Melville, Whitman, and James, to mention just the gay male classic writers, without the work of these two scholars. Matthiessen came up with the *American Renaissance* and James's "major phase," and Arvin, among other things, wrote memorably about Melville. They were both gay and engaged in relationships. Matthiessen's with the painter Russell Cheney is preserved in letters, published as *Rat and the Devil,* and is deservedly famous. Arvin was an early lover of Truman Capote's; you can do with that what you will. These smart and talented homosexual scholars created new terms on which the culture could read its most important gay writers, terms that expanded their importance and impact, but did not make reference to their gayness, or to the homosexual themes in their works.[5]

What they did do was to connect the writings to democracy and a specifically left kind of democracy, so that in both Arvin and Matthiessen, left politics exist to broaden and radicalize the perceptions of the writers they discuss. The problem of evil and the problem of social justice, the presentation of the classic American writers as not merely ornaments of the American imagination and expanders of its literary culture and soul, but as artists who somehow saw through the social order—elements in a radicalized modern consciousness—are contributions of these critics, in concert with non-gay critics. But the issue of politics as a kind of beard, in the place the homosexuality ought to be in their writing, is important to note, if equally important to forbear from judging.

What students of American culture learned from Matthiessen and Arvin (and others) was a view of the American literary accomplishment that placed the highest literary tradition within the best democratic aspirations. The closet functioned here to expand a cultural interpretation and to make at least putative room for a guarded identity, perhaps to make a better bargain for the gay imagination by trying to make a more just society and a more elevated literature. If Santayana's closet made him read America as a place to leave, Matthiessen's and Arvin's made them read it as a place to change. By keeping the closet's code and recreating the dimensions of the interpretive closet, that admirable generation contributed specially to the culture's self-understanding, from a point of view which has a special meaning because of the situation of the homosexual critic. But even this was a custodial act based on a key self-denial, one that continued the life of the interpretive closet and the tragedy of the personal ones.

The great American play *Our Town* was recently revived in New York, presented in the spirit of America's neo-traditionalist self-celebration, the original prairie home companion, an American classic. It is safe to say that this beloved play will not in the near future be billed as Thornton Wilder's presentation of the closeted gay doing the culture's work. And yet, friends and neighbors, that is what it is.[6]

The son of a genteelly poor, New England Protestant family, Wilder was stuck between the world of men and women, of business and art, between Christianity and paganism, between all the rocks and hard places of American genteel culture. His early works try to reconcile the ambitious artistic conscientiousness of his mother's world with the ambitious worldly conscientiousness of his father's, an attempt to reconcile Proust and the Puritans. By no means his alone, this odd quest was what Santayana had predicted American gentility would require and what the American empire promised the world: to give the human condition a happy ending. Wilder's version encountered great success with American readers in the twenties.

Wilder was homosexual. His life is the familiar and always interesting story of a brainy, ambitious sissy who had the wrong feelings and early on recognized them well enough to know that he had better straighten up, and who decided that writing was the way to advance and protect himself. From an early age Thornton knew what the world required of him, and he learned to take that knowledge into his self-consideration: that whatever his inside feelings, he had better create an acceptable outside and develop at least a twelve-mile limit around his feelings. He seems to have chosen early on the role of friend and helper, teacher and know-it-all. One of the most wonderful fluke publicity events from the '20s was the Alpine jaunt Wilder took with the bookish world boxing champion

Gene Tunney. Wilder was didactic and divided. Gertrude Stein remarked that he had two sides to his life: the theater and his puritan upbringing, between which he alternated, avoiding commitment to either. This noncommittal variance also represented his reaction to his own sexuality. Wilder said that his work was always about "the fear of catastrophe" and whether he could meet it.

In 1930 he published *The Woman of Andros,* which was about a courtesan's hopeless and unrequited love for a young man. He employed the device of a dead person's return to earth. It is not hard to read this book as a deep and pained exploration of someone in the closet. It is Wilder's "outest" book, and it was generally well received.

*The New Republic* asked the proletarian writer Mike Gold to review it. Gold, the enforcer of a socialist-realist sensibility, went to work on Wilder and, in a notorious attack, took him to task for writing about vaporous and elite ideas instead of reality. In "Prophet of the Genteel Christ," Gold attacked the religious gentility of the book. "Is it a vital religion? No, it is that newly fashionable literary religion that centers around Jesus Christ, the First British Gentleman. It is a pastel, pastiche, dilettante religion, without true neurotic blood and fire, a daydream of homosexual figures in graceful gowns moving archaically among the lilies. It is Anglo-Catholicism, the last refuge of the literary snob." Write real books about American reality, Gold advised.[7]

The controversy shocked the reading public, and most readers, even Hemingway, sided with Wilder. The attack is represented as a significant outburst of the left spirit of the times against the literary middle classes, and as having inspired Wilder's turn to ordinary American subjects. True enough, but to a closeted homosexual writer reading the review, the word "homosexual" sounds an alarm. Wilder was terrified. Days later, at the University of Chicago where he was teaching, Wilder read an undergraduate's criticism of a fellow student, and reacted with fury: "You shouldn't have done that. You shouldn't write that way about someone else. I'm sorry I ever said anything bad about anyone. Now I know how it feels." It isn't hard to figure out what was so terrible. What Wilder experienced was a homophobic naming. Whether Gold meant his characterization to apply to Wilder in a specific name-calling way is irrelevant. Gold certainly made use of the culture's code words for his own purposes. Wilder must have seen it as blowing his cover.

Absent the ugliness and tone of his own theory, Gold was pretty close. *The Woman of Andros* is the closest Wilder came to writing his kind of gay book, and it is not hard to read that way. Gold attacked him politically, this everyone knows, but the clincher was the homophobic reference. First in *Heaven's My Destination* and then with *Our Town,* Wilder determined to find a reality locating him so securely in the American heartland that he would be safe from the likes of Gold. *Our Town* was his response to Gold's attack, in overt claim and inside strategy.

*Our Town* strips American family small-town life to the basics. It is unusual in the century of *Winesburg, Ohio,* and *Peyton Place* in that it exposes small-town American life in Grover's Corners, New Hampshire, for the wonderful thing that it is. It is a kind of illustrated sermon given by the stage manager. He shares out the irony and superior view of common conventions with a preacher's familiarity and distance on what he, by definition and by calling, must endorse. It is a very powerful play, bound to move you or embarrass you; if it doesn't make you cry, it will make you squirm. *Our Town* requires no scenery. The stage manager runs things. He is a key figure for Wilder, who later played him on the stage, didactic, condescending, distant, controlling. "In our town we like to know the facts about everybody," he says, and he decides what the facts are and who gets to know them.[8] He is there to divert as well as to control. He appears to be the town's only bachelor.

The first act is about "Daily Life," the second about "Love and Marriage." The play is aggressively about marriage. The stage manager remarks that "almost everybody in the world gets married—you know what I mean? In our town there aren't hardly any exceptions. Most everybody in the world climbs into their graves married." Mrs. Gibbs says, "Yes ... people are meant to go through life two by two. 'Taint natural to be lonesome." When you strip away the layers of nonsense the play claims to be peeling away, apparently, what you get is the endlessly repeating cycle of birth and childhood, courtship and marriage, and death, all within the town, all within the family. The second act ends with the marriage of George Gibbs to Emily Webb.

Wilder apparently had trouble with the third act, the one about death. He devised a memorable act in which the young wife and mother Emily dies and joins the chorus of the dead Grover's Corners people as they sit on one side of the stage, balancing the living on the other, and talk about life for what it is. It gives the play's view of life an imprimatur of the distance of death. Emily tries to return to life for a day, her happiest remembered day, and finds out that people who don't live it don't appreciate it, don't notice it, do not see one another. *Live all you can* is one of the messages, but *life is wasted on the living* is another. An intense theatrical experience, the living and the dead, resolves into a kind of be-good-to-folks-while-you're-alive sentimentality to fend off a bitter chilliness about the possibilities of human connection.

There is some testimony about how Wilder came to write this third act. He was spending time with Samuel Steward, a young English teacher, later a tattoo artist and writer, a friend of Gertrude Stein, and Wilder's off-and-on affair for some years. According to Steward:

> I met him for the first time with Gertrude's introduction in hand, and Thornton gave me a great lecture about "normalizing" myself or at least how to handle my homosexuality and learning to live with it, and a lot of advice about meeting the problem; reading the great homosexual writers of the past. We talked all evening and walked all night in the rain. We walked and walked getting wetter and wetter. . . .

But Wilder had to show Steward great literary landmarks of Zurich:

> . . . then he insisted we stay up until dawn to hear the bells of Zurich as Max Beerbohm has described them. That was in my drinking days and I kept going into every café we passed. My feet were getting so wet and so was I, and I kept hollering for an umbrella. When daylight came I went home to dry out and fell into bed and slept all day, but Thornton went to his hotel and wrote the last act of *Our Town,* which begins with the grave-yard scene with the umbrellas. He confessed later that he had "struck a match on me," and that the graveyard umbrella scene came from my complaining about my walk in the wet.[9]

Wilder may have struck a match on Steward and the umbrella, but the spark was probably from somewhere deeper. Wilder knew he was gay, but he never integrated that fact into his life. He led a double life, a peripatetic switching among the scenes of his life, himself like his stage manager or his Theophilus North, mediating didactically, ambitiously, frantically, successfully, but never coming to grips, let alone coming out, keeping his distance.

Wilder wrote about Gide's journals in his own, of Gide's doubleness after mentioning his homosexuality: "Gide early in life lost the *true tone of voice.* All his vast intelligence is in falsetto—doubly tragic because his life is one long sincere effort to be sincere. One cannot even apply to him Cocteau's phrase: 'It is not possible both to be and to appear sincere': for one feels that his 'sincerity' had long since retired into a cave way down the depths of his being. And the grave implications of all this for myself do not escape me."[10]

The night before writing the last act of *Our Town,* he was filled with desire and apparently did not consummate his passion. The intensity of the third act probably reflects this personal circumstance; it seems to be brimming with feelings, the mixed-up feelings that must have moved Wilder on the rare occasions when the barriers of his compartmentalized life fell. Steward's umbrella and Steward were occasions for feelings to which the third act must not be reduced but which stirred Wilder's truest imaginings.

The third act retails the wisdom of the closet in duet with the slow motion of real life. It is about how you know what Wilder knows about Grover's Corners, what it takes out of him to know only those things America is willing to know about itself, the price he paid for success and safety. Its holds up for our reflection how people never know one another for who they are, not even our parents, not even when we ask them directly to notice us; it treats normal life as a procession that does not understand itself. Life is reduced to the inaccessible normal. It touches the grim truth that lurks in the ordinary but does not tax the ordinary with its special knowing. What Wilder calls "death" in the play is living death, the absence of communication, being unacknowledged, being outside, being inside the closet.

Even the natural things, the normal feelings Wilder has the play endorse and until the third act advance turn out to be incommunicable, unappreciated. The truth that underlies this is bitter and closeted. It is the homosexual's distance on the normal voiced by the dead people of Grover's Corners. To be alive in the closet among the straight is a living death.

The stage manager's description of death is resonant: "And they stay here while the earth part of 'em burns away, burns out; and all that time they get slowly indifferent to what's goin' on in Grover's Corners. They're waiting. They're waiting for something that they feel is comin'. Something important and great. Aren't they waiting for the eternal part in them to come out clear?"

Live All You Can. Shades of Marcher in *The Beast in the Jungle*. The dead have a special insight into the living because they no longer share the delusions or the hopes of that life. They view things from the point of view of the grave, as Santayana phrased it. They warn Emily when she tries to rejoin the living that it is awful, even if she chooses a happy day, because "You not only live it: but you watch yourself living it." And she tries to bridge that gap, to live though dead, to connect, to communicate. And failing, she realizes that the earth is too wonderful to be appreciated by the living. Wilder's conscious resolution reinterprets his feelings.

Looking at the two dramas that owe something to *Our Town*, we can see its individuality. *It's a Wonderful Life* takes the device—like *Carousel* and *Here Comes Mr. Jordan*—and much of the philosophy, but in the place of the stage manager gives us protagonists and explores, without naming, the angry ambivalence its sentimentality resolves. *The Glass Menagerie* takes the stage setting and the stage manager but allows that distance to be the distance of the probably-gay Tom on his family. *Our Town* allows neither the anger nor the distance to have their play.

Thornton Wilder, in his journals, gave a kind of license to this reading in his remarks about Gide and James, keeping in mind that "neurosis" for Wilder included being gay: "It is a predisposition to neurosis in infancy which awakens, spurs the intelligence—yes. With the passing of years, the neurosis becomes conscious of itself, with two results: (1) the subject feels himself as 'exception' in society; and (2) He is subject to the law of all neurosis, namely that he burns to tell and burns to conceal his secret."[11]

*Our Town* burns to tell and burns to conceal Wilder's secret, which is America's secret.

**PART II**

# LISTENING TO
# SOPHIE TUCKER

# ⚡ Criticism and American Cultural Repair

AMERICAN CULTURAL CRITICISM came first, American culture second. Europeans always had ideas about what America was going to have to measure up to. The land was theirs before they were the land's. Cultural criticism is what we have come to call the genres of Americans examining America in light of their expectations for it. Although commonly expressed in terms of objective issues—what effect does America have on the personality, what sort of literature has it produced, etc.—it is persistently a tradition of expression about how America seems to its self-consciously philosophic, literary, intellectual individuals.

Beginning even before the Puritan expectations for a "city upon a hill" lost out to an equally expectation-laden claim for a new world in which there was happiness to be gained, the tradition has partaken of the prophetic. It is important, however, that both the spiritual and material promises of American life, by which its culture was to be judged, new Eden or New Jerusalem, were a priori standards to which American culture was meant to measure up. The American cultural critic was born prophet and still aspires to the prophet's schematic life: apart from the crowd, moved by an inner voice, more often vindicated than appreciated, a paradigm of the demanding, opinionated, hyperattentive seer, surest when alone, truest when unheeded.

This essay was written for *American Literary History* 1, no. 3 (Fall 1989). Reproduced by permission of Oxford University Press. I am grateful to ALH editor Gordon Hutner for the opportunity to respond in this fashion to the several essays in the same issue on American cultural criticism. I have removed most specific references to the essays here, but they are well worth reading: Nina Baym, "Early Histories of American Literature: A Chapter in the Institution of New England"; Eric J. Sandeen, "Bourne Again: The Correspondence between Randolph Bourne and Elsie Clews Parsons"; Casey Blake, "The Young Intellectuals and the Culture of Personality"; Paul Jay, "Kenneth Burke and the Motives of Rhetoric"; William Cain, "An Interview with Irving Howe"; Gregory S. Jay, "Hegel and Trilling in America"; Sohnya Sayres, "Susan Sontag and the Practice of Modernism"; Jane Gallop, "Heroic Images: Feminist Criticism"; and Wilson J. Moses, "Dark Forests and Barbarian Vigor: Paradox, Conflict and Africanity in Black Writing before 1914."

More characteristic than prophets unheeded have been American prophets embarrassed by acceptance. Acceptance rather than rejection has created the baffling condition of American cultural criticism. It is clear that the eagerness of their audience to heed critical strictures, to accept their prophecy, to establish that American democratic culture has no place for the highest satisfactions of art, haunts the tradition of American cultural criticism, which has come to depend on the rewards of the critical stance. The critic has become the one left standing, criticism identified by unpopularity. The result is an American high cultural tradition which must explain success rather than failure, in which posthumous readership is a stronger proof of merit than the contemporary, and for which the democratic is a problem.

Cultural criticism invariably reflects what some individual wants or feels. It is not only thinking; it is thinking about how the culture within which one lives, works. It proposes the individual's response to the culture. This individual may take many authenticating positions, but the conceit remains constant and plays out the larger tensions between the democracy and the individuals, whose natural rights are an equal principle of its authority. Cultural criticism may take culture as its subject, but its creative act is the assembling of an opposing—now "oppositional"—self. Emerson's innovation was to construct the encompassing response by an individual to America from the Puritan and Jeffersonian and German models he inherited: "The American Scholar" does cultural criticism, but about American life, not just its cultural production. A decision to view from a singular perspective the lives that other people lead in a regime in terms of cultural productions is itself of significance. The assumption remains in force that formal, high, and, especially, literary culture provide the standards by which democratic culture should be judged, just as democratic politics must be judged by other politics—radical, royalist, agrarian, Marxist, socialist—and democratic self-consciousness must be judged by alternative modes, for example, Freudian, new age, religious.

At some level, cultural criticism reflects the individual's dissatisfaction and is almost always expressed in terms other than those the democracy offers, if possible one's own. The American tradition of cultural criticism, like any prophetic tradition, values vindication after the fact, invents martyrs, mistrusts consensus, and seeks betrayal. In the twentieth century, the grounds on which the individual might criticize or oppose the self to the culture have changed from broadly taken claims about the individual to more specific claims about the literary. They range from hopeful to beleaguered. They advance claims from a highly articulated "identity," or what one might call the abiding questions of democratic pluralism translated to an individual arena.

The tradition began with expectations and has had to confront, in the twentieth century, a real history, things to sort out. Much of the energy of the modern cultural critic has therefore been to describe the nature of the nation's literary history. Unlike Emerson who could imagine it, the genteel critics and their successors, like Van Wyck Brooks, Randolph Bourne, Lewis Mumford, Constance Rourke, Phillip Rahv, and Lionel Trilling, had to recast or canonize a tradition. The problem of the culture for such as these remained those genres and traditions that borrowed from an earlier prophecy, like Emerson's, but no longer satisfied the contemporary prophet. Cultural criticism became the fault-finding part of a tradition that began with as much to recommend as to criticize.

Alas, democratic reality seldom satisfies the critic's hope for it. It seems inescapable that American cultural criticism is what is left of a prophetic claim that always did better in the crying wilderness. It took root in the absence of a civilization and continues to guide that civilization best by pretending that most of what it in fact created and accomplished does not exist. How else to explain the almost dogged inattention by cultural critics to what most would agree is the great triumph of American twentieth-century culture, its endlessly compelling and widely admired popular and material culture, its songs, movies, gadgets, snacks, entertainments, and lifestyles, its proliferation of generic versions of the central myths of Western civilization. Some, like Edmund Wilson and notably Gilbert Seldes, did pay attention. But most cultural critics saw popular culture as a specimen, not a worthy and interesting production.

They were, rather, proponents of a different notion of American culture, one as unpopular as its Puritan, Jeffersonian, Transcendental forebears, but, unlike them, not troubled by the likelihood of its nonacceptance—rather, fueled by it. Cultural criticism is what the culturally ambitious intellectual might do to explain an interest in a culture by definition not shared by its people, and to enforce the critic's own distance from the bourgeois and popular cultures of the times. The cultural critic's true "text" is the civilization, not the individual expressions it produces. The cultural critic is usually someone who takes those expressions as a principal concern as well; cultural criticism is characterized by an interplay between the general and the specific American works the critic addresses. The popular and the respectable had no longer become something to control or assuage or attract. It had become the thing to be criticized and replaced with the life of the Western mind.

The tradition from which modern cultural criticism derives had been at pains to create a connection between its cultural authority and a democratic public, through such devices as the literary canon and such institutions as the schools and colleges. The very project of traditional American attention to culture, as Nina Baym recognizes, will result in certain forms of allegiance, forms that create a kind of culture: "if the didactic and rhetorical aims that shaped 'American literature' as a school subject as well as a scholarly subject continue in force, we may have no option but to replace the rejected story with another narrative very much like it. If we practice American literature in the classroom for the ultimate aims of forming students' characters and making them better citizens, we find ourselves to our surprise carrying on Whig goals, no matter how radical our claims; we walk in paths laid down by the first American literary historians."[1] Cultural criticism remains moral, that is, about justifying and organizing expressive and intellectual activity in terms of a connection to the general good of the American regime in order to cement a connection between knowledge and power that it assumes and wishes to engross. It begins in an ambition to connect America's superior individuals to the workings of its democratic regime.

The narrative propounded by American cultural criticism is rich in the irony of audience acceptance. From Edwards to Emerson to Upton Sinclair, defeat has been lodged more often in acceptance than rejection. American critics have felt, as Upton Sinclair did, that they aimed at America's heart and hit its stomach. They have found, as would Emerson, the battle cries of anti-institutionalism carved over the gateways and arches of institutions even more venerable than the ones he attacked.[2]

In one sense, the historical interpretive project of American letters can be seen to have been the erection of a cultural criticism to guide a nation in need of direction. The feminist account of the development of American cultural and literary studies gives a context for its well-known attempt to make a canon of oppositional views. The Emerson we study is a rebel who was defeated by his acceptance by the genteel middle class. In another context, the twentieth-century history of American interpretation might be seen as the attempt to locate a criticism uncontaminated by acceptance and unhappy because of the conditions of a democratic capitalist regime. This envisions an intellectual and artistic life untroubled by the problems of patronage and audience. This is an artist's understandable ambition, and a prophet's fate, but it is a problematic foundation for a cultural criticism in a democratic society. This surely has been the great merit of the contemporary critical project, the reseeing of classic texts in terms of what principles of selection their anointing reflected. The canonic ambition may account for much of the attraction of Tocqueville, the influence of Santayana, and the taste for American writers undigested by the mass of readers, like Herman Melville and Henry James. It also may have generated the power of Perry Miller's embattled view of the Puritans, not as Vernon L. Parrington's small-town, narrow-minded hypocrites, but as prophets of piety and demanding spiritual discipline, the perfect lights by which to read the failure of liberal, middle-class, modern culture.

One might almost come to the conclusion that American cultural criticism is the punishment that America's modernist, dissatisfied, radical, unread, self-conscious youthful geniuses visited on the happiness America afforded its fortunate in the name of art, not justice. One big difference between politically and culturally based criticism is that the political can take up the cause of those to whom justice is denied, of those who are oppressed. It also forges an ideal connection between the complicated intellectual discourse and the interests of the masses. Cultural criticism, separated from ideals of democratic justice, must argue that its own literary standards are somehow better than the common and sufficient in themselves and, by the way, oppressed; this is almost impossible to do without institutionalizing a moralizing, canonic reflex. Cultural critics are also political but in a particular way that emerges from reading Phillip Rahv and Mike Gold in tandem.

The attempt of made-up minds to control American experience comes a cropper not only when their admonitions go unheeded, but crucially when they gain attention. The zealous and literal-minded redactions of Jonathan Edwards by followers such as Samuel Hopkins foredoomed the delicate poise of his philosophical and practical synthesis. Van Wyck Brooks's appropriation of Santayana's category of a "genteel tradition" transformed it from a briar patch into the parlor. The privileging of the democratic, feared by Tocqueville, has scuttled most attempts at traditional cultural control. If the regime itself has had to grow into democracy, the American culture has always been more democratic because more resistant to traditional control. Its democracy has offended tradition without necessarily ennobling equality. The cultural critic comprises the remains of the ancient hope that America would be the place where nature and culture, bounty and craft, invention and discovery would get human social matters right, at last. The Jeremiad of early New England, Jefferson's conceit of the natural aristocrat, Emerson's "American Scholar," the man of letters, the radical, the expert, Du Bois's talented tenth, "the best and the brightest," our own "public intellectual," all represent attempts to institutionalize knowing to control better what has always been understood to be a free society. The fear has remained the same, that a free people would ignore good counsel and license bad. The hope of connecting the naturally gifted to a disinterested view of the public good, and the fear of the danger the malevolent superman posed to free institutions have coexisted in the American imagination from the start.

The role we ascribe to the cultural critic was once understood to be a central and directing one, intellect allied to the course of a polity. For Jefferson and Emerson no less than for the Puritans, this was assumed to be the redemptive response to the hierarchies of unequal distributions of ability, and understood to be part of spiritual or political democracy. What is striking in the present understanding is how oppositional the cultural critic is as compared to these earlier incarnations. Jefferson expected, and Emerson still expected, the gifted individual to gain the public ear and achieve a creative relation to the public will. The cultural critic revealed in these essays must explain away gaining the public ear and is assumed to be ruined by acceptance. Surely this explains much of the continuing fascination with Randolph Bourne. The cultural critic is, it seems, prized equally for insight and isolation; the failure of criticism to take effect is also an emblem of its success. Criticism is, like literature, prized as an uncorrupted text, uncompromised by being acted upon, not valued for how many it reaches, in whatever diluted readings and forms; it must resist contamination by the popular democratic. The critic may write "we" but remains the singular first person. A suspicion of democratic consumption is a condition of this understanding of cultural criticism.

The role of the cultural critic expresses the convergence of two things, the superior individual's ambition and the culture's understanding of how to institutionalize that role. Americans have a famously curious history of feeling about intellectual giftedness. Anti-intellectualism leads Americans to under- and overvalue the importance of brains. Our culture's images of brainpower tell the story; Ichabod Crane, Jiminy Cricket, Ben Franklin, Einstein, the absent-minded professor, Dr. Strangelove, the schoolmarm, and the computer hacker suggest how wide a range. The society proclaims that education and individual development are important because a free society must attach to its common goals the best brains and train them toward democracy. This is Jeffersonian dogma, reflected in the various democratic elitisms that litter American history. Cultural criticism represents the nether side of utopian democratic elitism. Its office reflects the central and lasting difficulty a free society sees in attaching to its best interests its most talented people, and reveals a hidden embarrassment that the purposes of society are not defined in terms of its superior citizens and the finest human traditions, but in prevailing American majority culture.

Jefferson hoped to fix the natural aristocracy to the public weal. Emerson saw the American scholar as a kind of heroic man of letters inspiring a national culture of individuality. In fact, as these discussions of cultural criticism reveal, the literary-minded and intellectual-identified have become another American interest, contending for space, privilege, share, and control. Democratic society is notoriously hostile to its own braininess, dismissive of the practicality, worth, and common sense of its talented— *vide* Booker T. Washington to Du Bois. The arguments for the prudential experiential wisdom over untested and unreliable braininess echo through our history in the coarse tones of democracy, which does not know much about art, after all, but knows what it likes.

Cultural criticism has become a forum for discontent with American society that can be expressed in terms of civilization and taste. The career of the cultural critic features two characteristic phases. The first is a youth of utopian, contemptuous aggression in which a common cultural politics provides a critical viewing point of the culture. Much lasting cultural criticism is a revolt of the young. Then—as the Young Intellectuals or the New Humanists or the Agrarians or the varieties of '30s Left or the '60s radicals mature—there is a second moment, when they must choose whether they mean to live their lives in critical opposition. Walter Lippmann and Van Wyck Brooks chose not to.

Randolph Bourne did not live long enough for us to be sure, but it is hard to imagine him inside.[3] His views remain compellingly and almost definitively oppositional. It is hard to think of anyone, except perhaps W.E.B. Du Bois, who equaled Bourne's contentious, high-culture political dissent. He refused the society he criticized. Brooks and the others, after all, joined a culture with themes they sounded as trumpet-blast calls in youth but as harmonies in maturity, because shared. Brooks's later works are most unlike his early ones because they have found an audience, and his earlier trope of the writer in opposition to a culture is succeeded by books about writers set in their cultural context. Sometimes cultural critics, like Brooks and Trilling, got much of what they wanted. In interviews, Irving Howe expressed a muted wonder that he too had gotten a hearing, and much in literary and cultural life appeared to content him, perhaps in part because of that.

Nothing can dim the passionate disappointment of Bourne. He died young, and he was disabled, and he got little satisfaction. Like any genre, cultural criticism needs heroes who die young. But there is also Du Bois, whose long, illustrious career could not soften the at-oddsness of his race with this culture. For all the interpretive possibilities of family configurations and intellectual influences, it was Bourne's disability, which gave him the extra feeling of distance, that led to his criticism of the culture. Du Bois was likewise prevented from agreeing, from acceptance, by the doubleness of vision his racial identity gave him. The key moment in a career of cultural criticism seems to be when the ground on which opposition began in youth turns into something permanent. Should a tradition of cultural criticism evolve that prizes distance and individuality, it must rely on the permanence of distance, even if that requires the seeking of distance. Thus does American cultural criticism owe much of its force to the outsider of temperament, of sexuality, of physical condition, of gender, and of race. It is a cultural criticism that may be about literature but is expressive of a deep disengagement in American society and refuses the distinction between the political and the literary. Careers that privilege the literary chart a different and less oppositional course. The history of cultural criticism charts the use of literature as a test of the moral health of the civilization. It is an understanding worth thinking through.

The New England canon of American literature created as constant companion a kind of conscience to guide the development of character and citizenship and sensibility in a potentially licentious people. Thus did license become associated with unculturedness, and the power of culture aggrandized in the minds of those who had an interest in it. The purpose of the literary canon was to make good people from good books; even when the definitions of good books and good people shifted, their axiomatic relation persisted. This was what Santayana understood as the genteel. It helps us see how cultural criticism came to be about literature. It was Santayana, in his genteel tradition essays, who pointed out the consequences of that notion of philosophy and literature. What the institutionalization of learning in American democratic society did in the name of goodness, in his account, did violence to excellence and beauty of thought and expression. The generation of Van Wyck Brooks accepted Santayana's distinctions without really believing that they were bound by his understanding. They thought that if you changed the purpose of literature to the right one, less genteel, more vital, then the axiom of good literature creating good people could be turned to account. Like Parrington, they hoped to change the effect that literature would have but they stuck to a moralistic understanding of literature.

Lionel Trilling did believe that if America could be made safe for modernism, and if he could unseat Parrington, it would be a better place to be. The Trilling project is crucial to the tradition of American cultural criticism, because he in effect replaced the liberal tradition with a politics of literature that responded to currents in modern thought—Hegel, Marx, and Freud—and in art, not to main currents in American political life. By demeaning side-taking through a dialectic understanding, Trilling made a certain politics supreme, and it was one powerfully responsive to the good of the study of literature. The present state of literary criticism as a practice at once vital and institutionally sophisticated and also distant from the common reader has something to do with Trilling's project to remove from literary studies the reference to the good of America in any given time and to substitute an understanding of the civic as somehow being best tested in the literary.

This constituted its great improvement over the genteel tradition. There need be no American character formed by the world's literature, but the good people that great books would make would be conscientious and scrupulous, self-conscious and aware, as Freud and Marx as well as Austen and Joyce might make them. Literature could be trusted to improve humanity even if unrestrained by moralistic devices and untrained in civic or behavioral results. Good books make discerning individuals, discernment being what America lacked and required. If the foundations of the study of American literature are all mixed up with the New England ambition of social control, what did that social control attempt and achieve? Trilling's defense of *The Bostonians* endorsed the novel's attack on reform. It is worth remembering that the New England tradition, imposing itself on Americans in part through a literary canon, was a source, among other things, of abolition, the women's movements, peace movements, and other large and small attempts at reform. The attempt to tie these causes that judge but do not necessarily arise from American democratic or any untrained politics, is one cultural criticism still struggles with.

Replacing Parrington with Trilling resulted in consequential political changes. Trilling's recasting of the American canon in modernist, cosmopolitan terms attempted to purge American literature of the Parringtonian and the earlier moralism of its literary study. Perhaps the goal of truth, beauty, and modern cultivation, freed from the interfering claptrap of moral sentiment, is a good thing. The Puritans, Jefferson, Emerson, Dewey, and Mumford were saying that the unfettered intellect, the intellect freed of some connection to the democratic whole, could not be trusted to pursue the best interests of American democracy. However sentimental the connection, a tradition of cultural criticism that cherishes one is different from a tradition that dismisses one. The tradition of cultural criticism, as presented in these essays, tended to put literature where values and large issues of justice had been and to endorse the notion that by concentrating on literature you might talk as if everything were literature, with the skills and predispositions that such reading rewards.

There is a view of American civilization which stresses the continuity throughout the culture of shared genres and forms which surface in different ways at different levels. It is a map of appropriations and genres and forms from which the classics of high culture emerge, but over which they may lord. Canonized and canonizing cultural critics seldom recognized their own values and talents in the larger precincts of American democracy. They might or might not disdain their own influence within that culture, but they would not see themselves mirrored in it. They identified with what they canonized and not with democracy at large. They conceived of their passion for literature as outside the Madisonian system of competing interests. Instead, they divided what Jefferson and Emerson warned that the culture must never divide.

True prophets are few and far between. The consequence may be a trivializing of the capacity of cultural criticism to address the pressing issues of American civilization, which literature addresses, reflects, and may form part of, but which are not literary. We need a cultural history that repairs the division between the genres of cultural criticism and the rest of the culture. We need to find a way to make shared intellectual life in the different genres and languages of the culture welcome. The isolation of the cultural critic like Randolph Bourne is an emblem of the failure of a just society and of democratic comity, not a symbol of the power of a cultural critique. The goal of repair must supplant the pleasures of isolation.

# ◢ The Kind of Person You Have to Sound Like to Sing "Alexander's Ragtime Band"

IN 1910 IRVING BERLIN wrote a song that would sweep the Western world. "Alexander's Ragtime Band" remains the archetype of the American popular song, an appropriative, creole genre, in which the conflicting claims of European and African traditions are settled in songs and unsettled in interpretations. The songs reflect the status of the blending. The combination of African and Western is an unstable union, reflecting the riddled, horrific history of the formation of American racial culture.

The role of the artist in this appropriation, however, needs attention. The generic and creative artist chooses among available cultural traditions, in the American instance, largely among diasporas. The modern popular artist as broker in cultural transaction—a half-breed, a "white" black or "black" white, and, as the signifier of sophisticated cosmopolitanism—forms part of the subject of American popular songs. Their singer, whatever the stated subject (usually love), becomes a certain kind of person in the singing—much as the lieder singer must be a certain kind of singing person as a way of "becoming" what the song describes. That kind of person, the modern kind of person, as a creation of American cultural brokerage, is the kind of person you have to be to sing the song.

To some extent being the kind of person who can sing the modern song is the ingredient that modernism sought in its primitivism. Darius Milhaud found in Harlem's jazz what he missed in Broadway's: "the profoundly human value which it is capable of having and which overwhelms as completely as any universally recognized masterpiece of music."[1] While modernism was doing its appropriative thing, it was already beguiled—and divided—by the musical appropriations of the likes of Irving Berlin.

This essay is reprinted from *Prehistories of the Future,* edited by Elazar Barkan and Ronald Bush, with the permission of the publishers, Stanford University Press. © 1995 by the Board of Trustees of the Leland Stanford Junior University.

I am grateful to my colleague and friend Elazar Barkan for his invitation to prepare this essay.

They are the very essence of the modern, not least because they substitute cosmopolitan for provincial traditions. This story of Irving Berlin and "Alexander's Ragtime Band" concentrates much that was widespread in early twentieth-century taste and culture and is also an instance of how deliberate the connections between cultural traditions were and how conscious the modern choice among them.

The key challenge for the modern American songwriter was to make a song that white folks could sing, not in blackface, but in white face. The African American tradition was sophisticated and various. The cultural production typified by "Alexander's Ragtime Band" recognized the value of that tradition and a need to simplify and stereotype it. The American song in its golden age is the textual equivalent of a somewhat liberated place. The particular black people in the songs are given greater scope and more humane place than in Jim Crow society. But these are still givens, not rights, let alone equality. The white performer remains the vehicle of this tradition, inspired by and surrounded by blacks.

Some African American performers, like Bert Williams, Ethel Waters, and Paul Robeson, were given restricted place.[2] Individual African Americans or stylized groups appear in the American tableaux presented by popular entertainments toting barges and standing respectfully before the statue of Father Abraham in the Lincoln Memorial. (See Frank Capra and Robert Riskin's *Mr. Smith Goes to Washington* for the latter image.) Lena Horne's appearances in MGM musicals were fashioned so they could be cut from the prints to be shown in the South. But in general, the music was still about the omnipresence of the largely invisible and always subordinate black persona. This musical appropriation was an appropriation of the "primitive" because of its sophistication, because the African diasporic had the ingredients to shake up the American white European normal. The autonomy of the black was subverted by the songwriter, usually an outsider, frequently second-generation American Jewish—Berlin was an exception to this, being himself an immigrant—and formed part of the immigrant Jewish project of making America more sophisticated, more hospitable, and more tolerant.

North American elegance and sophistication and, it turns out, the musical element that moved the whole modernist-Africanist safari, was undertaken in code: the supposedly primitive was taken on in order to increase sophistication. The actual moment of canonic discovery involved a substitution of African American cultural complexity for something less complicated, resulting in an appropriative blend. The sophistication of this blend, verbal and intellectual as well as musical, was remarkable and often the work of songwriters working in the borrowed African American modes. Elegance and sophistication were the very elements that

African American and American popular musicians could reactivate by taking them back to the musical impulses that had inspired them. Song writers faked, imitated, and depended upon a black presence in the music and language of the songs to take ironic, sophisticated, earthy, comic views of American life, simplifying and commodifying what was specially available to the African American.

The invisibility, controlled rendition, or faked presence of the African and African American in American music was exactly what jazz came up against and what bebop challenged. The history of American music is in the shifting blend and unequal exchange of such appropriations and repossessions.[3] One key of modernism was an appropriation of what it took to be African to make a sophisticated music. The true sophistication did not reside in the taste for the "primitive" but in the very traditions being appropriated. The plundering of the African American tradition for its hard-won sophistication, which expressed in matchless fashion the ironic mix of participation and distance from American convention, was the crucial ingredient of the American song, its coded breeziness, its passion, its cool, and its room for improvisational freedom. The modern American moment, however, still preferred to assign that song to a white singer in blackface or, in time, to singers like Fred Astaire, whose incorporation of the African American was more subtle and less advertised.

The African American in the appropriative mix retains artistic advantage and ultimately drives the creative game. The canonic American choice was between an Old World and a New. In fact, the American choice was between several Old Worlds. The elimination of the Native American distinguished America's first few centuries. In place of the flourishing North American civilizations, the European colonial and successor states introduced waves and classes of immigration.[4] In place of native hierarchies, European Americans instituted distinctions based on race, religion, date of arrival, economic success, and so forth. The cultural history of this New World constitutes itself as a series of choices between available cultural traditions and among prototypical agents of culture.

Here are the words to "Alexander's Ragtime Band":

> Oh my honey, Oh my honey
> You better hurry and let's meander
> Ain't you going, ain't you going
> Up to the leader man, the ragged meter man,
>
> Oh my honey, let me take you to Alexander's grand slam, brass
>     band, ain't you comin' along
> Come on and hear, Come on and hear
> Alexander's Ragtime Band

Come on and hear, come on and hear
It's the best band in the land
They can play a bugle call, like you never heard before
So natural that you want to go to war
That's just the bestest band what am
Oh my honey lamb
Come on along, Come on along
Let me take you by the hand
Up to the man, up to the man
Who is the leader of the band
And if you care to hear the Swanee River played in Ragtime
Come on and hear, come on and hear
Alexander's Ragtime Band.

Irving Berlin had been fooling around with the melody that became "Alexander's Ragtime Band" for some years.[5] Russian-born Israel Baline had begun his career as a singing waiter and song plugger and realized that songwriting was the way for him to make his mark and Irving Berlin the name to do it with. (It is worth recalling here how Irving, Howard, Milton, Morris, Seymour, and Sidney became names associated with American Jewish males from immigrant families.)[6] Berlin had inspired facility and a good ear, but no musical training. He was as dependent on transcribers in his early work as so many of his compatriots were on scribes to write their letters. "There is the fellow who creates the song and there is the fellow who is a technical man, just the same as there is someone who's skilled at typing your letter. Now you may not be able to type your own letter, but somebody else can do it for you. But they can't make it up for you."[7] Berlin, of course, took dictation from the culture with his inner ear but that is what expressive cultural agency is, knowing how to take dictation from a culture in musical and lyrical shorthand. Berlin was Franklin-like is his genius and his keen ear for the democratic popular.[8]

Berlin had experienced frustration in his early career. He was a successful vaudeville song writer who wrote with other people, putting words to their tunes, but as he said, his hits were just passing things. He compared his work to Stephen Foster's: "folks are still singing 'Swanee River' and 'My Old Kentucky Home.' It's something to be known like Stephen C. Foster." The key to Foster's great appeal lay in his effective combination of the sentiments and melodies of American creole culture: his pastoral songs combine touches of African-American minstrelsy with doses of Euro-American sentiment; you can't have Foster without racial diversity, and you could not have Foster without racial hierarchy. "Darkies" add color to the music and the lyrics, setting off the sentiments about home and family that this composer understood as an outsider can understand the sentimental needs of cultures in formation.[9] Berlin shared Foster's ambition of creating from the outside—the driven immigrant was certainly an outsider—a music that would make room for him and appeal to the country's essence. However much he was beguiled by European things, Berlin knew that what made American music go was the African element. He wanted to harness that element in his music. He also knew that novelty was part of the formula: popular culture had to be new and traditional at the same time, like social Darwinism in America, new ways of saying things people believed.

Berlin fooled around with several formulas for a hit. He tried to liberate himself from co-writers and composers by writing words for a melody in the public domain. Mendelssohn's "Spring Song" emerged as "That Mesmerizing Mendelssohn Tune" (or "Rag"). In 1909 Berlin adapted the 1890s updating of this classic and added his own words: it is an invitation to hear that lovely Mendelssohn tune, a hit but nothing remarkable.[10] Irving Berlin was more than a *macher*, however; he really wanted what he perceived as Foster's permanence, the security of a popular genius, the safety of an American creative endeavor, and he was a phenomenally gifted songwriter who pursued his craft with the singlemindedness of genius.

Berlin had liked what he knew of black music. Although the ragtime craze had passed, he knew that "ragtime" as whites understood it was far from exhausted. Ragtime, as Scott Joplin, James Scott, Artie Matthews, and others had developed it, was a complicated, written-down music, arguably the most sophisticated blend of African and European American musical inheritance ever achieved—the stuff, its composers believed, of opera and concert halls. Berlin, like many white listeners, heard the lilting call of ragtime and yearned for its syncopations in the music they liked, not just that old concert-hall stuff. Berlin did not have the musical training to grasp the complexities of ragtime. He couldn't write it. He couldn't even read it. What he called ragtime was the syncopation and some of the chords, not the composed music or its elements.[11]

Depending on composer Ted Snyder for the melodies, he tried several versions of ragtime to Americanize, that is enliven, ethnic ditties: "The Opera Rag," "Sweet Marie, Make a Rag-a-time Dance with Me," "Yiddle on Your Fiddle Play Some Ragtime." The songs were not hits, but his method is significant. Berlin tried to mate ethnicities, to broker the exchange through juxtaposition, to take one group's beat and another's stereotypically ethnic behavior. This in essence tried to separate the black music from the black person's image, like Sophie Tucker's saga of trying to sing hot music in whiteface, not blackface. But it did not work, probably in part because Berlin could not make something real out of two artificial elements, a black music he could not master and a series of ethnic stereotypes he was equally ill placed to manipulate—not to mention a culture devoted to keeping African Americans visible in only restricted and demeaning capacities.[12]

The first thing Berlin solved was the music writing. He was a roughhouse pianist—Jimmy Durante was the classic of the breed—playing the black keys, which were easier to control. The "nigger keys" is what they were called; this apparently restricted Berlin to the key of F-sharp major: "The black keys are there under your fingers. The key of C is for people who study music," said Berlin. Biographer Lawrence Bergreen writes that "playing only the black keys deprived him of the ability to explore a wide range of musical subtleties. Nor could he embellish his tunes without harmonies. Without some way of manipulating his melodies, he would never be able to call himself a songwriter, and he would never be able to match the standard set by Stephen Foster."[13] Lucky for Berlin, there was a machine, the transposing piano. This piano could change keys when the player moved a concealed lever, the cotton gin of American music. George M. Cohan had three. It solved Berlin's musical problem, although he still depended on transcribers to write the music down. The music, he said, was in him: "I know rhythm."[14] What Berlin did, of course, was to take the rhythm and the harmonics of black music—music that Joplin, Scott, Matthews, and James Reese Europe, to mention a few, had elaborated with great sophistication into a written classical African American music—and plunder it for its beat and for its cultural meaning.

"Plunder" is what composers and writers do, of course, and Berlin's borrowings across American culture were standard operating procedure. But part of that cultural-production-as-usual must be understood as doing with African American music things that (1) African Americans were not equally free to do; (2) that, for purposes of popularity, reinforced stereotypes about black Americans that were restrictive and demeaning; (3) simplified to the point of crudity a flourishing African American musical tradition and culture; and (4) claimed credit for something borrowed not invented. By the twentieth century, it must be recalled, there was already a well-developed black American composing and performing tradition that included popular (dance music, church music, street music, work music) and formal expressions. Its masters were African American, but their mastery did not have access to the patronage and popularity that really counted. This stripped the music of the culture within which it developed. White American culture was not prepared to accept black musicians, except in the musical equivalents of its own racial images. Indeed, it was still the case that America preferred its black musicians not to be African Americans at all but white Americans in blackface masquerade.[15]

What Irving Berlin did was to take his own creative advantage of a situation for which he was not responsible. He was not motivated by conscious racism, but he did have a quality other than his genius that suited him to be the agent of this most influential of appropriations of African American music: its transformation into the rhythms and harmonic capital on which the golden age of American songwriting and musical theater could confidently draw. Berlin was the key musical figure of the American musical theater and popular song tradition. Asked to define Berlin's place in American music, Jerome Kern said he *was* American music. Savannah-born "southern gentleman" Johnny Mercer remembered as a child having asked his older brother Walter who the greatest composer alive was, "and he told me Irving Berlin."[16] Berlin was that good. But he was also able to represent American music because his black contemporaries could not, because American culture was in no way prepared to grant agency or cultural identity to African Americans.

The music that resulted from this mating is terrific. But what Berlin created and Jerome Kern, Cole Porter, George and Ira Gershwin, Richard Rodgers, Lorenz Hart, Oscar Hammerstein II, Harold Arlen, and Johnny Mercer distinguished was mastered by Thomas "Fats" Waller and Andy Razaf, Duke Ellington, and Noble Sissle and Eubie Blake. While their mastery was acknowledged, their work and autonomous creativity was discouraged, if not prohibited, because of their color. Berlin, Kern, and the Gershwins did not intend racism, as they understood it. A genuine part of their project was to eliminate what they felt was American race prejudice, to respect what they recognized as African American racial genius, to express a fellow feeling as victims of oppression. Berlin's extraordinary "Suppertime," a musical monologue of a woman giving her children supper while trying to figure out how to tell them that their father had been lynched by white racists, which he wrote for Ethel Waters, is still striking because it is so direct. The fact remains that even the racially best-intentioned song writers had to write music for characters like Porgy or Joe in *Show Boat,* which were specific set pieces, frequently wonderfully good, but inevitably assigning a place to the black people who sang them and whom they depicted. They adapted black music for white audiences, which generally meant using white performers. The original *Show Boat* had blackface performers, but American popular music had still no room for black artists.[17]

The serious worth of the ethnic project, the Americanization of the European, does not deserve to be understated, nor does the persisting and material animus of anti-Semitism. The Jews, for instance, who leap-frogged American blacks into acculturation and assimilation were not simply at fault. But, as they knew, their Americanization was an obstacle course with a finish line of relative equality; for native Americans and African Americans, that was not the case. In fact, the immigrants took over from the African American as acceptable "blacks." One might even speculate that, contrary to too much received opinion, one obstacle to black progress was black progress, the success American blacks had achieved in elaborating cultural institutions. Howard University preceded not only Brandeis University but the removal of Jewish quotas from the Ivy League.

One reason American immigrants could do so well is that they were willing to be white blacks. The African American Bert Williams was never as acceptable as Al Jolson as a coon-shouting performer for many reasons, predominantly the absence in Jolson of the inescapable racial inventiveness and irony that distinguished African American playing of the American racial game. When Jolson, Sophie Tucker, Tess Gardella, Jimmy Durante, Eddie Cantor, and Bing Crosby (in voice, not face) adopted some part of a "black" persona, they left behind the sophisticated cultural irony that always accompanied African American culture, that lurked in the rags of Joplin as well.[18] Berlin's assimilation of the black keys was coincident with the shifting of the culturally visible African American musical project decisively away from the institutions and purposes of African American culture.

What distinguishes the assimilation is the adaptation of the black musical impetus to a narrative song tradition that emphasized common American values, like Christmas, love, and Mother, and that had two distinct phases. The first, Irving Berlin's (and Tucker and Jolson's) moment, has second-class white people, Jews as white negroes, more acceptable aliens, whose parroting of American ideals was more successful or less threatening, and the barriers to whose Americanization were less strong. The deal seemed to be that Jews played the "coon," a caricature beneath most sophisticated black performers, and one that removed black people from the mainstream of a culture that did not want them visible. The immigrant assimilation was difficult, and prejudice—anti-Jewish, anti-Irish, anti-Italian, anti-Catholic—was persistent. But the cosmopolitan values immigrants represented managed to take hold, and the creative fact of the matter is that the immigrant playing black came to represent American cosmopolitanism because the European diaspora was acceptable in a way that the African one was not.[19]

The other thing is that the white simplified the African American. The music was simplified, and the implications of black artistic agency were simplified. Berlin's motto for songwriting was: make it easy to sing, easy to say, easy to remember, and applicable to everyday events. "Alexander's Ragtime Band" was all those things. According to Lawrence Bergreen, Berlin thought he would have better luck with the tune "if he included words that could help sell the idea of ragtime to audiences." The song took some time but, reversing the common pattern, caught on throughout the country: coonshouters and minstrels, Emma Carus, Lew Dockstatder, and Al Jolson took to it and it spread to England and Europe, and it became the best-selling song of its day, the song that established Irving Berlin. It was the quintessential song about the phenomena it represented, about white people's interest in black music.[20]

The song, a catchy raggy march, does not tell a story, like "Some of These Days" does; rather, it takes place. Let's go hear some hot sounds, I'll take you to hear this great new group, Alexander's Ragtime Band. Right away, we know a few things, ragged meter, ragtime, and the diction of the opening, *ain't you going,* tell us this is about black musicians. The lyrics are meant to be "coon shouted," and they are clearly about how anyone can Africanize him- or herself. The singer talks that talk as evidence not of his own blackness, because that much we do not know, but because he is familiar with the black side of town. The singer is an agent of cultural appropriation, as we say, or hip—he anticipates Norman Mailer's "white negro," the cool, and much of modern American successive youth cultures, which develop in relation to black style and which is the explicit narrative of jazz history—a tour guide to the wrong side of town.

Critic Gilbert Seldes judged Berlin's accomplishment acutely:

> How much ragtime had been sung and played before, no man may calculate; it had been heard in every minstrel show, and its musical elements were thoroughly familiar. What was needed was a crystallization, was one song which should take the whole dash and energy of ragtime and carry it to its apotheosis; with a characteristic turn of mind Berlin accomplished this in a song which had no other topic than ragtime itself. *Alexander's Ragtime Band* appeared with its bow to negro music and its introduction of *Swanee River;* it was simple and passionate and utterly unsentimental and the whole country responded to its masterful cry, *Come on and hear!*[21]

And the singer knows Alexander, a personal friend of his—this is a step beyond some of his best friends—but we have no reason to think he is "inside" the black culture he visits. He is, like Berlin, enthusiastic about the sound and anxious for us to get into the swing of it but not himself *of* it. The visit is mediated, the tour guide is hipper than we, cosmopolitan, in the know but not part of the culture being visited. It is hard to get the distinction, but even "bestest band what am, oh my honey lamb" is not taken as Alexander's own talk but the appropriated slang of the cool visitor. It sounds odd to us now but contemporary sources, such Carl Van Vechten and Blair Niles, suggest how the archaic blackspeak that we associate with blackface performers had some of the aura of the later white appropriations of black speech.[22]

What Berlin had done was to present the story of the song as a way and a persona for whites listening to black speech. It eliminates the voice of the black person whose music, recognition, and even friendship it appropriates, in whatever demeaning restraints and with whatever redeeming transforming ironies, and substitutes a presence that acts out a black person that whites can be. Both coonshouting and minstrelsy enable the elimination of the black person so that the white person can become the part of one he wishes to. The African American is occasional and peripheral to the appropriated African American persona. The black performer has the choice of a rigid restricted response stereotype or ghettoization, that ghetto being a kind of permanent minor league, the place white people go to hear Alexander's band play so they can copy it. The fact that the ghetto became a shrine for well-meaning whites, talented and black-acknowledging whites, has slight weight when the society and culture are structured racially. The black performer becomes the touchstone for the white appropriation of the song; from now on the game will be who gets to sing the song: how black a white person must sound and, in a subsidiary way, how white a black person must sound, to sing it. The manners for listening to African American music are as conventional as in opera or chamber music—there are body moves and snaps and shakes that distinguish the hearer. The African American source of these manners has also been appropriated as learned behavior by American whites.

Calling the bandleader "Alexander" was one of Irving Berlin's master strokes. It sounds right in the song and has the "darky" ring, but think of what else it does. Who was Berlin's Alexander? He may not have known from Alexander the Great, after all, but from Alexander the czar of Russia he must have known. And like the slaveholders, who degraded their slaves and the uncomfortably demanding aspects of their own classical cultural baggage by naming them Caesar or Pompey, Berlin names his "darky" Alexander. He thus rendered the threatening ridiculous, as he was later to do when he had the *goyim* marching down Fifth Avenue, showing off their fashion finery for Easter instead of rampaging on a pogrom on the Lower East Side. It is interesting to compare "Alexander" to Shelton Brooks's "Darktown Strutters Ball," a wonderful instance of a black songwriter writing a "coon" song for white performers, and a good song at that. "Alexander's Ragtime Band" may well be playing at the Darktown Strutters Ball, but Brooks's lyrics do not catch, as those of "Alexander's Ragtime Band" do, the distance white folks might have to travel to hear Alexander's band. Brooks's song can refer to a white-and-black or to an all-black event.

The success of "Alexander's Ragtime Band" was phenomenal and lasting. The song preserves in lively lyric and tune a perennial moment in American life, where white America had to go to find the best band in the land and all that "signifies," as Professor Gates has shown us. The terms on which that visit takes place have changed; indeed the history of

American music lines the history of that moment. The terms of the appropriative exchange have improved from the African American point of view. The broker's role has changed; it is a "target of opportunity" position in a cultural sense, although largely commercially still restricted. Berlin's success with it was ironically sealed by a persistent rumor that he had not written the song himself, but that he employed a "little colored boy" who wrote the melodies for him. Berlin's response was furious and curious:

> Songwriters don't steal, at least those of reputation don't. Why should they? But the public, by some freak of mind, would rather believe that the fellow who is getting the credit isn't the one who is doing the work. . . . Someone started the report that I had paid a negro ten dollars for it and then published it under my own name. I asked them to tell me from whom I bought successes, twenty-five or thirty of them. And I wanted to know, if a negro could write "Alexander," why couldn't I? Then I told them if they could produce the negro and he had another hit like "Alexander" in his system, I would choke it out of him and give him twenty thousand dollars in the bargain. If the other fellow deserves the credit, why doesn't he go get it?

The rumor didn't die; Berlin's publisher believed it.[23]

The rumor only specified in unproved allegation the cultural truth of the allegation, that Berlin had taken negro music and put it to his own use. That use transformed the music into what would be the standard text for the next generation's music. Berlin became "The Ragtime King" but remained baffled by the complexities of ragtime. He gave the name of a sophisticated music to some of its ruder gears. "I never did find out what ragtime was," he said. Berlin was offended by the notion that he needed a black person to write his music. "The reason our American composers have done nothing highly significant is because they won't write American music. They're as ashamed of it as if it were a country relative. So they write imitation European music which doesn't mean anything. Ignorant as I am, from their standpoints, I'm doing something they all refuse to do: I'm writing American music!"[24] So he was. But he took the name for the serious American music African American writers were writing and gave it to the more accessible, appropriated, and shared music he was writing. This may explain why Duke Ellington resisted the category of "jazz" and said that he was writing American music.

Berlin acknowledged the widespread rumor that an African American wrote his songs at the fortieth anniversary celebration of the founding of the American Society of Composers, Authors and Publishers (ASCAP). Berlin offered his remarks in a parodic medley of his own hit songs. It included these lines: "I'd like to express my gratitude / To a man in my employ, / I'm speaking of THE LITTLE COLORED BOY!" Berlin continued,

"Sweetest little fella / And can he compose! / No one's ever seen him / But he's Mighty 'Lak' a Rose! / He wrote—'Come On and Hear, Come On and Hear' and a / Hundred other hits!" In the audience that night was the songwriter many on Tin Pan Alley had credited with being Berlin's "little colored boy," Andy Razaf.

Andrea Razafkeriefo remains best known for his collaborations as a lyricist with Fats Waller on such songs as "Black and Blue," "Ain't Misbehaving," and "Honeysuckle Rose," and with Eubie Blake on "Memories of You." He was a very good songwriter of that golden age of songwriting; his career presents a classic illustration of the neglect, discrimination, and frustration African American songwriters endured during the heyday of a music specially their own to write. Razaf, whose experiences and creative output are indispensable to understanding the history of the American song and its cultural context, replied to Berlin in the *Amsterdam News* on 8 May 1954:

> Please permit me to comment on the legend of the "colored boy" who was supposed to write Irving Berlin's songs.
>
> As a writer who virtually lived in Tin Pan Alley from 1913 until 1948, and who owed much of his inspiration to Irving Berlin, I, for one, would like to see this ridiculous legend placed in a coffin and given a permanent burial.
>
> Berlin, as a writer, is to Tin Pan Alley what Louis is to boxing, Edison to inventions and Einstein to science. Their kind of genius comes along once in a lifetime. Few writers can write a great tune and a great lyric. This guy does both—and how!
>
> Of all his breath-taking list of socko hits, I'd be happy to settle for just two of them—"God Bless America" and "White Christmas."
>
> Yes, if such a "colored boy" existed, many would-be writers today could really use him. To think of it, I could give him some part-time work, myself.
>
> In closing, I would like to say to anyone who still insists this legend is true, that if a "colored boy" wrote Irving Berlin's songs, then a "white boy" wrote mine![25]

Berlin wrote his own songs—although he could not write his own arrangements. He did the culture's work, brokered the exchange, denying autonomy to the very part of the music that entranced the world, trying to limit the thing that made it music, patent it, name it, own it, control it, apply it, use it. Like Sophie Tucker, who made a point of removing her glove so her audience would know this "colored gal" was white, Berlin resented having his work attributed to a "colored boy." The music he wrote, however, invited the thought, and its most interesting composers and performers had to cope with it because the libel expressed apocryphally the cultural situation he made his success from. The white black person succeeded the blackface performer. What that person learned from the music was not the syncopation fix Berlin imagined, but a taste, the most sophisticated taste Americans could have, one that competed with and replaced the European sophistication that had been the hallmark of American cosmopolitanism since Jefferson and Franklin. The Old World like the New was finding out about Africa.

The African American path not taken by majority American popular and formal culture remained thwarted but by no means deserted. What Berlin and his fellows, black and white, did was to establish the canonic text or blend or, as they say, standard for American popular song. It was characterized by an American foreground, the plantation South, the country, the city, abroad in European, Asian, and African locales, and a European–African American backstory. The American musical, like the generic song, was always balancing operetta with contemporary American lingo and up-to-date reference. This process juxtaposed the subtle ironic American democratic, streetwise, African American language with a more formal inherited English lyrical language.

Different mixes were achieved. Kern was the most European and Arlen the most Afrocentric among white songwriters; among black songwriters, it is harder to say. Ellington let whites write the words often as not, and created a body of song about which the standard thing to say is how little the words measure up to the music, but about which it might be more accurate to say that he wrote music that preempted lyrics. Waller and Razaf, like the Johnson brothers, Noble Sissle, and Eubie Blake, wrote terrific songs but were prevented by the Jim Crow culture from gaining anything like equal access to the kinds of opportunities that made songwriting a lucrative vocation for white men with talent. These conditions still limit the reception of the work of such remarkable African American songwriters as Curtis Lewis.

Two rough paths emerge. White writers keep going back to hear Alexander's band and get that inspiration, while black writers develop something different, the application to the standard accepted, appropriated text of the very energetic, ironic, rococo, racial, coded artistry that escaped Berlin. Until the atom bomb and the emergence of bebop and the civil rights movement, American popular music established itself within the song's circumference, the song as Berlin set it, seeking rhythmic and setting updates from blacks. The line of white black wannabes in this culture is extraordinary. "Alexander's Ragtime Band" is interesting because it signifies the fixing of the "classic" (as they now say) American song, the text that would stabilize racial harmonies for a generation.

What ensued, of course, was a history of exchange. White artists and black artists had something in common, something shared, a place—unlike the movies let alone literature and life—where America developed cultural exchange. It was Louis Armstrong, of course, singing his monumentally deconstructed and rhythmically restored version of "I Can't Give You Anything But Love, Baby," who captured the moment of exchange with an irony that subverted the blackface purpose and launched jazz's reappropriation of African American music. Improvisation, not imitation, is freedom. And freedom is what even the best song of that era must deny the African American. The freedom to improvise, to change the melody, to reinvent the words, to alter the nature of drama and self-presentation, to play a new game on the given ground—this freedom is what African Americans before the Second World War were still denied.

Look for black people in American culture in that era, and you'll find them alive in music, especially playing instruments and surrounding certain white stars, not incidentally musical stars. Mae West sounded like she learned it from Sophie Tucker (or whoever taught Sophie), but she knew enough to hire Duke Ellington for a movie to accompany her, and to keep black women around her to allay some suspicion and get her into the mood. The American blonde had more African American in her composition than meets the eye. Peggy Lee, Marilyn Monroe, and even Doris Day borrowed from their black sisters; Peggy Lee sued Walt Disney for stealing her song stylings, stylings she learned from Billie Holiday and Lil Green.[26]

The greatest white black man of them all (before Elvis) was Fred Astaire. He remains the classic singer of the Berlin, Kern, Gershwin, Porter, and Arlen song. He presented black-inspired rhythm in singing and dancing at its most complete and evolved. His vaunted style shares African with Anglo American roots. In white tie and tails, Fred is somewhere between master and servant, always at ease but never quite at home. His memorable and embarrassing blackface homage to Bill "Bojangles" Robinson in *Swingtime* ("Bojangles of Harlem," by Dorothy Fields and Jerome Kern) is alarming because the good song and the terrific dancing are mired in weird, degrading settings and associations that set off the artistic connection between these two giants and express Astaire's own and through him the majority culture's debt to Robinson and the African American traditions he represented. Astaire got to be what Robinson could not—except in the movie *Stormy Weather,* which is a fictionalized biopic about a black entertainer like Bill Robinson—because, and it is that simple, Robinson was black in a racist society. Bojangles could dance with Shirley Temple because the society trusted with its girls and boys the black men from whom it kept its women and its citizenship. Young and old black men were welcome, but the prime of adult African American man was not on screen except in chains or some other slave drag. To dance with Shirley Temple was, of course, *pace* Graham Greene, to dance at a distance from acknowledged sex. Fred Astaire touched the women he didn't kiss more than Errol Flynn the women he did. And Astaire's romantic, sexy moves were borrowed and forbidden to those from whom they were appropriated.[27]

Lincoln Kirstein identified African America as the source of American elegance in remarks that follow the journey of "Alexander": "[Carl Van Vechten] helped me explore the marvelous dark continent where shone those magnificent palaces, the Savoy Dance Hall and the Apollo Theater. It was a Harlem then oddly unresentful, open and welcoming to the Prince of Wales, to Miguel Covarrubias, to Muriel Draper, and to all writers and artists who recognized in its shadows the only authentic elegance in America."[28] The African American had access to elegance, an irony that keeps one aware of the double standard behind the stated connection between having class and being good. The black knew as a condition of life (not just a canon of taste) that you could be as good as could be, have style, and still remain an outsider; this also meant being unacknowledged and unranked. The lie of taste in a racist society is first and foremost the connection between individual merit and accomplishment. The irony that gives almost automatic subtlety to the most ordinary racial exchange also lends movement to the most static of postures, and a hint of danger to the safe. That very irony is the hallmark of American sophistication, which sees the real truth behind the lie of a racially ordered society yet, it must be said, does not seek recourse in revolution. The elegance is circumscribed by the appropriative setting. One is an agent of a cultural element rather than a free agent of self. Elegance is always distinguished by formal limits and style. The American elegance plays the details of such style and rules against the free and open democratic range of feeling and against the democratic human type. American sophistication piques rather than lays down a rule. But it is a piquing that is deeply formed by and knowledgeable about the rule and committed somehow to something other than a simple personification of it.

The black American knew the rules, had better know the rules better than anybody. Historically, however, black Americans were not able to be what they mastered so completely. They had to caper in between the formal ministrations. Thus the immigrant playing black is a more sentimental creation that the black playing black. African American elegance derives from this situational irony, which makes any African American utterance at once supportive of and ironic about the rules. Compare, for instance, what Kern and the Gershwins did for Fred Astaire with what they wanted to but could not do for black performers. Paul Robeson struggled with the limitations of the generic situation in *Show Boat*. "Old Man River" is a memorable aria, right up there with "Summertime." But it is an aria, in allegorical setting, imposed rather than free, and Robeson's achievement remained circumscribed. Astaire had the freedom that the African American created in music and in tone, but the text served him well. But Astaire like Mae West had to keep black people around. Singing and dancing "Shine on Your Shoes" in *The Band Wagon* (MGM, 1953), Astaire is partnered with a black shoe-shine man, the wonderful LeRoy Daniels, who has rhythm and cool and lends some to Astaire's lively, rhythmic, if somewhat archaic tap. It is a great scene that dramatizes what "Alexander's Ragtime Band" canonized, the source of the hip white in the actual contact with the black. Given the insistent racial hierarchy of American society, such totemic contact was a kind of renewal and its best art, the songs of Berlin, Gershwin, and company, keep coming back to it.[29]

The attempts to stage the authentic scene itself, for all their interest, suffered from the inevitable deadening weight of the nature of black status quo in white America. Virgil Thomson and Gertrude Stein's *Four Saints in Three Acts* shared the problem, as did Gershwin's *Porgy and Bess* and Scott Joplin's *Treemonisha*. This is not a put-down. These were cultural productions that did not allow for artistic any more than civil freedom. The black white like Astaire or Mae West, or earlier versions who borrowed from the black to be free whites—sexually charged and physically expressive and rhythmically free, more playful, more all sorts of things—opted for a kind of freedom. They expanded what the society already granted its racially privileged.

The black choice was widened as well. The text, the American song, the appropriative blend created places for African American artists to improvise and reassert their agency and the independent interest of the African diasporic commentary on these cultural goings-on. The way to hear it is to listen to Louis Armstrong, Sidney Bechet, Coleman Hawkins, Henry "Red" Allen, Art Tatum, Lester Young, and Billie Holiday and the way they performed the songs that emerged from the great "Alexander's Ragtime Band" moment. The quality of improvisation they brought to the proceedings asserted the true character of African American sophistication, which unsettles the song with the surprising appearance of its destined singer. The key to jazz as it evolved within the larger American cultural marketplace is that its story, at least until bebop, was the liberation of African American creative energies within the set form of the American popular song. Its genius was in part original and also lay in its imposed ironic improvisatory commentary. Jazz narrated an American setting that would not yet acknowledge it. Bessie Smith's 1928 version of "Alexander's Ragtime Band" returned this hybrid original song to its truest sources and expressed the musical impulses Berlin borrowed. Hers was a relatively straightforward blues reclamation, magnificently earnest of things to come.

# ⚡ Some of Those Days

IN *NAUSEA* JEAN-PAUL SARTRE told the story of a historian, marooned and blue in the French sticks in 1932, who took some comfort from sitting in a bistro and listening to a recording of what he considered an American blues song. Antoine Roquentin's feeling of *nausea* expresses the existential butterflies in the stomach of a modern man, manifesting a degree of self-consciousness about life that makes even daily choices almost impossible. This somatic version of a metaphysical and cultural dilemma finds temporary surcease when Roquentin listens to an old recording of an American jazz song. He hears it with an extraordinary intensity that seems to supplant his inner emptiness with bearable emotion, with real feeling that makes him feel real.

He remembers the song from American soldiers whistling it in the First World War, and it becomes the entire focus of his existence when it plays:

> The vocal chorus will be along shortly: I like that part especially and the abrupt manner in which it throws itself forward, like a cliff against the sea. For the moment, the jazz is playing; there is no melody, only notes, a myriad of tiny jolts. They know no rest, an inflexible order gives birth to them and destroys them without even giving them time to recuperate and exist for themselves. They race, they press forward, they strike me a sharp blow in passing and are obliterated. I would like to hold them back, but I know if I succeeded in stopping one it would remain between my fingers only as a raffish languishing sound. I must accept their death; I must even will it. I know few impressions stronger or more harsh.
>
> I grow warm, I begin to feel happy. There is nothing extraordinary in this, it is a small happiness of Nausea: it spreads at the bottom of the viscous puddle, at the bottom of *our* time—the time of purple suspenders and broken chair seats; it is made of wide soft instants, spreading at the edge,

A version of this chapter was first published in the *Western Humanities Review* 41, no. 3 (Autumn 1987).

like an oil stain. No sooner than born, it is already old, it seems as though I have known it for twenty years.

The music challenges the everyday. It stills the meaningless with a sudden moment of meaning. It will replace the noise of despair and settle Roquentin's nauseated stomach. Listening to the song gives Roquentin some missing sense of life:

> I am touched, I feel my body at rest like a precision machine. I have had real adventures. I can recapture no detail, but I perceive the rigorous succession of circumstances. I have crossed seas, left cities behind me, followed the course of rivers or plunged into forests, always making my way towards other cities. I have had women, I have fought with men; and never was I able to turn back, any more than a record can be reversed. And all that led me—where?[1]

Roquentin's feelings have a history of their own. The complicated articulation of his sense of things is an example of the way in which self-conscious (historically, white) listeners have described their transport with jazz and blues and Afro-American music. It has moved a whole class of people who have no stomach for the modern world and yet take to the modern avant-garde. At the most serious and silliest levels alike, racial communication is carried on through music and the picturesque posturings of self. For societies that comprise difference to hold together, there have to be pageants that proclaim what *we* know about *them* and *they* about *us*. These are strictly regulated kinds of knowledge, but there is something in music that abets illicit communication between socially separated lives. It is hard to talk about, however, because the argots of the divided worlds, which the sharing of music brings into a somewhat altered contact, are not meant to express that sharing. But white people acting, singing, talking black is a subversive genre in life and art, long after the society has committed itself to black people's being allowed and encouraged to sing, talk, and act white.[2]

The song Sartre has Roquentin hear is all refrain. The verses of that song, "Some of These Days," which was composed in 1910, tell the story of a pair of country sweethearts. One day the "laddie" tells the "girlie" he is going away, and her heart just about breaks. In the first verse he leaves and she warns him with the refrain, and in the subsequent verse the warning comes true and he regrets having left. For all its scenic, pastoral quality, the song has the comic edge of a smart and realistic woman lurking inside that "girlie." One key element in the persona of the blues or blues-imitating, the black or the *blackface* or *blackvoice* female blues singer is her distance from the Victorian-maiden epigone of the virgin as victim. If someone is going crazy over lost love in her world, it is not going to be she.

The African American or lower-class woman was allowed to be realistic about the world in a way the white virgin lady heroine never was. Melodrama placed unrealistic females into fantastic gothic situations of harm, while comedy allowed realistic women to encounter and outsmart real-world dangers. The blues was initially seen as comic; its poignant moods simply took until later for white ears to recognize. Black speech seemed scary and strange and funny to whites, even during the twenties, like immigrant speech, like city speech, exotic.

"Some of These Days" folds the woman of passion and instinct who can take care of herself into a milk-maidenly country lass. It is a song of feeling and warning; its protagonist knows her worth and makes it clear that she means to have her way, having let him have his. The couple were more than sentimental sweethearts. For all the pastoral verse, this is a song about a man leaving his woman. She sings that he'll be sorry because he'll miss her loving and not just her love, and, as the second verse makes clear but the refrain implies, she's not about to wait for his return. As the young man leaves, she sings:

> Some of these days
> You'll miss me honey.
> Some of these days
> You're gonna be so lonely.
> You're gonna miss my hugging.
> You're gonna miss my kissing.
> You're gonna miss me honey
> When I'm far away.
> You're gonna be so lonely
> For you only
> 'Cause you know, honey
> I let you have your way.
> And when you leave me,
> You know it's gonna grieve me.
> You'll miss your mama
> Some of these days.[3]

We may have trouble nowadays recognizing the sexual directness of this song. It is essentially unsentimental and angry, expressing more the feelings involved in a situation of sexual betrayal than the sentimentally elaborated balladry of the time could convey. She's mad, but she won't die from it. He'll be sorry. The words make a bow to the old tradition, but the singer of this song is that lusty, direct woman who was still a suspect creature, more a denizen of the lower depths than of the limited demimonde America hosted. Lillian Russell, remember, sang "Mah Evening Star" in dialect, but it was a lilting and tender, wistful song. The woman of "Some of These Days" was not about to die for love of that rat. As Roquentin understood, this was "the song of the Negress," an expression of that unbridled passion and sexual directness that Western civilization, in the guise of Victorian morality and intellectual second-guessing, had schemed to rob the human animal of.

Hold on a second. *"Stop the music!"* as Jimmy Durante used to interrupt. "Some of These Days" was not a blues or even a jazz song particularly. As Hayden Carruth notes in his introduction to the translated *Nausea,* "It is unfortunate that Sartre chose to call by the name of 'jazz' a recording that, from Roquentin's description of it, most musically minded Americans will recognize as commercial pseudo-jazz."[4] And yet Sartre clearly was not aware of this; his choice was his mistake. It mattered to Roquentin and to his creator that the song was written by a Jew and sung by a black woman. From their relation to the medium of the blues song arose a view of authenticity and meaning in the modern world. This rendering of the situation of the modern bourgeoisie remained an element in that aspect of Sartre's writing that has influenced Western culture's view of its own encounter with the traditions and peoples it colonized and considered "other." It juxtaposes the natural, unrefined, authentic feelings of the outsider with the too-self-conscious European intellectual or bourgeois self, who must feed as the Jewish songwriter on the black singer to convey anything like the real, the natural, the passionate, the fire down below, that which is authentic in human feeling.

The song was written before World War I, but Roquentin's fantasy of its creation by a Jewish composer (someone like Irving Berlin or George Gershwin) feels like the twenties. Ironically and wonderfully, Sartre's imagined subduing of the black beat by a Jewish writer for a "Negress" to sing reverses the real-life situation. In fact, a black writer (Shelton Brooks) translated a black beat into terms a Jewish singer (Sophie Tucker) could perform for white audiences. The song provided the audience with that patented experience—a safe passage to the ground of natural feeling conducted by the tour guide of modern life, the simulated or sanitized black.[5]

Time was when Americans knew "Some of These Days" as the signature song of the great Sophie Tucker, the Mary Garden of Ragtime, the last of the Red Hot Mommas, one of the great vaudeville and show-business stars of the century, one of the shining female stars, one of the first American Jewish stars. She made several recordings of "Some of These Days," including at least one from the mid-twenties, the one Roquentin probably heard, a version which did not include the introduction to the song. She appeared in Europe, and her records were sold there. The hand-book of the Smithsonian Collection of American Popular Song, which be-gins with Tucker's 1911 recording of the song, describes what the singer Roquentin probably heard when he thought he was hearing "the Negress":

> This song and its performance demonstrate the changes occurring in Amer-ican music in the first decades of the twentieth century. In both text and music, it reflects the emerging American vernacular styles. . . . There is only a hint of jazz feeling, but the way the horns are played provides a clue to that developing influence. (Both this song and Brooks's 1917 hit, "Dark-town Strutter's Ball," became the basis for many jazz performances.)
>
> "Some of These Days" also became the theme song of Sophie Tucker (1884–1966, b. Sophie Abuza), who made this, the first of her four record-ings of it, near the beginning of her six-decade career as a popular enter-tainer. She is at the peak of her form here, using her powerful chest regis-ter to excellent effect. . . . Tucker's voice and interpretive mannerisms clearly reflect her continuing association with black singers and musicians. In "Some of These Days" she gives a fluidity to the song's rhythmic patterns by singing off the beat, and in the repeat of the chorus she incorporates an assortment of vocal "breaks" so reminiscent of blues singing. She plays with the tempo as later singers would do, and there is no subtlety in her singing. She opts instead for dramatic effect, and her robust projection, when heard from the stage of a theater or cabaret, was dauntless and powerful.[6]

The pseudo-Negress Sophie Tucker *was* show business. Lenny Bruce would satirize her as Mother Tucker, the old-broad madonna of the sen-timentality and hokum of trouping. Tucker, for good or evil, pioneered what has come to be an infestation of self-regarding show biz and end-less appropriation of the current in the service of the entertainer. Sophie Tucker also pioneered the leavening of American Victorianism with the rude and ribald remark, with a humor based on sexual candor and her own appetites, her self-described physical ungainliness, and straight-from-the-shoulder, woman-to-woman talk about her disappointments. It is apt that Bette Midler uses Soph as the persona of her dirty jokes. Joan Rivers probably knows how much she still works in Sophie Tuckerland. Sophie sang and talked dirty in a kidding, homey way. She made a point of her own size and bad luck: "nobody loves a fat girl," she wailed, "but oh how a fat girl can love." Along with Mae West, she opened things up for the down-to-earth and the candid, getting arrested for her shimmy, offend-ing bluenoses all over the place and making a point of it. Like most great music-hall entertainers, Sophie made her act out of her life. She did not respect the distinction between show business and life's business and always tried not so much to bridge as to fill in the gap. Her art was like life and meant both to stem from it and respond to it, to make it better, but to include within the art enough of life to make the art count, connect. She was shameless, as all great popular artists must be.

An ambitious immigrant Jewish daughter, Sophie Tucker was determined to make a home for herself. The conditions of trouping meant that she had to make America her home sweet home and in every performance come to grips with the issue of assimilation: how much of a woman, a Jewess, a singer, a city slicker, would this or that American outpost embrace, how to get noticed and yet not be rejected, how to be remembered without being ostracized, how to make it in the new world. *What do they want and what will they take* form the American popular artist's litany. And Sophie had to represent not only herself but also Tin Pan Alley and the mythical city that sent out its imperial foot soldiers of song, dance, and personality to the hinterland to entertain and make of this random people something more homogeneously, and so more profitably, cosmopolitan.

Cultural enterprise *is* imperial, dispatching its preachers and its touters to drum up the market for its goods. Universities and burlesque wheels, television networks and presidential administrations alike create emissaries of their views to woo and entertain and excite a response in their audience. Entertainment socializes a democratic people with our constantly shifting and always privately enterprising commercial cultural values. There is no such thing as culture in this country that does not market itself, well or badly. People must want it for company in life. Sophie Tucker understood this. She had talent and ambition. She took her work seriously. She happened along at a good moment for her extraordinary impersonation of a crowded crossroads of American cultural values. And she understood that to distinguish between life and art was to risk losing her hold on her audience.

Sophie did a great deal of philosophizing in her act. Most of what she shared was experiential wisdom about love and life. Her unique blend of Jewish daughter and black mammy and, finally, Jewish grandmother with a past and an attitude was a pungent and authoritative vehicle for her reflections and a reminder of how interesting a woman she was. She was sometimes political, however, and—as with most show people—the surest goad to her politics, her liberalism, was society's attitude toward entertainers as socially suspect and its puritanical censuring of their acts. Show biz promoted an American society advanced by liberal politics because show business is hooked on novelty. The progressive political motto of entertainment is the old saw "Change your act or go back in the woods!" Of course, the conservative impulse is reflected in the equally potent show biz dictum "Don't fuck with a hit!"

Sophie Tucker was self-consciously political in the sense that she felt entitled to sound off about current events. Her autobiography contains many instances of this. She understood the politics of her songs. About the sentimental "My Yiddishe Mama," which she sang in Yiddish and English, she wrote:

> Even though I loved the song, and it was a sensational hit every time I sang it, I was always careful to use it only when I knew the majority of the house would understand the Yiddish. However, I have found whenever I have sung "My Yiddishe Mama," in the U.S.A., or in Europe, Gentiles have loved the song and have called for it. They knew, by instinct, what I was saying, and their hearts responded just as the hearts of Jews and Gentiles of every nationality responded when John McCormack sang "Mother Machree." You didn't have to have an old mother in Ireland to feel "Mother Machree," and you didn't have to be a Jew to be moved by "My Yiddishe Mama." "Mother" in any language means the same thing.[7]

This is clearly reasoned liberal *meltingpotismo* and it bears analysis. It is shrewd about practical matters. Sophie did not go around America singing in Yiddish unless Jews were a majority in the theater, but she dreamed of the day when all people, Jew and gentile, could sing together about their mothers.

In Paris in the early thirties, Sophie found herself in the middle of a riot between Jews and anti-Semites, caused by her singing "My Yiddishe Mamma," which became the song many Europeans identified her with: "Several years later, after Hitler came to power and started the persecution of the Jews in Germany, I heard that my records of 'My Yiddishe Mama' were ordered smashed and the sale of them banned in the Reich. I was hopping mad. I sat right down and wrote a letter to Herr Hitler which was a masterpiece. To date, I have never had an answer."[8]

Her autobiography was published before the true scale of the Holocaust was widely assimilated, and this may account for the tone of Sophie's response to Herr Hitler, like Chaplin's *The Great Dictator*. But it also shows the characteristic limits of the entertainer's politics, which are based on the blurring of distinctions between life and art. Sophie Tucker's art is not on a scale to comprehend such enormities.

But in one instance Sophie Tucker opined about a subject she grasped keenly, the state of American freedom, in her 1920s song "Fifty Million Frenchmen."[9] A blend of Montesquieu's *The Persian Letters* with "How You Gonna Keep Them Down on the Farm after They've Seen Paree," the song begins with a report from France: "they say the French are naughty / they say the French are bad. / They all declare / that *over there* / the French are going mad" (emphasis added). The song goes on to bring its point home:

> When they put on a show and it's a hit,
> No one tries to censor it.
> Fifty Million Frenchmen can't be wrong.
> And when a book is selling at its best,

It isn't stopped, it's not suppressed.
Fifty Million Frenchmen can't be wrong.
Whenever they're dry
For brandy or rye,
To get it they don't have to give up their right eye.
And when we brag about our liberty,
They laugh at you and you and me,
Fifty Million Frenchmen can't be wrong!

Sophie Tucker had fashioned a stage self as a sex-hungry, sentimental, good-natured, upstanding, big-hearted, *zaftig* broad whose emotions were out front. She fought the enemies of free expression because they were the enemies of self-expression, which was the vehicle of her art, which in turn was the distribution of urban values throughout what remained a small town, rural America ... sort of.[10]

Being Jewish and singing jazzed up (that is, black-influenced) material were central to her performance. She was a pioneer of the classic twentieth-century American show-biz mix whose immortals included Al Jolson, Eddie Cantor, Fanny Brice, and Jimmy Durante. Its performers' trademarks included a highly individualized personality playing a familiar character within recognizable settings and situations. The characters were universal human types with broadly painted strokes of ethnic and other variations. Their vital assimilation of American culture enlivened the familiar with elements of surprise that gave these lasting stage personas their initial kick. It was big-city and shamelessly sentimental, but also hard-edged and jazzy in delivery, the one-liner and the patter bringing the slicker pace to the outposts of America, infusing America with a cheeky and even subversive energy.

The immigrant's assimilation of American values always had an edge. My immigrant grandfather wanted to be a Mason and unwittingly mastered many too many degrees his first weekend of initiation. The examiners asked him, "Mr. Rosenberg, why are you in such a hurry?" He replied that it was "an old American proverb, Washington said it, never put off until tomorrow what you can do today!" Franklin probably said it, but they were all Washington and Lincoln to my grandfather. And in our family this was a story of the *goyim* trying to hold grandpa back because he was a pushy Jew, and of his clever turning of the American two-headed coin to our advantage, and of our ambivalance about all of it.

We were raised to imitate them, not him, of course. Our politics had the innocent purity of belief, and they lost sight of Max Rosenberg's realization that in this new country you could sometimes win by sticking their professed ideals to those guys, although this required that you proclaim your loyalty to those ideals relentlessly. We were stuck with the professed ideals, floundering in them, exhausted with having to find the energy for them, good old helpless idealism, phobic about motive. (Trying to hold society to its professed ideals as my grandfather did was a historic method for the black struggle for equality.) The idealism about one's own professed principles that leads to righteous behavior is the least stable and most vulnerable of beliefs, and the person who is principled is always prey to the trickery of someone clever enough to play on those principles, for good or ill.

In the immigrant entertainers' bag of tricks there was a shameless willingness to use America against itself, so to speak, to gain admission. Their ambivalence about what you would have to endorse in order to belong led to calculations concerning how much of yourself you could afford to be, what was advisable to shed, and what you might even want to keep in your own heritage. The resulting mix gave some of that entertainment its edge. Urban entertainment was always in major ways at odds with the prevalent values of the heartland it had to please. "Mother Machree" and "My Yiddishe Mama" might lubricate the dry ducts of Protestant America, but they also heralded a cultural change. And the greatest change was in the intimacy it introduced with what had once been distant.

For this style was heartfelt, personal performance that thrived on the communication between audience and performer. It was old-fashioned in the sense that it raised to a national scale the same qualities that characterized a subculture. It might get gussied up, but it was plain in essence; and while topical, it was technologically somewhat conservative. Ted Lewis and Sophie Tucker went out twisting their theme songs to the young people's beat of the rock era, just as Barbara Stanwyck made a picture with Elvis Presley. There was always a way to accommodate the moment. And it featured immigrants and poor people, the way prize fighting did. This live popular entertainment was the way from rags to riches through the public consciousness and tolerated a rougher-and-more-tumble kind of impersonation than the movies were ready to do. You could be recognizably Jewish and be a vaudeville star at a time when Jews rarely had significant roles in films. And they sang and danced in the Afro-American-derived mode. There was lots of other stuff mixed in, but the decisive musical addition was ragtime, jazz, syncopation. Call it what you will, this recognizable *americano* music, it was another adaptation of the black for the titillation and surprise and entertainment of the white.

There was a moment around the turn of the century when American popular music was syncopated to a black beat. It appropriated much from the Afro-American tradition, including cakewalking and ragtime, and especially from the conventions of blacks entertaining whites. At the same time immigrant musicians to some extent took over from black performers in playing to white audiences. There is probably a connection between this replacement and the imposition of racial segregation and separation during the 1890s. *Plessy v. Ferguson* had its entertainment corollary in the rise of a new class of white entertainer.

White Americans seem never to get enough of the music and clowning of blacks. It is a complicated attraction and one that continues to grow. It is perhaps *the* American acquired taste, that complicated and ambivalent taste of whites for blacks, for their patois and for the charades of dominance and nostalgia that this involves. Remember how much of the music is about sex, the forbidden American subject; remember that music is warmed by the fires down below, that it is notoriously iddish.

The music also presented the set piece of nostalgia for the aristocratic past. The American operetta is quintessentially Southern: hoop skirts, flirtations, quadrilles, and a sentimental vision of a class society and a healing view of the almost fatal Civil War that sweeps the true conflicts under the rug. It is something every generation of Americans has to learn; the song of the South may change with the generations, but it remains the story that must be learned. It sorts out race and class and war and honor and the aristocratic alternative to the democratic, the ancient to the modern, the slow to the fast, the connected to the alienated presents. The Old South was where it was different back then in a way that suits America to fantasize. It is our Valhalla and the scene of some of our deepest, most soothing, and enraging cultural dramas, and its intense importance in popular entertainment and music cannot be overstated, particularly before the immigrant story was accepted as worth telling. The role of the darky, colored, negro, black in this ensured some sort of black visibility to a white-run society. The blackface entertainer took some of the job away from the black and became the darky. That was step one; step two was the blackvoice and black-stepping white entertainer who succeeded the blackface.

The songs reflect what was important about the drama: moonlight and magnolias, fields of cotton, paddle wheelers, and so forth, the rhythms of desire and the eccentric dance of submission, all mixed up in that steamy southern country brew that had so many variations. This was where American popular song started, and it came to be able to absorb and use the inspiration of Afro-American music without referring to it directly, although that reference was always a resource. The first thing the music had to do when it changed, be it Elvis's revolution or Irving's, Graceland or Tin Pan Alley, was to reconnect itself openly to its black sources.

This had the ironic and interesting effect of freeing white performers from the need to impersonate blacks while not blessing blacks in any substantial way. Blacks were still imprisoned by stereotypes when performing for whites and, before the twenties, often prevented from performing at all. American popular music had adapted its African American inspirations to the needs of white Americans and could create its song at last with white people. Blackface gave way to blackvoice, and blackvoice became a kind of learned white voice. The twenties reopened select white audiences to some black performers, especially in all-black shows, such as Lew Leslie's "Blackbird" reviews. But the situation remained restricted, and the weird story of the period was the liberation of the blackface performer, a simulated drama of racial and artistic liberation within the context of stereotypically racist, conventionalized, and marvelously vulgar musical entertainment. Sophie Tucker was a monumental figure in that transition. She somehow made the music more palatable to Americans, who were beginning to discover it anyway. She began with what was called "coon shouting," a phrase which expresses the combination of demeaning epithet and source of entertainment that characterized the culture of that era. "Coon shouting" was inevitably and purposefully degrading to the black people whose style and humanity were being plundered. It also refers to the genre in which Sophie Tucker and so many others sang. In fact, Sophie Tucker coon-shouted her way to fame.

Tucker's career began and continued to develop in this groove of borrowed black as the best available vehicle for an unassimilated personality. She was born in Europe and grew up in New England, the hardworking and rebellious daughter of a hardworking but luckless Jewish family. She left a failed marriage and a young son to make her way in show business, going to New York in the early 1900s and getting a job singing in a big eatery. Her autobiography, *Some of These Days,* of course, tells about her first vaudeville engagement, an amateur night. Having cleared the preliminary hurdles, Sophie gets her chance to sing for the impresario:

> The pianist beat out the tunes and I did my best with them, keeping my eye glued to Chris Brown, lolling back in his shirt sleeves, hands on hips, chewing a cigar. He looked bored as hell, but when I finished he nodded. "O.K. Use the first three we tried. You can go on."
>
> My chance had come.
>
> I stumbled out of the door conscious of the envious looks of the others who had been turned down or were lined up waiting a chance to be heard. I felt dizzy: hot and then cold. Behind me came Chris Brown's voice, calling to an assistant: "This one's so big and ugly the crowd out front will razz her. Better get some cork and black her up. She'll kill 'em."[11]

And she did.

But Sophie describes this big personality-loaded Jewish woman's having to express her very size and feelings and need for attention and gottasing inspiration in the persona of the blacked-up coon singer. And in an interesting passage, she describes mastering the stage persona of the blackface girl shouter. She accepted the judgment that she herself was so big and ugly the audience would only accept her as the image of the most downtrodden of Americans, who was not a Jewish immigrant after all, but the fat, lusty, sassy, moaning, eye-rolling, funny Missus Sambo, Madame Bones. Soph recalls how bad she felt for herself, but like the good trouper she was, she learned the ropes and seems not to have worried about the politics. On her first real gig, she accosted the booker:

> "Let me leave off the black," I pleaded—"Try me out the way I am and see if I don't go over." But he wouldn't hear of it.
>
> That's how I became a blackface singer. "World-renowned Coon Shouter" was how Joe [Joe Woods, her booking agent] put it on his notices. On the Park circuit I was also billed as "Sophie Tucker, the Ginger Girl, Refined Coon Singer." ... And on my first New York date in December 1907 as "Sophie Tucker, Manipulator of Coon Melodies."[12]

She felt a loss of identity, but Sophie Tucker was ambitious and determined to work her way up to being a headliner. This meant for the time appearing in blackface, and her book gives an almost surrealistic version of the true hurts of the black person as they are experienced by the fake black person, with young Sophie crying as she wipes off the staining makeup and getting used to the public shining black face she must wear to earn the appreciation of white audiences. The songs she sang even then would have been the broad, syncopated, or sentimental songs of Dixie and loving and betrayal and lust, the comic edge of blackface being the ticket to the fires down below in the still-puritanical American hinterland. It was OK to depict funny, outlandish black people as experiencing human passion and the hardness of human fate, and to express the unsentimental feelings that are in so many of the songs about wayward men and suffering women, hard times, and missing my home, basic emotions for which America had no better patois.

Indeed what Sophie Tucker made of the "darky" laments was one of the first popular immigrant lingos, known now as show biz, but as Jewish and Irish and Italian as it ever was heartland and whose principal cultural function seemed to be translating into acceptably comic English the emotions and dialect of black-faced aliens brokering for the native aliens. When Americans were ready in the twentieth century to enjoy some of the warming fire, they had to take it prophylactically from "their" blacks. And show biz grew up to provide it. And the stuff within the African

American impulse in its white American stereotyped version was essentially sex and feeling, expressions of love that in America were so Protestantly restrained. You could get warm in the vaudeville embrace of Sophie Tucker, with her Jewish animation and her subtext of feeling in her blackface straitjacket and her blackvoice passion.

The fledgling Sophie runs into George LeMaire of the team of Conroy and LeMaire, headlining blackface comedians. Kid, he tells her, you don't do your makeup right, and he proceeds to give her the blackface lowdown: "Up North they don't know anything about the high yellow. Here you're either black or white." Is this street wisdom or stage wisdom or what? LeMaire teaches Sophie about pacing, and sure as shooting, she was getting good: "My greatest difficulty was convincing the audience that I was a white girl. My southern accent had got to be as thick and smooth as molasses. When I would pull off one of my gloves and show that I was white there'd be a sort of surprised gasp, then a howl of laughter. *That season I started interpolating Jewish words in some of my songs, just to give the audience a kick*" (emphasis added).[13]

One of the interesting things about blackface is how important it is to reassure the audience that the performer is white. For the blackface singer to convey the scary message safely, we must know she is white. And so at the very moment that Sophie began to perfect her blackface, she had to make sure people were not color-blinded by her disguise, and, wonderfully, she began to realize what a kick it would be for her to add her Jewishness to the mix. Picture her, big, blackfaced, leather-lunged singer, black in song style and accent, revealing herself to be white—remember that this was the reversal of the drama of miscegenation as in *Show Boat*—it was a comedy of relief, not a drama of social confusion. Sophie's Yiddishisms, like one-liners, peppered an American stew with urban melting-pot, street-smart wisecracks.

Sophie's own drama underscores the interest of blackface. It keeps her down. Why, she wonders, must she appear in blackface? What did she do to have to pretend to be so black and blue? "I'd worked so hard. My hands were smooth and white now. No one would suspect them of long association with the dishpan and scrub pail. My own hair under the wig was a mass of burnished gold curls. Nature and my fine Crimean ancestors had done that for me. They had given me, too, my smooth, fine skin, that was pleasingly white now, since I had learned to care for it."[14]

"I'm white, but it's inside, so that don't help my case, 'cause I can't hide, just what is on my face . . . .[15]

Tucker's blackface dilemma is an uncanny marking of where American racial relations were. The black person had to be *white* inside, and only a blackface white man could give the white folks what they wanted from a black. The blackface performer stole from the black something that the black would not have been allowed to use. The dilute sensual freedom that was an essential part of what Americans accepted from ragtime and jazz, and other values that blackface began to locate if not really formulate, would not have been tolerated from real blacks. That very decade's going to Harlem "in ermine and pearls" and even Carl Van Vechten's *negritude* sensibility, which it kidded, were the most advanced sort of taste. Even then, the first was the occasion for the creation in Harlem of the African American Potemkin Village of the Cotton Club, and the second was occasioned by a privileged alienation from the society that held mixed blessings for the African American who might want a regular old American life. But Sophie Tucker wanted to be herself and regarded blackface, which had been a vehicle of her career, as restricting. She was sure she could do all she had done in blackface better as herself. And it came to pass.

A Boston appearance heralded by posters advertising "Sophie Tucker: World-renowned Coon-Shouter" courted disaster when the trunk with the makeup and costumes failed to arrive in time for the matinee. What was Sophie to do? The manager tells her, "Go on in your street clothes, the way you are. A good-looking hefty squaw like you don't need black make-up." More nervous than ever before, the real Sophie Tucker walks out on that stage and tells the audience in what was to become her heartwarming, straight-from-the-shoulder, Mother Tucker style: "You-all can see I'm a white girl. Well, I'll tell you something more: I'm not Southern. I grew up right here in Boston, at 22 Salem Street. I'm a Jewish girl, and I just learned this Southern accent doing a blackface act for two years. And now, Mr. Leader, please play my song."[16]

Sophie was out of blackface and in the pretty treacherous territory of being a woman, *hefty squaw* indeed! But blackface had outlived its usefulness to her. She got to keep the music and the intonation because, of course, nobody in those days sang the music people wanted to hear without somehow doing blackface. Listen to early Bing Crosby or Mildred Bailey and Jolson or Durante. The singing of the black music, using black intonation and wording, was a matter of inflection, like learning a foreign language or, better, learning a new style, putting on company manners. In plain fact, the white appropriation tended to be the mastery of a part of the black style that had developed to please the master anyway, the assumption of the mask blacks used to please whites. The comedy and pathos of submission and ostracism, the constant comedy of the alleged black inability to learn to be white—because not allowed to be fully human—suited the immigrant vaudevillian especially. But not for long.

The depth of the African American aesthetic, its true genius, was much harder to capture, and the story of that exchange is the story carried on not by Sophie Tucker but by Irving Berlin and Fred Astaire. The black-face singer gave voice to universal emotions in a cultural language developed by the American negro as a placating, survivalist, ironic, and theatrical expression of oppression. It expressed what was tolerated and expected and looked for by white in black, as well as what freedoms and ironies and angers and pride and accomplishments could be included in the deal. This was an American language and one full of the rich and terrible history of an oppressed race. To get it into shape for the American public, it had to be learned by a class of "coons" whose shouting would be amenable to white society.

A touch of the centuries of woe and a history reduced to cavorting and mockery. Can you imagine Jews watching the Hebrews mocked by Egyptians doing Jewface for the Pharaohs? No longer allowed to be the Jews on parade themselves, they must witness the Torah reduced to an entertainment that allowed Egyptians to add a bit of Jewish flavor to their own lives. Sophie Tucker's own happy emergence from her blackface cocoon cannot alter the essential melancholy and bitterness of this story from the point of view of the person whose face she has shed and whose life she no longer needs to plunder but whose song, you better believe it, she will continue to sing. She remained an imperishable interpreter of the old coon shout of blue ridges round my heart waiting for the Robert E. Lee Mammy mine hmmm mmm mmm. But the impulse of what that once depicted changed; and with the changes in black art and life and in white expectations of it, new blends replaced the old, leaving the old darky tableau not so much racial as show-biz nostalgia, longed for by old troupers the way the good old oppressive times they depicted were longed for by the former masters. To these must be added the burgeoning numbers of whites who fantasized having been masters.

Sophie Tucker was a constant, self-mythologizing autobiographer. She would introduce a song with her story about it. The introduction took the place of the song's introduction and was about her own connection with it. This is how Sophie was telling her own story by the 1920s:

> Life is a book, so they say, of records on each page.
> I turned my first leaf when I went upon the stage.
> The road was rough and it was tough especially for a girl alone.
> Heartaches, sighing, nights of crying, for my folks at home. Why,
>     I remember . . .
> Way back when, way back when, I was a young Connecticut lass,
> I was just as green as grass, had lots of nerve, no class.
> And the men I met then, they were some sweet bunch!
> Said a star they'd make me, right away they'd try to date me, but
> I had a Yiddishe hunch.

> And then there came a day for a job with pay, I wondered if I'd
> make it.
> Only twenty beans, but when you're broke it seems a fortune, and
> you take it.
>
> And then there came along,
> one fine song.
> I hope you'll never forget to remember me when you hear . . .[17]

The fine song that came along was "Some of These Days." Notwithstanding Sartre, it was written by the black songwriter Shelton Brooks.

The way this song came along is curious. Sophie became a headliner and enjoyed the services of a maid, Mollie Elkins. Mollie Elkins, who was herself African-American, met Sophie Tucker when she worked as a maid to fabled Follies beauty Lillian Lorraine, and Sophie was a young unknown, the "patsy," about to get her big break in the Ziegfeld Follies of 1909. Mollie befriended Sophie and gave her advice and encouragement. When Sophie stopped the Follies cold in Atlantic City, she and Mollie hugged, and she vowed that she'd take Mollie as her maid when she made it big. But as luck would have it, Sophie's success with the preview crowd angered the show's star, the great Nora Bayes, who made Ziegfeld take Sophie's solo spot away. Crushed, Sophie turned to Mollie, who counseled her:

> "There's other shows. Do your one song, Patsy, and when the season's over
> you'll get a chance in another show. You'll see. It'll turn out all right. If
> you've got the goods, and you have, there's nobody can take your chance
> away from you."
> What a wise Mollie. And what a lot I owe her. She kept me from feeling resentful and bitter. She made me see that this was just one of the tough
> breaks that show business is full of.[18]

This was not only good advice, it was specifically good survivor advice, a kind of wisdom highly developed out of necessity among American blacks, leavening the impatience of ambition with a feeling for the intractability of the world. It is also, as so much of that wisdom was bound to be, better given away to someone whose heart would not be broken by the devil *ex machina* of racism. It was updated advice of a black mammy to her white child.

After the Follies, Mollie became a source of support for Sophie, helping her out, bucking her up, sometimes feeding her. And sure enough, when Sophie became a headliner, Mollie became her maid and companion. Their relationship parallels the relationship at the core of Fannie Hurst's *Imitation of Life,* in which two women, one black and one white, band together to make their way and gain success, with the white woman essentially fronting a business based on the black woman's down-home know-how.[19] Their relationship, although conducted according to American urban racial rules, is genuine, valuable—and in some important respects, equal. If you separate the contemporary elements from the historical romance of even that retro classic *Gone with the Wind,* you will find in the relationships among black and white women a level of actual reciprocity and connection in the world of women within a world of race and class. The real give and take of mother-daughter relationships often surfaces in black-white female relationships, just as real sororal feelings surface among rivalrous, friendly, or even the mother-daughter relationships so common in women's genre fiction.

The women in Hurst's novel do not inhabit the relation of a lady and her maid, although their roles seem to be that of lady and maid, and their household is divided into those conventional, racially understood spheres. In the movies as well, the intimacy and exchange in the relationships between Mae West and her maids, as well as others, was more about making do in a tough world for women than about nostalgia for a caste society. Sophie Tucker's relationship with Mollie Elkins lasted Mollie's lifetime, and its form had to do with conditions beyond their control. Mollie was one of the Tucker career's key *people,* as we now say; she was good at it, unlike Sophie's several husbands.

Tucker's intimacy with an African American woman shouldn't surprise. Much of her own style was taken from black women. Alberta Hunter remembers Sophie Tucker's coming to watch her work: "Sophie Tucker came to hear me do 'Someday Sweetheart' and 'A Good Man Is Hard to Find.' Later, she'd send her maid Belle for me to come to her dressing room and teach her the songs, but I never would go, so her piano player would come over and listen and get everything down. But I was crazy about her as a singer, and she influenced me."[20]

This is the confusing reality, the same one where Louis Armstrong could be so crazy about Guy Lombardo, where the relationships from which culture grows thrived. The "Belle" whom Alberta Hunter remembers may well have been Mollie Elkins. Tucker may well have learned "Someday Sweetheart" from Hunter; there is a resemblance in their styles. Sophie Tucker's picture appears on the sheet music of the song, but that doesn't signify. Race separated. "Someday Sweetheart" by Spikes and Spikes, "Sophie Tucker's sensational hit," was published by the famous Melrose of Jelly Roll Morton fame, and Morton claimed to have written that tune. Sophie could make a hit out of the song because of her capacity, though a white woman, to sing like a black woman, but not too much so. Alberta Hunter, like Ethel Waters, could also sing like a black woman but not too much so, as apparently could Florence Mills and Josephine Baker.

On the contrary Bessie Smith. Her greatness was indelibly and uncompromisingly racial, as blacks shared and defined it. It was not aimed at a white ear, which might not only miss the beat, not quite understand the diction, but blanch at the feelings and the carryings on. Her singing is the ultimate accomplishment of what Sophie Tucker was imitating. Their singing of the same songs is instructive. Bessie's versions of "Alexander's Ragtime Band" or "After You've Gone" have an authority, a power, and a feeling that slow them down and transform them into something very deep, that return them to the very impulse that informed them. Sophie's records are jazzy and lively and fun, but the feeling isn't in the music; if it is there, it's in the words and her experience of a woman's lot, often sentimentalized by the passing of time.[21]

The way Bessie Smith sang those songs restores to them the initial impulse that inspired them. And it was Alberta Hunter who was more like Sophie Tucker, an entertainer with a real or learned origin in black music and blues, except that Alberta Hunter, like Ethel Waters, really could and did sing the blues, which Sophie Tucker did not and could not. She imitated blues feeling, and her "blues" were rather those folksy parlando introductions, which have more to do with Jewish than Afro-American expression. But the relationships between black and white women, especially in show business, were interesting. Alberta Hunter stayed at the Dreamland and was not about to toddle on over to the Sherman Hotel to teach even a singer she admired how to steal her stuff. Sophie ended up sending her maid, whose job pretty clearly included scouting and lessons in blackvoice.

Mollie Elkins and Sophie Tucker had a relationship, as told in *Some of These Days,* that really mattered. Theirs was a story much like Fannie Hurst's premise of lasting mutuality within conventions of power. It included much exchange and business partnership and lasting mutual consolation and a partially shared philosophy, that culminated in a moving deathbed parting. The white woman's success protects the black, whose relegation to instrumental status is never questioned, but the black woman's support helps the white who is a less centered, albeit a racially luckier, person. Fannie Hurst's *Imitation of Life,* of course, works out the racial tragedy in the dramatic story of the light-skinned black daughter Peola and her tragic alienation from her mother and her race.

It seems that Sophie Tucker's relations with women were, in general, better than those with men, who tended, with some major exceptions, to exploit or otherwise disappoint her. Mollie looked after her all right:

"Some of These Days" is one more thing I owe in a way to Mollie. I was riding high in Chicago, palling around with a fast crowd, too full of myself to pay attention to a lot that was happening around me. Many songwriters used to bring me their work, beg me to try the songs in my act and plug them. Every performer is besieged with that sort of thing. At first, you hear them all, you're so fearful of missing a good thing. But after a few years of it you get careless. I guess it was that way with me. One day Mollie came and stood in front of me, hands on hips, and a look in her eye that I knew meant she had her mad up.

"See here, young lady," said she, "since when are you so important you can't bear a song by a colored writer? Here is this boy Shelton Brooks hanging around, waiting, like a dog with his tongue hanging out, for you to hear his song. And you running around, flapping your wings like a chicken with its head chopped off. That's no way for you to be going on, giving a nice boy like that the run-around."

"All right. I'll hear his song," I promised. "You tell him."

"You can tell him yourself," said Mollie. And she brought him in.

The minute I heard "Some of These Days" I could have kicked myself for almost losing it. A song like that. It had everything. Hasn't it proved it? I've been singing it for thirty years, made it my theme song. I've turned it inside out, singing it every way imaginable, as a dramatic song, as a novelty number, as a sentimental ballad, and always audiences have loved it and asked for it. "Some of These Days" is one of the great songs that will be remembered and sung for years and years to come, like some of Stephen Foster's.[22]

Of course, no matter how she sang it, some things are apparent about the song. It is a pseudo-blues song, like Stephen Foster's a drawing from the African American well. It translates into clear American English and into a plain heartland setting the blues lament that Roquentin heard in that dim café on that antique French phonograph. Shelton Brooks set the story of two sweethearts amid the "simple life of country folk." But the full-throated lament the woman sings is rich with feeling and anger and warning. It is passionate, but it organizes a musical impulse that is more fluid and comes from a different context. Removing the blues and making a song of them makes for a lot of good music—consider Harold Arlen and Ted Koehler's Cotton Club *oeuvre*. But it is removing something from a culture, its habitat, and putting it in a stage zoo, where its own purposes can be characterized but not served.

To the extent that cultural expression is culturally specific communication, its presentation as entertainment within a larger culture is already distorting. When the larger culture is oppressive of the smaller one, makes demands that the smaller culture present itself to the larger, within ritualized modes of exchange, and insists on and needs that culture to express itself in terms that justify, explain, comport with, and justify its oppression, as well as please and reassure its oppressors, that is distortion indeed. Black entertainment is always a threnody of damage, self-protection, pleasing, and coded genius. The white pleasure in the black is full of the forbidden, the dangerous, the need for reassurance, and the desire for destruction. The black is symbolic beyond redemption to the white, the white dangerous beyond trusting to the black. The cultural exchange founded on this nexus was still in the early twentieth century substantially unmodified by progress. When you are on exhibition in the cultural zoo, you cannot control the motives of who comes to look, and the best and worst intentioned alike have equal access to the imprisoned creature. It is always sad and poignant to see the glories of a culture caged for show to its captors and rulers. And this dynamic remains an inherent aspect of the relation of African American to American culture.

The story of Sophie Tucker suggests how immigrant individuality might impersonate black reality and act out a charade of upward mobility still denied blacks. Sophie Tucker began in blackface and shed it to emerge with her own skin and curls, blessedly white and twice blessedly blond, adding her Yiddishisms to the blackvoice, and like America itself, taking the impulsive energy of the African American folk culture and its musical genius and making a pop music out of it for others to dance to.

Sophie Tucker's near monopoly of "Some of These Days" extended to Europe, where her recordings were known. In the thirties, she played a concert hall near The Hague to a thunderous reception. Sophie buttonholed the promoter:

> "Wait a minute," I said to him. "There's something I can't get through my head. Outside of a very few people who may have seen me in London, and those who know of my phonograph records, nobody in Holland knows who I am or what I can do. How, then, could I rate an ovation of seven minutes?"
>
> "Dear Miss Tucker, if you could understand Dutch, you would have heard the words the entire audience let out in one gasp at your entrance: 'My God! she's a white woman!'" It seems the Dutch had thought from my phonograph records and my syncopation and deep voice that I was a colored star. The Dutch shopkeepers advertised my records: "By the American Negro Singer Sophie Tucker."[23]

Sophie understandably fails to explore this wonderful misunderstanding. It helps explain why Sartre heard what he had Roquentin hear. It was, of course, the point of her singing style. It was her stage style that played on the deception, and the Dutch applause is white applause of a sort Americans understand, although it was no longer quite cool in America to have that obvious a reaction of the solidarity and relief of racial recognition.

Sartre didn't know any of this, apparently. Yet he made up a story that takes a cue from the weird phenomenon of blackvoice. In itself, as Roquentin himself says, it isn't such a big deal that Roquentin got so wrong who was singing what. But Sartre did have his character experience the ersatz as the real, without knowing that it was, ironically, the bourgeois version of the *really* real that old Roquentin was taking heart from. Right away, this should remind us that the really real, the authentic if you like, is a subjective experience rather than an objective category. Sophie Tucker was not an authentic black woman, and yet her singing of a regulation coonshouting number, Shelton Brooks's interpretation of a genre whose purpose was to fit the African American beat to the conventions of the American popular song, did convey to many listeners the feelings they associated with African Americans.

The pseudo-Negress was not merely a popularized racist figment. The exchange between races that goes on in the unequal situation is a creative and lasting one, however unjust and unlikely, and however valiantly opposed. A culture based so squarely on the difference between white and black will have to learn not to dismiss the difference but to see it differently, enjoy it decently, celebrate it democratically. This is true of all differences in pluralist democracy. Getting rid of the culture of racism, sexism, or homophobia does not make the differences on which these attitudes are based disappear and, indeed, was never meant to. You are not supposed to have to stop being black or female or gay, or experiencing what it has meant to be so, in order to have your rights as an American. Hard as this is in law, it is even more difficult in culture.

Sartre understood that the Jew is to some extent a creature of the anti-Semite. His writing about *Anti-Semite and Jew* makes a philosophical statement from what was already evident in *Nausea,* and which was so influential in the theories of race and revolution and personality of Frantz Fanon. How long that creature lasts generationally and in the racial heart is another question. In America, the exchange among white and black found especially sensitive mediators in Jews. Jewish intermediaries did paradigmatic but ambiguous work in the brokering of white and black American exchange.

Johnny Mercer of Savannah learned from Irving Berlin, late of Russia but forever of Tin Pan Alley, how to make the connection between black and white new and exciting again. Jews were prominent in teaching Americans about America, using blacks, among others, as a text, scared to use Jews, needing stand-ins. They patented a pluralist, tolerance-based liberalism that was liberating and also confining. That exchange is not a simple one. You can't understand its dimensions or possibilities from the Sophie Tucker version alone. What can be seen, however, is that the notion of authenticity remained important in modern liberal politics, because it was the notion that expressed what the liberal worried modern life sacrifices to injustices in contemporary society; it is the $x$ that seems to be missing when you take up a liberal critique of life. It makes the identification with the oppressed while stopping short of making common revolutionary cause with them; but it also devises means of making revolutionary cause with them, which is why liberal and left culture have so much, often antagonistically, in common.

The conservative believes that if everyone accepted the near fit of social hierarchy and natural hierarchy, things would be as good as they get in this life and we could comfort one another and endure. This notion inevitably harks back to some status quo ante. It also gives traditionalists a rationale for enjoying and protecting what has traditionally been their own good fortune. The liberal confers authenticity to express the sense that it is by entering into the experience of the other—finding oneself in the parts missing from bourgeois life, relocating the spirit and soul in especially the victims of the prevailing system—that we will find our real selves and the proper fit between the social and the natural.

The judgment of authenticity is a response to the people whom an analytic understanding of modern society sees as outside the benefits of our community, and authenticity is a fiction that makes it possible to connect with them. To prefer the outsider is a consequence of dissatisfaction with your own lot. It also reflects a definition of your own lot that goes beyond yourself to include the neglected, the outsider, the other, parts of yourself, people in the world. This has Christian and hard-boiled sources: Saint Francis, Hemingway, the private eye all treat the outsider and other as possible completions of the self. This is a liberal problem. To believe that the outsider has something you want may begin in political courtesy but quickly risks becoming patronizing and exploitative. This because the outsider may value what you are tired of and disparage; but also what you value in someone else's exclusion often turns out to be the very badge, oppression, and misery of that exclusion. You may find yourself uncomfortably envying the bondedness of the oppressed and the expressive community that developed among African Americans in the course of their survival of oppression without knowing how to avoid sentimentalizing the horrors to which it was in part a reaction.

The notion of authenticity will not lead to settled cultural politics, since the identification of the other as authentic is a repressive identification, no matter what. The authentic may have to become the primitive or remain the oppressed to serve the liberal taste, since "authentic" boils down to what they have that we do not and think we lack. And the receptivity that makes it possible to encounter the different with hope and interest may also lead to surprise at our own stubborn interests or to the neglect of what might be valued in our own cultural core.

Roquentin's appropriate falsehoods, in Philip Larkin's phrase,[24] are the problem. That he mistook white for black and black for Jew in his

Frenchman's tin-eared enthusiasm for American culture is just one of those things. It helps see deeper into the structure of the experience itself: that intense and widely shared need to experience through music a charade or shadow or portion of African American life. Perhaps this was sought as a clue to the world the Europeans had been ruling and were beginning to lose control of, as a new phase in the complicated but not always faced up to interrelationship between that world and the European culture that swelled so proudly from its gorging on the rest of the world. The American empire received the European and the African heritages in much more directly confronting measures. The white need for the black and the white exploitation of the black to fill that need makes one of the central stories of American, hence modern, culture.

A last story for Roquentin and for all of us who have listened so intently to Afro-American music in all its guises. A friend of Mildred Bailey remembered watching her listening to a record of Duke Ellington's "Black Butterfly" at her farm in upstate New York. "She sat at the kitchen table with a single candle blowing in the wind from the open door. The shadows on the maples outside the door danced all over the kitchen walls, and Mildred played the record over and over again as if afraid the trees might stop blowing if the band did." [25] What it is, in the end, is what it feels like when you listen to it.

# N  Fred Astaire

NOBODY'S GOING TO give you an argument about Fred Astaire. If American foreign policy could summon the kind of consensus Fred Astaire does, it would be the American Century again. And there isn't much new to say about Astaire; his dancing, his singing, his seeming effortless perfection, his matchless grace and good humor and style; the way he . . . .

Most of the great movie stars didn't *do* what they did on the screen. Sometimes, athletic or musical prowess buffered that realistic downer of a thought, but the image of Wayne on horseback or even Mae West in a boudoir does not really mean that what they were doing up there was actually being done. Except when they do their own stunts, there is always this trick, the crafty portion of art, a use of what is authentic in a star to make a kind of story work. Who James Stewart or Katharine Hepburn were had a lot to do with the characters they played and brought to life. The greatest stars did concentrate their own experience of life into their aliveness on the screen. But even if they were like that in real life, they didn't actually have all those adventures they did in pictures.

Except for Fred Astaire. He remains the original exception (other dancers and singers—Rooney, Garland, Kelly—approached him), the movie star whose accomplishment was that his movies are almost documentaries of what he could do better than anybody else. They are cinema verité stories about Fred dancing and singing and romancing Ginger Rogers and the other girls, breezy, friendly, stylish and wonderful, imagined and real. Other ineffable stars leaned on the things that they appeared to be in order to convince us they were doing things we watch them "acting." Fred Astaire did what we see him doing. His only deception was to make it look easy.

Astaire movies did not aim at realistic stories, because Fred himself was on the level. Theirs was a truth constantly authenticated by his mastery, and there was no illusion about it. When, in some of his pictures, effects are used—the slow-motion dance in *Easter Parade,* the rotating room in

---

This essay was originally written for the *Los Angeles Reader* to coincide with a retrospective of Fred Astaire movies at the Los Angeles County Museum of Art. I want to thank Richard Gehr for giving me the chance to write about Fred Astaire and Katharine Hepburn for the *Reader.*

*Royal Wedding*—they simply extend the exhilarating and breathtaking effect of his more straightforward dances, the machine gun in *Top Hat* or the duets with Ginger. At the core of Astaire movies was always Fred Astaire doing to surpassing, heart-stopping, time-stopping sublimity what only he could do.

Astaire's mastery was especially interesting because it was so understated. Making mastery look easy is hard enough. Making the most stylish, aristocratic mastery accessible was something else again. He has spoken of his love for Douglas Fairbanks, and the Astaire character resembles the Fairbanks character, especially the early one scripted by Anita Loos, whose physical prowess was never compromised, but existed within the setting of a breezy, friendly American fellow. Gene Kelly also descended from Fairbanks, from the showier, more self-conscious Fairbanks of the swashbuckling epics, whose athleticism required exotic and heroic fantasy settings. It is an interesting difference and a reminder of the rich continuity of moving pictures.

The essential grace of the Astaire prowess resembled that of Chaplin and Keaton. They shared more than an isolated if glorious coordination, a quality that connected their movements to the fortunes of their characters. That grace defines masculinity in the Astaire pictures, almost perversely insisting on the very quality that made dancing so suspect in an American man. Gene Kelly's dancing incorporates an American man's awareness of the ambiguity of male dancing in our culture. Fred Astaire conceded nothing to it. The resulting performances established a true and natural standard of being, with a lighthearted dispatching of false models of convention and order. Fred seldom faltered.[1] There was that characteristic Astaire movement, the feint toward imprecision or mistake that formed part of the drama of so many of his dances; but he always stumbled into a higher art. His generosity to us was to match his extraordinary ability with a manner that deprecated it without subverting its beauty.

Like most of the popular masters, he surrounded his mastery with approach. You do think, watching him, that you could do it too. It is part of the experience of Astaire pictures that the street outside is full of people singing and dancing in the inimitable Astaire manner. Everyone tries it, thinks he can do it, but the fact that you can't never embitters, because it keeps the pleasure of his pictures going. It's as if he is right here teaching you how. The Astaire dance studios were superfluous; the movies teach you the joy of life by making it seem as if you can do it too. So you stumble with a laugh. Think of the great moment in *Swing Time,* when Astaire pretended to Ginger that he couldn't dance—"Please teacher teach me something, nice teacher, teach me something, I'm as awkward as a camel and what is worse . . ."—with its advice worthy of Ben Franklin to "pick yourself up, dust yourself off, and start all over again." Her good sense warns her that Fred's poor mouthing is a come-on. But how well he rewards her moment of weakness; and so it is with us. His superiority is never nasty; it is essentially generous, giving one the sense, however ridiculous, that it is within our power also; that is what they mean about the universality of art. And this is what Thomas Jefferson was imagining when he wrote to John Adams about the "natural aristocrats" that America could train to serve the best interests of democracy, a palatable superiority to emulate and attend to.

And Fred takes that to the beautiful reaches of a democracy; everything he does has the ready feeling of the familiar about it. Somehow it is awesome but never strange. Astaire's regular-guyness made him kin to Stewart, Cooper, and Grant, but different too. It had to do with his being less beautiful and more certain that a specific setting (and the skills that attend it) was required for him to shine. In that sense, unlike Stewart who argued for a natural small-town order and more like Grant, Astaire was a city fellow who made the case for a certain sophistication, for the beautiful *things* of this world. Astaire's skill, acquisition, and his success with women (and with men) were earned, in Grant's case forgiven, in both deserved and democratically carried off. Even his style: think about how he lets us in on his putting on his top hat. All those Astaire moments of perfect elegance have companion gentle, funny numbers where he puts on the ritz, gets an invitation, and has us join him in preparation and in anticipation. You believe that you could be doing it too, even as well as he. It is a meritocracy that Astaire validated, a meritocracy shorn of effort and failure; a wonderfully refreshing and generous American fiction, especially coming in his heyday, which was, after all, the heyday of the greatest American popular art.

Astaire was a vaudevillian, a professional entertainer, making high art without a touch of the highbrow. Almost all his pictures contained moments that lampooned and distanced him from the cold, heartless versions of the aristocratic style he redeemed. His pictures needed those funny posing Europeans, the snooty butlers, Edward Everett Horton, and the silly pretensions Fred shattered with a tap or two. *Damsel in Distress* was not much of a movie (no Ginger and a bloated Wodehouse plot), but the majordomo who has to run outside to shriek operatic arias is the perfect counterpoint to Fred's invasion of olde England to win a rather dim Rapunzel with his American goods. *Nice Work If You Can Get It* still does what so many Astaire numbers do: they scatter the trappings of culture with the tap of a foot to the rhythm of jazz. As Fred understood the world, dictators would be better off (and we too) if they'd "zoom, zoom now and then" (*Slap That Bass*). Having got rhythm might not be everything, but Fred's rhythm seems to summon up tremendous possibilities for the pursuit of happiness.

Part of what made Astaire so convincing was his text. He didn't have to be realistic about America since America was still a place Americans believed in and recognized. They fought for a place in it, not a piece of it. America was in him and Ginger, and in their songs and music and attitudes. They needed no realism to bring it forth; everybody knew it when they saw them. The Rogers-Astaire pictures, like Jane Austen novels, were about courtship and love, and they touched on comic and serious emotions and realities: money, jealousy, erotic response, pride, prejudice, obstacles; they featured contrary models of unhappiness and failed romance. Fred and Ginger made mistakes, and the love they would finally find amounted to something more than desire. They found in one another something real and erotic that ultimately separated them from the rest of the world; the dances gave them a place to be alone together. Astaire dancing was the closest thing to making love in the movies. Remember the moment in *Gay Divorcee* when they danced to "Night and Day." It remains a breathtaking vision of love, the physical union transfiguring, almost unbearably beautiful and romantic— no wonder the pictures had to rest in between their dances—and after the dance, spent, Fred guides Ginger to a seat and . . . he offers her a smoke.

Fred Astaire sang more of the best American songs first than anyone, because all of the best songwriters jumped at the chance to write for him. He knew how to sing them. His good-enough voice was peerlessly good at uniting the swirling elements of American song. He could do the operetta stretch, but the very thinness of his high register kidded and eased the attitudinizing of the operetta into just the right self-deprecating kind of romantic singing. "The Way You Look Tonight," so funny in the picture, *heard* is a great example of this. But in all his yearning songs there lurked a passion, banked and also freed from the stilted conventions, but with enough left of effort to remind us of how noble those emotions were.

Fred could sing words. He never muddied the diction. The Billie Holiday covers of his songs (recorded a few months after his) made deeper inroads into their richest meanings, but Astaire always got the story right, what the songs are about, and they are about the most wonderful things. Fred sang the many stages of love: on his own, *No Strings;* recognition, *A Foggy Day;* flirtation, *Isn't This a Lovely Day To Be Caught in the Rain;* the many moods of love, *Night and Day, The Way You Look Tonight, A Fine Romance, Let's Call The Whole Thing Off, I'm Putting All My Eggs in One Basket, Things Are Looking Up;* and heartache, *They Can't Take that Away From Me;* the serious, *Let's Face the Music and Dance;* and the stoic *Never Gonna Dance,* the first of Fred's mad scenes. The point is that Astaire expressed in eloquent song and perfect time the surpassing renderings of love. His singing of them gave them life they still enjoy. His unorthodox voice channeled their orthodox meanings.

And then there's the rhythm! Astaire's songs—surely Berlin, Kern, the Gershwins, Porter, Fields, Lane, Lerner, Mercer wouldn't mind my calling them his—are one plausible siting of the melting pot. They took the rhythms of America, especially the precious treasure of African American jazz, and did that great thirties thing, blending many traditions into something Americans could all share and like without homogenizing. Billie Holiday's incomparable records of those songs make surpassing listening, if only to hear how easily she reclaims them for a deeper jazz, displaying the songwriters' care for what they borrowed. Astaire's own borrowed beat was always true, never dull, and still shines through. When Fred cut loose singing a jazzy ditty and dancing up a storm, like Schwartz and Dietz's "Shine on Your Shoes" in *The Bandwagon,* he worked close to the bone of the best beat in the world. The African American beat of his day animated jazz when it was still—for good or evil—hinged hopefully to a notion of a national audience. In his singing, in his dancing, and in a certain carefree, hip ease he made a point of this a part of what makes a American, despite the inevitably troubling setting and the hierarchy that complicates his partnering.

"Bojangles of Harlem" in *Swingtime* preserves a terrific song, the presentation of which we see as painfully stereotypical in its conventional racialist condescension, a proper homage to the great Bill Robinson by his own fettered times, and unsettled by Astaire appearing in blackface. Comparing it with the pastoralizing dirge of the seventies singer-songwriter Jerry Geoff Walker, "Mister Bojangles," an important song in its day, one gets something of the point. Walker's Mr. Bojangles is a drunken victim of a racist society, dilapidated and noble in suffering, a pathetic figure who can still dance across a cell. It is a sweet but uncomprehending song that reduces to undignified and unimaginable misery one of the most buoyant and successful Americans artists of the century. "Bojangles of Harlem" does an older-fashioned thing. Dorothy Fields and Jerome Kern set the story of Bojangles in a Harlem where "they may not know who's President, but just ask them who Bojangles is" and that, like Fred's blackface, strikes us as loaded. But time passes and the real point of the song emerges again, the breathless admiration the dancing conveys, African American dancing that is a flowering genius. Fred's dancing, so different from Bojangles, so indebted to him, pays the tribute of a master to a founder. The blackface and the slighting references to Harlem can be faced as how they did shows then; they are a crucial reminder to the enthusiast about the old times. Astaire's dance is just the thing that Nina Simone demanded in her searing recording of the Walker song, interpolating "respectfully": "I heard them *respectfully* ask please, Mr. Bojangles dance." Respect and delight were the keys of Astaire's one attempt to pretend to be the thing that of course he wasn't.

But Astaire was hip. And hip meant working closer to the black back-beat than any other white star and, along with its naturalness, assimilating its incomparable elegance. The Astaire style mixed the casual and the faultless. The furnishings and surroundings in his pictures, the extreme art deco beauty of the Astaire-Rogers RKO pictures, the improbable, matchless, luxurious beauties of MGM ... but almost all the things in his movies looked marvelous. As did he. Astaire extended Chaplin's deceptively contentious relation to the material world. His own special relation to clothes endures. He had a unique way with things and the political, moral, social, and physical laws that govern them. Recasting vaudeville sand dancing, he spread sand to dance Ginger to sleep; he defied gravity and time. He danced on chairs and tables, and redecorated while dancing.

The trick to the undimmed elegance of his personal style was that he made it personal, suited to his needs—that is, to his movements. *Putting on My Top Hat* explained the dress uniform of the privileged—in the Depression yet—as if there were more and less to it than the ceremonial, the luxurious, and the exclusive; it was dressing up for a tour of the posh. His pictures about rich and lucky people (in *Swingtime,* his nickname was "Lucky") made sure to entertain and connect with serious hope, and the outsider looking in with us was always some real part of Fred. This wasn't the voyeuristic soap opera about peering into the lifestyles of the rich and famous, like *Dynasty.* The elegance was richer, the standard purer, and the appeal not voyeuristic but encouraging, because the message seemed to be that money isn't everything if you have it. Fred led us to believe in every way that we might understand the rich, the successful, and the lucky in love because the world will reward excellence, virtue, and American breeziness, and because to be those things is the highest incarnation of the ordinary. He was the ordinary man transfigured by extraordinary grace and talent, but never transformed. He might have worn a high hat but he never high-hatted anybody.

What can one say about the dancing? It astonishes and delights, it grows out of the setting, it authenticates the character, it seems to me to make life worth living. Its theatre was not cathartic but deeply encouraging. The great dancers and critics have paid their tributes, and it seems worth adding only a few things. Rooted in Fred's character, dancing was what he did: how he did it, with whom, and to what music tell the stories of his movies. The "la belle, la perfectly swell romance" with Ginger was bound to end, because the marriage was going to be about life and not love, and Fred's dancing with Ginger is perfectly and ineffably about love. She gave him sex and he gave her class is what Hepburn is supposed to have said, which was shrewd of her. But I think that at their best, they resembled Depression American kids whose happiness had to thrive in the most private of splendors.

Their being together, which was everything to their movies, however got up in international art deco settings, was always set in emotional America, where two kids could still find one another and share a matchless romance, where the tempests in their teapot might loom larger than depression or war, where their magical chemistry generated a world of their own. Henry Fonda and Sylvia Sidney, say, knew that *they* made one a criminal and would take everything away. Fred and Ginger knew that even if the best things in life aren't always free, even *they* couldn't take everything away. So they didn't kiss, so what? Fred knew that they had gone beyond the clinch. They had in fact unclenched the clinch and demystified that steamy moment of American prudery, with something that still stirs a wistful recognition in our human hearts.

Of course, Fred had a marvelous life after Ginger, and there are many superb moments in those pictures. I especially like him dancing with Rita Hayworth, and he seems to me to have given Judy Garland some of her few peaceful moments. Their duets in *Easter Parade* were a joyous high point in American entertainment. The stories of the Astaire pictures became complicated. The search for the right partner magnetized them, and it sometimes exposed him to embarrassments and mismatings. The way to watch an Astaire picture is to watch how (and sometimes whether) the numbers extend and enhance the plot. The music and dance still cue the meaning in his pictures. The movies with Rogers surrounded those moments and were advanced by them and finally in *Swing Time* with "Never Gonna Dance" achieved that self-referential moment in which there is nothing outside the song, and it tells the picture's story.

But the stories of Fred's later pictures shone with deeper tones, darker moods. He drank; he got angry. His fantasies were liberated in searches after ideals of pleasure. Often his romances didn't work. Life was not so swell. Fred got older. One after the other, the pictures documented the terrible truth about getting older, that life is not so hopeful. For the demanding especially there is much disappointment and even tragedy, and trouble a little less rhythmic than a good song.

But, at the same time, people do get better at what they do if they have talent and work at it. If Astaire deepened and his message roughened, his skill kept developing. As an older man, dancing with younger women, like Leslie Caron, Audrey Hepburn, or on TV with Barrie Chase—Johnny Mercer's "something" gave—he charted new conventions of what romance really is. He was a lot more mature and daring than American entertainment usually likes to be. There were sides to his growth, suggestions of the roué, moments of drama and intimations that all was not well in the world. Many of the pictures rather sink than fly. His partners kept changing, and their stories never attained the timeless truth of Fred's with

Ginger. And then, you get it. *The Bandwagon,* watching Fred dance with the bootblack, almost animating Cyd Charisse, fooling around with Jack Buchanan and Nannette Fabray and Oscar Levant and "By Myself," you realize something. Sure he is older. But he is also getting wiser and better. Friendship and profession count for more, experience too, and character.

Fred seemed to prove that you can live a life and get better at it, even though you understand it and suffer loss and change. He showed how age can be beautiful, and that it can attract respect, interest and, yes, love. And once again, you leave an Astaire picture encouraged that you can do it too. He was a hero. He faced the music and danced.

# ⁄  Katharine Hepburn:
## "The Heiress of All the Ages"

WHEN YOU FIRST see her, you can't stop staring at her, because you've never seen anybody who looked like that before; and yet, you know you've seen her before, in a Sargent portrait, in some old house, in what Henry James novel? You know you'd never confuse her with anyone else. She seems so completely like herself. She individualizes the world she's in; it starts turning around her. And even if you don't know that, she does. Breeding, talent, looks, brains, the words all spring to mind but they don't add up to her. You have to see her, you really do, listen to her talk, watch her move, and there she is, just like you thought of her before you saw her.

Of course that's how they became stars, those people. You see them, and you think you made them up, dreamt them up. One thing the good old movie stars did was make artists of their audiences, haunting us after the fact so we granted them imaginative life. We observe them and participate in the mixed fiction of movie and star, set them free in our minds, and presto chango! They are more real to us than anything should be! You experience a Jimmy Stewart picture from his insides out. Even though they change and he changes, it's him changing all right, you know who he is, in the way Adam knew the world when God let him name its contents.

We know what we know about the stars from their pictures. Books, articles, and interviews and all that celebrity journalism are just after the fact filling-in; celebrity gossip is willed ignorance masquerading as knowledge. The real person is not the real character, no matter how much we try to tie down our ballooning sense of them with facts about their impersonators. Bette Davis wasn't even *Bette Davis,* not to mention Julee Marsden, Margo Channing, or even Baby Jane Hudson. The real character is that driven, tested, testy, modern, nerve-wracking, unfree woman she managed to project from the thicket of those old Warner's pictures. Nobody really knows how it's done. Its collaborative, commercial, endlessly reported, mass participatory character makes us think there must be an answer, but in that regard the movies are an art, mysterious at the core.

---

This was written on the occasion of a retrospective of Hepburn films, again, for the Los Angeles *Reader.*

Movie stars carried the main load of our speculations about the art, because we saw and (since 1928) heard them. Their sitting is not concentrated as for a painting, and their voices are not abstracted from the voice that inspired the songs, as in music, and their selves are not trapped safely in the controlled medium of writing. The movie star is subject, object, and medium, despite everything we know about the scores of skilled craftspeople who make the movies and the often remarkably talented people who write, direct, shoot, and produce them. One seldom calls the movie star a genius. Chaplin or Keaton qualified because they made their movies. Irving Thalberg or Orson Welles, perhaps, but not Garbo, Cooper, or Gable. Yet it is often as not the star, like Katharine Hepburn, who incarnated an older notion of genius, which thought of genius more as the characteristic propensity of a form or a nation.

It isn't surprising that we look in star lives for the continuities and complications that smooth out and ground what we get in spurts from the movies. Once, in Charlottesville, Virginia, a pleasant gent, finding out that I was an American historian teaching at what people really did call "Mr. Jefferson's University," shared with me his earnest wish that more Jefferson letters might be discovered. Silly me, I would be just as happy without more because there are already too many for one to make sense of that wily titan. Of course, my new acquaintance meant a letter that would prove that yes, Jefferson was or no, he wasn't sleeping with his slave Sally Hemmings. Evidence seldom settles the most tantalizing questions we have about the characters, historical or imaginary, who live in our minds. Surely their ambiguity is part of their timeless appeal. All I'm saying is that you won't find the real story of Barbara Stanwyck in her life as a person. She dwells in her pictures, and there's precious little elsewhere to settle our thoughts about her.

There are other ways to understand our sense of the star's abiding reality. Like Benjamin Franklin, Gary Cooper hid his superiority in a deceptive modesty. Jimmy Stewart extended the range of his small-town character just as the America that fostered him had to. Robert Taylor seems to have learned the lesson from the Cooper of *Morocco* that the only safe way for an American man to be beautiful, if he isn't clever enough to act his way around it, is to sleep or not shave. Rip Van Winkle slept too, although he slept through something even more challenging than the consequences of his own appeal to women. Barbara Stanwyck remains the most real of the stars. Her women weren't vehicles of social intention like Sylvia Sydney's, or titanic expressions of ambivalence like Davis's. They lived recognizable, if theatrically heightened, lives. Her Stella Dallas is as believable a life in the American version of a class society as you are likely to see, not least because the melodramatic soapy setting has more to do with class barriers than the analytical acumen of more socially conscious pictures. Marlene Dietrich was as fabricated as Stanwyck was real, which reminds us of how wide a range the movies featured.

The art in which these memorable characters found themselves was commercial, and often the pictures stink. But the star characters give weight, theme, emotion, form, and raison d'être to their movies, and their relation to the stories is unsettled and unsettling. That is much of the appeal even of bad old pictures. You come away not only laughing but also moved by somebody who is in them, who the picture would better have been about; so you make up the real story of the movie in your head, and that is often what you remember. In Noel Coward's *Private Lives,* Amanda comments about the effect of a popular song, "strange how potent cheap music is." Similarly, the best thing about movies may not be the coincidence of their excellence, but the unresolved mystery.

The movies seldom rise to telling the real stories of the actors whose own reality shines through the conventions of their movie settings. And yet, the conventional settings are what we owe their ineffable magic effect to, and it is hardly likely that a more realized art could have done any better by them. So there they are, placed in those movies, exciting our curiosity. And that's why it's worth thinking about who Katharine Hepburn is, that interesting, irritating, unforgettable character she created in her movies, the fullness of whose life story is unequaled among screen lives.

The operative thing about Katharine Hepburn is that she is interesting. Especially when she was young, you wondered about her. In this she is like the heroines of the English and American novels. We meet Hepburn the way we meet Jane Austen's Emma Woodhouse, finding out right off the bat that she is "handsome, clever and rich." It isn't surprising that her most satisfying screen alliances have been with Jane Austen–like protagonists, resembling Elizabeth Bennett. In her screwball years, she regularly got a kind of Mr. Darcy in Cary Grant. In her chastened middle period, she found a Mr. Knightley in Spencer Tracy. The men she ended up with deserved her because they had tangled with her and could match her confidence with their common sense and, often, a knowledge of her character superior to her own. Their view of reality stays steadier than hers, and her dislocating effect on them moderates their attachment to their common sense with her uncommon sensibilities. Their maturity pays her the tribute of admiration, patience, and love, extracting in turn a devoted willingness to share a life for two.

The thing is that Hepburn, uniquely among women stars, starts off with substantive ideals about life; ideals in other female stars usually boiled up (or down) to sex: when, whether, with whom, with what consequences. Her movies showed Hepburn believing that she might have the world, make it better, that she knows what will make it better, that she can remain unsullied, not virginal. There is always the sense that settling on another person limits what the world can give, and that for Hepburn that limitation was more relevant than for most people. Intimate involvement risked her limitless possibility and her essential independence. She was an aristocrat, she loved liberty and overcame an innate distaste for equality. She was uncommonly superior, someone whose possibilities life seems certain to reward with grand completion.

Hepburn has always been hard to imagine reduced to domestic circumstance or romantic idyll. The world was her work, her oyster, her field, her concern, and she was certain that her job in life was to be who she was meant to be. The lights that shone in the Hepburn eyes were her ideals. She incarnated that persisting glory of the new world, the special flower of old time America, the American girl.

We meet her in *Bill of Divorcement,* as we meet Isabel Archer in *Portrait of a Lady.* The circumstances hardly matter in the face of her utter fascination for the interested audience. Go see the picture and try taking your eyes off her, no matter what you think of what the movie has her say and do. This is, of course, the very thing Henry James knew about Isabel Archer. The first Hepburn script was lame theatrical claptrap. But she got the right father, for John Barrymore was as close to an aristocrat as the movies could muster before Hepburn. The picture gets the conventional world of her silly mother and her feathery fiancé, the inadequate circumstances of this princess, out of the way. She belongs with Barrymore, alone in that big house from which she will emerge sprung from gothic excess into the world in her subsequent pictures.

*Bill of Divorcement* observed Hepburn in chrysalis, undistracted by anything other than the (brain) chemistry of the story, which is not as old-fashioned in our day of the revival of genetic predisposition as it only recently seemed. It also serves to underscore what a good daughter she was, Antigone-like in her loyalty and in her discernment that loyalty to her ideals was the proper filial duty. Her sacrifice of herself to Barrymore's insanity teaches her about character, and conveniently rids her of the stifling inheritance of her class. She may have seemed for a while to be a democrat's fancy of an aristocrat, like Claudette Colbert and those other screwball heiresses, whose desire to leave their families expressed a desire to be down with the rest of us, the soothing sacrifice of the uncommon to the common. Time would show that this wasn't Hepburn's idea at all. The source of her quarrel with her privilege was its lack of originality, which may account for the unenthusiastic audience response to *Holiday* and *Bringing Up Baby,* movies now so much admired.

In her RKO pictures, we see the intense, idealistic, inattentive Hepburn making choices, trying to be an actress, pilot, queen, artist, wife, woman, man, boy, girl. Her likeliness in so many ridiculous roles, and what they

have in common, reflects an awestruck sense of the possibilities of this compelling, embarrassing, intelligent, opinionated, cocksure, vulnerable, high-
minded, candid, all-wrong beauty. They keep trying to find a place for her.
When the movies go wrong, you may believe that maybe it is the world's
fault. Hepburn is hard to fault in her endlessly convincing individuality,
the Emersonian tip-off to true human excellence. It's not like the Depression convention that the world is against you. The world just isn't good
enough for Hepburn, or at least not any world you can get down in film.
Her secret history in this period resembles part of the real story of *Portrait of a Lady,* the world's insufficiency for the heiress to its possibilities.
There are some outstanding exceptions to the rule. *Stage Door* is worth
seeing for Hepburn's collaboration with Ginger Rogers, two characters who
almost never meet in movies, or in life, as if Emma Woodhouse shared a
novel with Becky Sharp, having it out until the movie goes soft. *Morning Glory, Mary of Scotland, Christopher Strong, A Woman Rebels, Sylvia
Scarlett, Quality Street* amplify the Hepburn character in generally bad
pictures. But they allow us to get to know her without much distraction.

Two pictures stand out. *Little Women* remains the closest thing we have
to a look at what Hepburn would have been like playing the New England
Emersonian young woman she summoned up and probably resembled. She
also suggests a Jeffersonian natural aristocrat, unburdened with money or
sentimentality, less genteel or conventional than the William Dean How-
ells heroines were to be. Josephine March is an irresistible character, with
all the spirit, generosity, and talent in the world. Literary scholars do go
on about the American Adam, but surely Jo March is right up there with
Whitman's self, Emerson's transcendent eyeball, and Thoreau at Walden,
an echoing American original. Hepburn breathes life into that noble and
much maligned New England woman of independence and principle, the
kind of woman who taught the freedmen during Reconstruction, the pioneer suffragettes, feminists, and social workers, Margaret Fuller, and
everybody's teachers, those trenchant defenders of art and idealism in the
commercial republic. Her eyes shine with New England's lights. She cap-
tures the essence of a national heroine, one whose bravery, feeling, and
intelligence, whose love of art and whose moral seriousness amount to
her rightful inheritance. Christopher Columbus! *Little Women* is one terrific movie.

*Alice Adams* is another good one. Softening Booth Tarkington's wonderful old book about small-town snobbery only at the end, it gives Hepburn a chance to play a plainer kind of girl, whose ideals are touchingly
bounded in the horizons of heartland and family. Alice is a ruder ideal-
ist than Hepburn usually brings off, but her extraordinary insides do
wonders toward making us feel the plight of this loyal, aspiring girl. She

brings conviction to some rather unpleasant conflicts as Alice yearns, poses, suffers, and apes. We get from Hepburn a sympathetic understanding of some pretty difficult emotions. She enacts the earnest desire for improvement, an instinctive feeling for appearances, the frustrations of people who feel themselves to be finer and more sensitive than the families and class circumstances into which they are born, the subtler pains of perceived social disadvantage that have crazed so many Americans. Hepburn gives the character lasting dimension; her fineness, her ideals, her intense willingness to be out of key make it possible for us to sympathize with Alice. Nor does she flinch at being seen as like Alice. We therefore have time to appreciate the tender situation of high hopes and spirits stifled by small-town life. Even loyal children can be ashamed of their families, and through Hepburn we can recognize their awkwardness and pretensions as the sad and touching human aspiration they are. *Alice Adams* is also the closest thing we have to a good movie of what Sinclair Lewis was writing about in *Main Street.* While keeping faithful to Tarkington's gentler story, Hepburn (and, of course the director, George Stevens) suggests the fate of the high-spirited and idealistic not born to advantage, adrift in God's country.

Which is why Henry James took Isabel Archer out of America and wrote stories about American girls in Europe. Hepburn's Alice tells us why Charlotte Stant Verver dreads returning to American City at the end of *The Golden Bowl.* It also explains the expatriate's fear of the journey home. You don't have to read Henry James to appreciate Katharine Hepburn. But she was the kind of person James made the subject of his art too. The power of her early pictures stems from our civilization. Her character is a fiction of the highest, if also uncertain, order, sometimes helped by her films, but always there in her.

For a while it looked like Hepburn might have a happy life. Like Isabel Archer, she seemed in films like *Bringing Up Baby* and *Holiday* to have found her milieu and her mate. Those screwball classics, in the Hepburn versions, resonate with *Pride and Prejudice,* not the MGM version. The right marriage doesn't bind her. It strips away her manic hilarity, removes the need for the eccentric independence, her sauciness, really, and she finds that her ideals can be shared. One of the joys of those two pictures is the happy feeling we have that Hepburn hasn't really given anything important away, that she has found something suiting her aristocratic splendor. *Holiday* ends like *Pride and Prejudice* with a marriage that doesn't so much defy convention as remind convention of nature. If only . . . .

*Holiday* and *Bringing Up Baby* did not find audiences, and they ushered in the painful episode of Hepburn's being labeled "box office poison" that almost ended her career. It is possible to imagine why the Hepburn character didn't find favor. What she stood for never mustered an audience of the size Hollywood respected. Myrna Loy and later Greer Garson occupied that territory. Her characters, not sentimental even when the pictures are, her sorts of values and ideals weren't shared. But unlike the other Hollywood women, Hepburn hadn't really surrendered, or even married; she never fell, she soared and said so. Her superiority to the general lot stood unmitigated and unapologetic.

The vehicle for her return, *The Philadelphia Story*, is the negative side of *Holiday*. A much-loved picture, it is about the interest people have in that conflation of character and actress, "Tracy Lord" Hepburn. The movie also ritualizes the Hepburn character's humiliation, the need to make her sacrifice her ideals. Like Emma, Tracy is interesting and mistaken. She is narcissistic and ungenerous to others, judgmental, and imperceptive. Tracy Lord's faults are a catalogue of what was always true about the Hepburn character, but seen not as ideals but false notions of self and society. So that Tracy can remarry Cary Grant's character C. K. Dexter Haven, he must manipulate her. She has to learn that she was wrong about pretty much everything. It is a very unpleasant story. She is punished for her ideals, which are mocked and distorted from every point of view: patrician, self-made, common, female, male, paternal, familial, public, and private.

Her torment is supposed to be the making of her, but I think that the key to its success is that what was remarkable and irritating about Hepburn has been tamed. After this, her pictures usually had an element that diminished or subdued her individuality and superiority, removing their challenge to the audience. It is not surprising that this Hepburn mated so well with Spencer Tracy, who mocks her ideals and makes her realize that they won't do in the real world. He is probably right, and they are terrific together. But I still love those ideals.

The assumption that there is something ridiculous about her then clings to Hepburn. She starts to eat a lot of crow. She collaborates in her own surrender. What is so good about *The African Queen* is that both she and Bogart give things of importance up for each other, and he knows enough to trust his life to her high ideals. Usually, she has to give up her illusions and the guy gets her, and sometimes she doesn't even get him. The older Hepburn played a woman men seem to love to blame and hurt and mock or pity, and their obvious interest in her and even fear of her doesn't mean that all this punishment hasn't affected her, too. She would henceforth carry the banner of the spinster, the martyr, the do-gooder, the ancient queens and eccentrics that have always offered havens for the American woman who insisted on the superiority of her ideals. What a pity she never got to play one mate in a Boston marriage. She and Tracy, like William Powell and Myrna Loy, showed a public possibility of adult marriage, a movie echo of Franklin and Eleanor Roosevelt. On her own, Hepburn played some suggestion of Eleanor Roosevelt. Apparently, John Huston told her to play Rosie in *African Queen* like Mrs. Roosevelt. But the impersonation only specified an errand to which she was fated.

The unforgettable Hepburn performance in *Long Day's Journey into Night* brings her disappointed ideals to bear on text of ideals as illusion. It is her Blanche DuBois. Surely one reason Hepburn is not ideal in Tennessee Williams—think of her Amanda Wingfield—is that his women are southern and their ideals are sexual and conventional and their independence and strength are the very marks of their failure. Hepburn, being from New England, is exactly the other way around. Right and wrong, things bigger than you and me, the ideals that made so much of the possibilities of choice and freedom, the American possibilities inspired Katharine Hepburn. She was a New England incarnation of the Jeffersonian aristocrat, a superior being who knew it and meant to lead the world by the lights of her ideals for the good of the democracy. The way to get a Jeffersonian (or a liberal) is to attack her ideals, even if they do make this world better for those who rudely live in it.

The uncommon Hepburn character paid dearly for her evident superiority and for everyone's interest in her. That is why one may prefer her first films with all their faults. Her ideals still burn in her as they remind us why James chose what he saw as the American girl and what we see as the American woman for his stories of the disappointments of choice and the havoc life plays with the birthright of freedom and possibility. Emersonian idealism does make rather a mess of things if it is not confined to a motto on a sampler or carved in a college arch, where it can inspire rather than instigate. Katharine Hepburn's character nevertheless touches depths and situations that lots of Americans have thought and written and suffered over. If the early pictures are especially sweet now, it is because one may still long for the company of that American "girl" who interested James and whom Philip Rahv should have known was right there up on the screen during all those *Partisan Review* years: "the heiress of all the ages."

# From Ohio to the Big Rock Candy Mountain: Los Angeles as the Terminus of American Democratic Culture

*There will always be an abyss dividing Los Angeles from San Francisco. Theirs is a classic feud which has its basis in the origins of two widely different types. We of the north are descendants of argonauts in whom initiative and physical courage were requisites before they ever started their dangerous adventure. But the Angeleno came to his city after the railroad had been built, his trip generally a timid retreat from some community of the Middle West where he wasn't smart enough to make a living. On reaching his goal, this migrant found himself competing with others no smarter than himself, so he was able to prosper and, groggy with the astonishment of unmerited success and titillated by perpetual sunshine, he blossomed forth, manufactured gaudy clothing, freak architecture, rowdy exhibitionist religion, and all the other devices which only a brain devoid of moral stamina and good taste could conjure up.*

Anita Loos, *A Girl Like I*

*Our first day in Los Angeles, Baby and I shared a cab with a man who called it the New Italy. Since then I've heard it called the New Greece, the New Palestine, the New Dawn and the Last Frontier, and found one name as apt as the other. Why leave a city that allows us to live wherever we care to imagine we're living?*

*In those days hardly a day passed without our city being described as an oasis in the desert, and the desert meant the Depression, strikes, communists, war, any kind of bad news.*

Gavin Lambert, *Running Time*[1]

---

The essay was delivered at the opening session of the University of California, Santa Barbara, Interdisciplinary Humanities Center conference on February 24, 1994, "Los Angeles: City of Exile."

LOS ANGELES sprawls in the modern consciousness much as it sprawls on its own site. A complex, confusing human metropolis, L.A. represents the current state of the American experiment in constitutional democracy, economic capitalism, cultural pluralism, and, especially, individualism. What New York once meant, both in terms of ambition and decay, is now L.A.'s to mean. Its vistas are implanted in the minds of the world, its values and its eccentricities, its recent civil comeuppance and natural disasters have a grip on the world that can't help looking to Los Angeles, which manufactures the simulated realities that characterize modern media culture, just as Detroit once manufactured cars.

The subject of Los Angeles wants definition. Like Alexandria, Jerusalem, Athens, Peking, or Florence, it is home to significant cultural work, human creative energies that interpret, decorate, imagine, and describe as well as build, invest, trade, and care for, as well as cheat, steal, murder, exploit, and lie, as well as tend, succor, love, and console. Los Angeles is America's world city, as much a city of the future as a metropolis of the present. It is a fundamentalist city, a center of visionary competition, a city populated by people from many different cultures. It is also the ultimate locus of American individualism. By *Ohio,* I mean white Midwestern middle America; the *Big Rock Candy Mountain,* of course, is that culture's dream of pleasure, the buzzin' of the bees and the cigarette trees. By giving these remarks the individualist spin, I am emphasizing the white American Protestant and *faux* Protestant experience of Los Angeles and that of many others who have managed to garner a share of that privileged experience of self-focus.

It turns out that one comes to L.A. in order to become more of what one is. But what one really is was never, as Emerson always said, the thing American conventional culture was very good at helping a body to know. The key experience for the Anglo population of L.A. has been an intense engagement with the premises of their identities, with a surprising variety of results. This sketch suggests some of the elements and contexts of that history and advances a case for thinking about L.A. in terms of its interesting realization of the chaotic promise of the Declaration of Independence.

When Frederick Jackson Turner proclaimed his frontier thesis of U.S. history five score years ago plus five, he argued a connection between the westward movement of northern European peoples and democratic political institutions. From the Anglo-Saxon forests to the Wisconsin woods, representative institutions spread with the energy and initiative of the westward-moving settlers. Like Madison, Tocqueville, Greeley, Faulkner, and so many others, Turner recognized in the aggressive, nomadic impulse one common element of the American democratic character. The inability to settle down may have transformed itself into the culture of the road, the challenged attention span, and the endless self-inventions of what we call American culture. Self-invention is hardly a modern innovation; it was a founding principle of our civilization. And when the European nomads were on the march, heaven help anyone in their way. Be they equally aggressive nomadic peoples or settling sorts, they fell victim to the propulsive metabolism and imperious sense of mission of this traditional Euro-American restlessness.

Another key element of American democratic culture, one Turner recognized, but which others in response to him have emphasized, was the accompanying need for order and especially for order in the face of the loosed forces of movement. One reason the New England Puritans have served so successfully as an emblematic instance of U.S. history is that their zealous experiment in transplanted theocracy freed human energies and ambitions that had been purposefully and hierarchically restrained by traditional European civilization. The very coming out to New England required that qualities of independent ambition and self-interested motive be released, for spiritual as well as material entreprenuerialism; hence the Antinomian heresy. The availability of the personal as an American category in turn required a new level of energy in creating a suppressive community, a system of enforced theocratic order that might restrain the breaking away of individuals from the newly ordained biblical commonwealth. One can read New England history before the American Revolution as the constant raising of stakes by the agents of religious and political community in the face of a populace excited by a vision of life that centered around the prospects of the self and family in material terms and in the here and now.

The War for Independence only certified the connection between movement by groups of determined individuals across the American continent and the constant attempts to retain or to channel the consequent disorder. That old classroom chestnut, liberty versus order, remains interesting because it does appear that the distinctive challenge of the American regime to the history of human civilization was its particular encoding of the twin impulses of individual liberty and community order. Another old chestnut—Charles Beard's 1913 economic interpretation of the Constitution—reminds us that the Declaration enshrined liberty and the Constitution interpreted that liberty in terms of the need for stable political community. James Madison did construct an ingenious formulation in *Federalist Ten*: extend the sphere for human selfishness and you may manage the most dangerous issues of faction. For Madison this was the likelihood that the poor would know how to organize to take from the rich, and thereby make restless liberty the servant of reasonable political order. Lodging selfishness in restlessness and compromise of self interest, Madison made the play self-interest stand for order.

Democratic institutions mediate between the pulls of these two staples; on one hand democracy is meant to enable individual freedom, and on the other to orchestrate the community of individuals whose anarchic or organized groups proved equally worrisome to sage heads. The focus of American energy on the material, the accepting of the entrepreneurial, the capitalist, and the accumulation of property as the stable measure of worth, and the success of individual and society do not contradict the essential connection between individual freedom and the materialistic impulse. The critics of the material understanding of freedom, those who emphasize the Jeffersonian language of serious happiness or the Emersonian understanding of the soul, criticize the unfortunate limitation of freedom by the material metaphor for it. They seldom venture beyond the figurative to the political understanding of material individual freedom as the capitalist myth of freedom or the religious understanding of materialism as the necessary guise of a godless freedom.

It is worth making the point as well that what Turner described as an effectively peaceable westward democratic movement was not peaceable. American democracy was in fact, as it appeared to its victims no less than to its critics, a licensing of some of the most dangerous of human energies and had anything but peaceful results. The decimation of native peoples, the enslavement of Africans in America and the subsequent racist regime, the refusal of citizenship and equality to women, and the environmental consequences of the stampede west were among the things ignored by the democratic celebrationists. They had to ignore them in order to see things the way they did; their values and hopes fueled equally this selective vision of democracy. In this they resembled their subjects.

It may be that all of these movements of peoples are better seen in global historical perspective. Certainly the movement of peoples, forced, voluntary, group, individual, over time and moment to moment, is an essential element in understanding the United States and, indeed, in revising its history. The United States specialized in the movement of some and the refusal of movement to others; mobility has always been a kind of American privilege. Turner and so many others of his time and sort were prescient in fretting that the closing of the American frontier somehow mirrored a closing of American democracy as they understood it. As more and more Americans reached a final destination, they have had to live with each other. The issues became less those of starting up than of getting along, especially as the old hierarchies of race, gender, class, and ethnicity have lost their sway and individuals of all sorts have lost their reticence in demanding voice and equality. The American city has been presented by historians as the crucible of this process, none more than New York.

In sketching this interpretive history of L.A., I am continuing the Turnerian focus group with one difference. Recognizing that it was the white northern European settlers who, in Turner's view, carried the makings of civilization with them, I start from their experience—although it is worth noting that in the 1830s many Californios already shared a republican ideology with their Anglo future fellow citizens.[2] The only difference is that I am identifying this democratic Typhoid Mary contingent not as universal everybodies but as particular somebodies. The effect of the transcontinental movement on the ethos and culture of this democratic American core group reassured the likes of Tocqueville that political community was possible in America, however little you yourself might want social community with the Americans. But Los Angeles turns out to have been the metropolis whose history is the working out of the restless, self-inventing, even anti-social individual impulse. Perhaps not uniquely, but surely distinctively, L.A. has been the site of the logical development of that movement of peoples Turner and others linked to the fate of American democracy.

Los Angeles is among many other things the place where these American white Protestants lost their bearings and found their feelings. In that blessed and troubling Jeffersonian moment of lost and found and hide and seek, lies the story of Los Angeles as the Mecca of the middle American whose surprise at exchanging Ohio for the Big Rock Candy Mountain continues to resonate. If you try, you can hear it, for L.A. is the seashell in whose chambers echo the American voices—the ones Jefferson liberated, Emerson empowered, and Whitman heard, the ones Frederick Douglass and Susan B. Anthony challenged and Lincoln apotheosized, the ones Henry Adams despised and Eleanor Roosevelt believed, the ones Duke Ellington captured, and the ones our therapists and channelers, gurus, preachers and pollsters, personal trainers and psychics interpret, the ones our colleagues theorize and deconstruct. For Los Angeles is, among many other fabulously articulated things, the American individual sounding board, not exactly stripped of identity, but always pressured by the odd centrifugality of the City of the Angels to the individual, the self, the you and the me.

It may be that to talk about L.A. is really to talk about a region, in the sense that the once very different places on the eastern seaboard do appear to us as connectedly if not uniformly *back east*. I urge here that one consider L.A. as the emblem of a region that may indeed include Orange County, the Inland Empire, Palm Springs, and more. I do think, however, that L.A. is distinct from Santa Barbara and San Francisco and the other Bay cities, which retain a character that the individual lives lived within do not diffuse or disperse. Santa Barbara and San Francisco have been updated, of course; their high Protestant tone has been softened, but they retain ethos even if that ethos is somewhat less restrained than it was.

Unlike these cities, Los Angeles lacks consistent tone, overarching definition, something outcropping and shared. What it has instead is a congeries of groups and individuals, a metabolism, a melting and stewing and bubbling without a cauldron or a pot. In L.A. the slime and mulch of its human energies have spilled all over the land, a spreading of things uncontained and uncontainable. If this image doesn't work for you, think of almost every city block in the good old city of the future: from east to west one sees staggering hopes, stylistic ventures, a series of big, beautifully conscious monumental or design-coordinated buildings that lurch and diminish into a mini-mall, a bunch of shops, or some other style, an assemblage that indicates not eclecticism but the lack of urban planning will.[3] L.A. has failed to impose its collective will in the only way cities really do, by putting up buildings that define the style and the density; the streets of the good old city of the future confirm our sense that it lacks shared community.

Earthquake, riot, or rain may bring the people of my city together, but what unites Angelenos is our particle of social or individual truth. In this sense the L.A. police, the *industry* as we call what others call Hollywood, the endless spiritual cults and social groups, and countless individuals are as close as this metropolis gets to sustained civic identity. The significance of this for American democracy is that some shared civic morality was necessary for the survival of the Union, but the traditional means by which such civic identity can be enforced were explicitly denied to this regime in the Bill of Rights, which in effect disempowers the systematic coercion of national identity as other nations have done it. That makes the American history of such efforts the intense, exaggerated, paranoid story it is and can be seen nowhere more clearly that in the factional character of such efforts and ideology in L.A., which brought us the John Birch Society, Ronald Reagan, the Hollywood Ten, fitness, and gurus galore. The point is that L.A. is where Americans find themselves out and have to face the splintered energies of the political founding. L.A. is where the exaggerated impulses of this polity and culture are reflected back at Americans en masse, in groups and to the self. L.A. is the laboratory of American democratic culture, freed from its restraints in creed and civic uniformity.

Four elements seem to me to describe the character of Los Angeles as a ramifying American place. The first, sketched above, is that it represents the terminus of the European westward sweep across a continent. Whatever that ends up really meaning, it does represent something. I would suggest the image of Constantinople rather than the land's end viewed by scholars who read Turner's confusion about movement as the necessitating urge for American century expansion. Constantinople because European crusades in the name of their punitive creeds encountered in the fabled East an intoxicating destination, one that reoriented the successor culture to Rome back toward the rich fields of non-European civilization, an ancient gateway where new bargains would be struck with the temptations and the peoples of this world.

Second, this frontier terminus was transforming. L.A. is where Americans encountered the lands of their desires, and it made them crazy, in the same way that the lands beyond Europe made Europeans crazy; think of T. E. Lawrence, think of Morison of Peking, think of Livingston when you think of American migrants to L.A. This also explains the persistent feeling on the part of the rest of the country that there is something dangerously Lotus Land about L.A. It represents a different category of urban danger from New York's corrupt hell. In New York or Chicago some *they* will corrupt you; in L.A. you will give in to yourself. In this sense it represents the contemporary version of the tempting, lazy South, and we have to agree with Mrs. Stowe's memorably staunch character from *Uncle Tom's Cabin,* Miss Ophelia, about what the southern clime and its mixed people need in the way of a dose of Yankee conscience and energy. In another way, L.A. has come to represent what Europe was for several earlier generations, the site of transforming temptation, such as Lambert Strether experiences in the Paris of Henry James's *The Ambassadors.*

The culture of conscientiousness that pervaded middle-class white Protestant American life was always linked to the fate of the polity by the belief that the moral restraint the common good might require would be endangered by the temptations of the flesh and even more by the temptations of an attitude that accepted the flesh and the spirit as integral to and properly the property of the individual. American conscientiousness, whether high New England or Jiminy Cricket, is about keeping a voice in the white American head that says *no* to the offers of freedom in the insistent whispering of desire. The Emersonian version of the conscience recruited that inner voicebox for a deeper and more independent inner voice, not necessarily relativist or licentious but certainly not conventional. That was Emerson's radicalism, and the co-opting of that radicalism into a brake on his Victorian audience was both a social triumph (the Emersonians did lots of good after all) and a falsification of the dangerous promise of individual liberty. The particular corruption that L.A. offers is its interpretation of freedom as desire and the unembarrassed accumulation of goods and status, but quintessentially its cult of the body, and the companion liberation of an understanding of the spirit as dwelling in the flesh.

We can see that this was also what was at stake for Emerson and his Transcendentalists: they turned toward the Asian and to the regimens of health and rearrangements of relations among women and men as part of their break with Puritan things. This theme also runs through the works of Henry James, whose characters are caught between the sacred rage and the fire down below. But the Transcendentalists and Victorians never did manage to break the flesh barrier, except in regimens and stray arrangements. The South remained the pornographic American landscape with its sexual melodrama of slave and master and mistress and its varieties of bondage and hideous sexual excitements. Nor were these pleasures uninteresting to the Yankees: remember Henry Ward Beecher's slave auction at Plymouth Church? The Jeffersonian has always the potential for a non-Christian understanding of the soul and the body: his substitution of happiness for property was a significant one. The Emersonians established that there was an American spiritual method, one that might involve a critique of materialism and mass democracy but that recognized convention as the engine of conformity which must result in the failure to be individual. However prudish Mr. Emerson and his century, the implications of his views were inevitably sensual and personal and wayward and sexual. And their natural destination was L.A.

A third element of the special character of the metropolis L.A. has become was its racial and ethnic character. The odd racial triangulation of most of U.S. history, in which white people thrived by eliminating the native American and subordinating the African American, does not describe the racial encounter in southern California. The native Americans suffered their familiar, horrific fate, but the African American presence in southern California was not the social touchstone it was elsewhere. Despite considerable and persistent racism, black Americans had an L.A. history in which they were not the singular example of social marginalization and degradation. The racial mixture of southern California included significant Asian American groups, especially Japanese and Chinese, and what amounted to a host population of Spanish and Mexican Californians, who not only had settled California before the Anglos but continued to move back and forth between the Californias and Mexico in a pattern of migration and settlement that the national borders of the 1840s and 1850s neither reflected nor enforced. The attempt of the Americans to turn California Mexicanos into an *immigration* population and then into a *migrant* population across borders suggests real and figurative strategies of displacement. The comparison with the assimilation of Jews or Italians is vividly telling; it was too dangerous to allow Mexican American assimilation, despite the plain fact that Mexican Americans had assimilated to southern California, and done so before or at the same time as the European immigrant groups whose inclusion in American democracy is a staple of celebrationist lore.

The white Californian-American immigrant, especially to Los Angeles, was in effect a colonial, an agent of a country that imposed itself on the terrain and earlier peoples of southern California, but was not, as in New England or the Midwest, quite able to replace them. The existence of a racially mixed and ethnically diverse host culture confused the American immigrants even more. They claimed and clung to their own ethnicity, as

Americans, white Americans, western Americans. They needed for the first time to say *Hey, I'm from* OHIO, and to make a sign to stand at the cafeteria lunch table to make friends. The migrants to L.A. had, despite their white American nativity, to conduct themselves as an immigrant ethnic group. They turned out to have a style and a culture we can identify as such, the ideal American ethnic style. For the price of a Hawaiian shirt and certain attitudes toward barbecues and leisure, you can be a Californian, and your kids will benefit in teeth and surf and height. Like all other American groups, of course, this free association had barriers, and the barriers were stringent with respect to nonwhites. This process, along with many others, created the terms of L.A. identity. The need to acknowledge themselves as American in a context that differed from back home, that needed to be settled and governed, to which they had come for their own desires but which also had this culture of sea and palms and sun and other peoples, indigenous peoples they could lord it over but couldn't exterminate, whose connection to the land they could not destroy, although they tried to and did seem to supersede.

I am not here presenting a nostalgic picture of a colonial paradise under whose wafting palms my Ohioans discovered themselves and did no harm. There is a real, important, powerful, and tumultuous racial, class, ethnic, and economic history behind the cultural interpretation I am venturing. The southern California lure did have a colonialist rhetoric—its promotional literature was amazingly like the literature of colonization that was produced to induce early modern Europeans to migrate to the New World—but it is no good reviving it. The feeling L.A. gave its Anglo immigrants was that they had arrived in a paradise they might claim, a resort. The facts suggest that they went about making it their own with customary racialist ruthlessness and lack of political consciousness.

This process created the terms of American L.A., a democratic identity that has its roots in the challenge desire poses to a culture used to preferring its desires in terms of power rather than in terms of satisfaction. The racism of Los Angeles was real enough, but its effects were disorienting to a people used to the structuring certainties of racial, gender, and other systems of privilege. The racist in southern California, often known as the police department, became the arm of interests whose power was in some ways both unchecked and dislocated. In this city, the police, like the newspapers, like the big businesses, like the movie studios, found too little in their way. They could influence, organize, steal, and end up just being the thing they were trying to influence. L.A. was a frontier town in the sense that its big interests and leading citizens created an official vigilante culture. It kept order without establishing order.

What resulted from all of this, and much more I have not discussed, was a view of the individual that on one hand fulfilled the Jeffersonian and on the other shook up its accepted meanings. The Jeffersonian-Emersonian individual was always a high-minded construct, an image of freedom that gave no ground to the traditional fears that to free the human being was necessarily to free the beast in the human being; natural rights in this view inevitably risked releasing human nature and its unchecked natural impulses. The breakdown of social restraint in L.A. is too familiar an experience of atomistic social dissolution to require detailing here. But a few things are worth noting: the thank-you notes you don't have to write, the self-improvement that is the cultural staple, the profusion of intensely singular visionary cults, the way in which individuals in southern California venture out on Ms. MacLaine's limb or any number of others. Joan Didion.

The consequences of that breakdown are powerful for the experience of freedom and are the fourth distinctive element of the city's culture. In L.A. we have the paradigm of a people that on a large scale seeks to satisfy itself from the inside out. That it finds the guide to those inside answers from externalized, commercialized sources is not to the point. The method is the key. And the consulting of an inner self that is free of organized conscience is the L.A. method. Robert Schuller, for instance, came from the rockiest-ribbed of midwestern Calvinist denominations to found his reassuring empire of Christian optimism in an abandoned drive-in movie, one his Richard Neutra structure and Philip Johnson Crystal Cathedral memorialize.[4]

The phenomenon is neither hard to grasp nor really controversial. What is less clear is how to take it seriously culturally. Is this something other than dissolution, is it crumbling of human possibility into trivial human potentiality? Is this a freedom from restraint that in turn gives rise to a culture of new restraint, both of which thrive in L.A.? The politics of the self do not, after all, differ along political lines; the individual moves from creed to creed. The key to the position is that *me* who takes it up.

There is another way of understanding the flake factor in the development of L.A. It is but one of the elements in L.A. life, and may or may not turn out to be the fundament of a city where one might argue ethnic and cultural concentrations will outperform individualist ones. Indeed it may turn out that L.A. is the place where we shall find out how American pluralism plays: will it be a negotiated arrangement of multiple identities based on community interests and nondissoluble identities, or will the individual be the trump card most students of American democracy have tended to think, whether they saw the game as won or lost.

A powerful challenge to the understanding of individual freedom that has emerged in the last generation has been the lesbian and gay movement for equality and equal protection of the laws. However much it borrows from the classic African American civil rights struggle and was directly inspired by the feminist struggle, the gay liberation movement has one essential difference. It is an inside truth of identity that it proposes, one only discoverable by using the Jefferson-Emerson method of searching one's self for one's gyroscope. This movement has already transformed the terms of American individual liberty; the battle rages in our politics.

The important point here is that this movement—with its important derivation from the truths of the body and the spirit, and which depends on the thorough repudiation of everything traditional Protestant American culture teaches—was a phenomenon of Los Angeles. The Mattachine Society began in Los Angeles. It was the creation of a group (significantly including Communist activists) around 1950 who happened upon the extraordinary connection between American individual democratic freedom and their own sexuality. It is taking generations for the movement to spread, and its history has been taking place throughout the nation, but the particular shape of L.A. culture and its implication for American democracy can be seen in the simple thought of what it must have taken for some people to decide that being homosexual was exactly a category of inside individual truth, exactly the kind that needed to force itself on the conventions and received truths of American tradition. And that truth, as Walt Whitman had seen, was a truth about the body as much as about the soul.[5]

The people who formed this small but historic movement had the help of left ideology and the experience of being homosexual in a society that could even turn against white people if they were *faggots* or *dykes,* in the process weakening their ties to traditional American views. But it took a different leap to get them into the great beyond of gay liberation. I want to conclude with this image of a movement for individual liberation based on the truth of individual desire, that the body and its desires and the spirit and its needs must be acknowledged. It is the Whitman endgame of Jefferson and Emerson, of course, but it is also the best example I know of the particular challenge that L.A. makes to the Anglo-American history that claims it. The gay liberation movement makes perfect sense in retrospect as identifiably Los Angeles in its roots.

I do not know whose this city really is or should be. Who can say what the future is for this particular empire of ours or how our constitutional regime will fare. It does seem clear, however, that a principal interest in the examination of Los Angeles as a "city of exile" is its hosting of the particular exile of the middle American and what that American found out about her hopes and fears in the absence of a traditional culture that was a container for them. My own guess is that the key is the equation of *anglo* with "free enough to be a student of one's own self," which means the owning of *anglo* particularity and the dispersal of what has been gained under the false premises of its universality. Too, the future interest of L.A. resides in the transformative possibilities of movements like the gay and lesbian one, which cut across all other identities and make pluralists out of anyone. But that's another story. This story, such as it is, ends with the realization on the part of a very small, mid-twentieth-century clique of queer individuals that the inside truth of desire was indeed the Jeffersonian payoff.

# PART III

# DOING SOMETHING ABOUT IT

# ⚡ STALKING THE BLUSHING ZEBRA

In 1993 I BEGAN to write occasional opinion pieces for the Los Angeles *Times*. I came to their attention as someone who could contribute a "perspective" on gay rights, and that has been my principal subject, although it is not the only area on which I have things I would like to tell the world. I continue to find the chance to write these pieces rewarding. I'd like to think that the kinds of things I write contribute to the conversation, if indeed there is one, about issues that much concern me.

I lucked into this opportunity as the result of the characteristic determination of Richard Rouilard, a protean and irreplaceable instigator of the gay and lesbian interest in American journalism. Richard deserves more than the brief mention I can give him here. He was an inspiration, a legend, a caution, and a hero. Nobody who enjoyed the pleasure of his company and the privilege of his attention will ever forget him. I am one of countless people Richard encouraged and, as in my case, pushed to things they might never have dared on their own. Himself a brilliant editor and truly individual voice, Richard came to the L.A. *Times* after a historic and memorable stint as editor of the *Advocate*. It didn't end well, but whatever the consequences to him, the state of gay and lesbian journalism will never be the same because of what Richard Rouilard accomplished. At the *Times*, Richard concerned himself with more than the limited services his new employers had in mind. And, together with other like-minded and open-minded *Times* people, Richard arranged for a few gay writers to submit sample columns for the op-ed page. The paper printed one of mine and then another and so got in the habit of being receptive to my efforts.

183

Richard and I were friends, and being his friend meant being the beneficiary of his ambitions for one. He gave me invaluable advice about how one does this sort of writing. He goaded me to expect and even prize being edited. He tried to teach me the ropes of a more popular style of writing than I had mastered—or ever really have—and to resist my academic's habits. He shared with me his wide acquaintance with and passionate convictions about gay issues and his incomparable feeling for the passing moment, the stringent demands of the "real world," and his joyous and helpless enthusiasm for the theater of life. Thanks to him, I had the chance to practice writing for magazines as book editor of *Genre* magazine for a year, to my great benefit if not the magazine's. Even a few years after his death, Richard is the journalist and the editor I have in mind when I am working out an opinion piece. And he is still the friend whose good opinion of my pieces I crave and whose company I miss.

I had the equal good luck of collaborating with Michael Nava on a book about gay civil rights during this time. Michael decided that we were going to write *Created Equal: Why Gay Rights Matter to America* after the tumultuous effect on all of us of the demonstrations lesbians and gay men staged in response to Governor Wilson's cynical veto of California gay rights legislation he had promised to sign; his pseudo-moralistic betrayal of lesbian and gay citizens' rights prompted several days of public activism, in itself infrequent among gay Angelenos. Michael's writing and accomplishments speak for themselves. I was his fan before I was his friend and am proud to remain both. His idea that we should write this book led to a happy collaboration and an abiding friendship. His thinking and our years of memorable conversation inform much of the writing here.

My sense of the issues discussed owes much to the writing and conversation and examples of numerous activists in the lesbian and gay cause. I have tried to keep in mind that I was not chosen to represent a various population; nobody elected me spokesman for gay issues. The relative scarcity of our voices in such places, however, contributes to the perception that any one gay person's views are representative. I have tried, therefore, to steady my own individual views with a sense of responsibility to represent lesbians and gay men fairly. I also tried to blend issues of general interest with those of particular importance to lesbians and gay men. The significance of gay rights and the facts of our situation form the major theme in those essays. I kept trying to find new ways to raise the central issue of why our rights should concern our fellow citizens. I would like to write even more about my own experiences. When the *Times* published a column about a woman's first use of lipstick, I proposed to my editor that I would like to write a column about mine. She thought I was joking, and I decided to let her. My mother would *plotz*. But I am hoping to write more columns about the lives we lead and the feelings we have.

Writing opinion pieces has been confusing and often frustrating for me. Shifting my emphasis from the performance style of the academic, in which the limited readership is compensated for by the presumption of their interest, to the demands of journalism, where you really have to try engaging the reader, has not been easy. In this as in so much else I am beholden to my principal editor for the op-ed pieces. Mary Heffron Arno, articles editor for the opinion page at the L.A. *Times,* has been a fair and helpful editor. I have been able to count on her to edit my pieces with the readers and the news principally in mind.

Opinion pieces in newspapers like the *Times* are a very specific genre. The op-ed piece is tied to the news. It is intended to present opinions and not to host rigorous debate, let alone lead to a conclusion. There is stiff competition for the space, and it is the editors' job to decide what merits it. I am grateful for the willingness of the *Times* to print as many of my articles as they have done, especially given the intermittent interest in gay subjects in the media. I have never been told what to say. The how-to-say-it decisions have been, in the main, ones I understood the reasons for. An editorial decision not to print something of one's own never goes down well. But I have been handled with considerable care and, even more important, I recognize that Mary Arno and her colleagues are in earnest in trying to represent the diversity of Americans. They take seriously their responsibility to print unpopular opinions like mine about significant injustices, like those lesbians and gays are routinely subjected to.

There are things I have learned in writing these pieces that mark my differences with the ways in which opinion pages work. I understand their need to key to current news. I also realize that they have columnists who supplement news with analysis. I think, however, that there are subjects, like mine, where there are fundamental issues of right and information that opinion editors should sometimes keep in mind as a corrective to the habits of their demanding work. I want to emphasize here that I am not criticizing individuals. I am especially concerned with the issue of "balance," which is central to editorial thinking.

Balance is sometimes a good notion, but it must be seen in a truly balanced way. The *Times* continues to fall into the trap of equating homophobia with what they see as pro-gay writing. It is very important that views contrary even to mine be given fair play. James Pinkerton, for example, is a columnist with whom I do not usually agree but who represents views that people like me need to understand and consider. But too many times gays are confronted with ignorant and bigoted attacks not on our views or stated agendas but with our very right to exist.

The column "First, We Demand Recognition," published on July 16, 1993, for instance, was suggested by a senior editor in response to my remonstrance on this point. I was given the chance to write a two-column assessment of the issues raised by their notion of "balance." The resulting redaction of my two columns into one was fair enough, and reflected respectable decisions from the newspaper's point of view. But it was paired with an irresponsible and ignorant counter opinion, which claimed, among other things, that lesbians do not like sex. To equate an earnest attempt to examine issues like balance with an uninformed diatribe, which had nothing to do with the issue, concentrates the problem. What other group continues to have to justify its very right to exist? I think the column states the issue clearly and believe the situation it describes still persists. I think this is not an issue of good will but inherent in the very structure of opinion writing. As a professor, I know the danger of getting into the habit of thinking that you know about anything that comes your way. Editors, like professors, must resist the built-in temptations of their job because so much of what they think they know about, they do not. People in responsible media positions need to educate and re-educate themselves about the sexual minority. Uninformed tolerance is not the same thing as fairness or balance.

A second problem comes from the very notion of identity-based, diverse, multicultural voices that has made my writing possible. The editors have their own views about what voices get to express what sentiments about what issues. Thus, my several attempts to write a column about needle exchange and safer sex for the *Times* did not really fit my category, and in my view made it easier for them not to print an opinion about something they had a public responsibility to air. They, it is only fair to say, believed that my columns on the subject were not newsworthy, well done, or otherwise worth printing. I do not raise this to quarrel with their judgment. Rather, I think the problem is that having come to their attention as a community voice, I am therefore so regarded and restricted by the issues that complicate contemporary cultural politics.

In 1996 I participated in a panel discussion among op-ed writers for the *Times* at a conference of opinion editors from across the nation. It was interesting to realize that all the other panelists claimed not to represent any views or agendas but their own. I have no such luxury because I am a representative, whether I like it or not, despite the fact that I neither merit nor claim such a role. And I do think the real justification for my punditry is the routine injustice and persecution to which lesbians and gays are subjected. One editor asked me a revealing question. He wondered how to keep the argument for gay rights from becoming repetitive and boring. My fellow panelists nodded vigorously and chimed in about their search to be fresh and keep the public interest engaged. I had no choice but to say that he would probably have advised Thomas Jefferson in the fall of 1776 that the natural rights and created-equal stuff was already stale, and couldn't he come up with a new angle. The editor was a gent about the exchange and took my point. But the problem is a real one. Gay rights do not really fit the opinion model because we have to argue for the rights we have been unconstitutionally denied in the face of denial that significant violations could still be happening and an avalanche of demonstrably false information that is frequently represented as equivalent to our evidence-based claims. You can be sure that my columns were subjected to much sterner standards of evidence than those of anti-gay writers.

Personally, I have trouble with the level of generality and the limited space for developing an argument in op-ed writing. This probably says more about my unsuitability for such writing than about the opinion genre. But it does flag a problem with the notion of opinion. I did a radio show with Orson Bean after the column "Holiday Lavender Blue" was published (below, p. 225). The column was printed as half of a point-counterpoint between me and someone who has no qualifications for writing about gays, except shameless and self-promoting bigotry, although she really did tell me that some of her closest friends and family are . . . I was not happy about the whole thing but felt obliged to do the show. I was stunned. Yet again. There was no attempt to address the issues raised. Instead, the host talked about gay marriage and how men might next want to marry horses, and so on. What was really troubling, however, was the absolute disregard for any notion of evidence or rational claim. Having an opinion increasingly seems to be a variation of the diminished-capacity defense.

The exalting of "opinion" barely conceals an impatience with the hard work democracy requires. Informed opinion is what democracy requires. Otherwise debate is as crude and destructive as the ignorant screaming that now passes as debate. I have been fortunate to have many old friends whose disagreements with my views on this subject have required me to think them through. I know what rational debate can be and try my best to seek its discipline, or at least not to duck it when the occasion arises. But what passes for opinion nowadays is part of the corruption of our public life. The very sorts who go on and on about the victim defense use the right to free expression of opinion in the same way. They disregard even the pretense of evidence for their views, insult anyone who won't accept their claims, and refuse responsibility for what they do say and its baleful effects by claiming the "opinion" defense.

In the course of preparing this collection, I also experienced an unwelcome side of writing opinion pieces. I began to write about an issue that is really unwelcome in newspaper opinion pages and have had to rethink my own relative ease in getting views on lesbian and gay rights published. The reason I have had the opportunity to publish these pieces is that the

*Times,* like some but by no means all major American newspapers, decided that lesbians and gay men qualified for representation among the diverse groups that people our city and our nation. My stubborn, sunny, liberal disposish encouraged me to think that I would be able to raise hitherto forbidden subjects. I failed to realize that my freedom of expression in this respect resulted from a decision that gay and lesbian viewpoints should be aired; it did not mean that the taboo had been removed from all stigmatized points of view. I realized this when I began to write about the issues of needle exchange and safer sex in relation to AIDS and other sexually transmitted diseases.

My columns on needle exchange, all but one of which are being published here for the first time (I've always wanted to write that!) explain themselves. I have been troubled, as have many others, by the state of public policy in relation to AIDS as the affected populations, domestic and worldwide, have grown and the numbers of people at risk have continued to skyrocket. The hopeful reaction to new combination drug therapies that have reduced the AIDS death rate among certain groups has muffled real concerns. These include the long-time effectiveness of those drugs, the real and present danger of infection, and the continuing issue of the justice and efficacy of the health-care delivery systems currently in place.

The only sure way to prevent the spread of AIDS is abstinence from both unsafe sexual contacts and intravenous drug use. But abstinence has a very poor track record, especially as a component of public health policy. What works is needle-exchange programs, and what works is energetic public education and ballyhoo for safer sexual practices. That these things work is not in dispute. But each is a politically sensitive issue, so sensitive that politicians and the media have in effect banned their discussion. This is not the place to venture a discussion of the ways in which American society refuses to look candidly at sex and drugs. But it is the very place to state that in the time since I began writing about these subjects in earnest, neither I nor most others who are concerned with the issues of needle exchange and safer sex have been able to get our views published in such major newspapers as the Los Angeles *Times.* I did get "Needle Exchange Can Save Lives" published in *Newsday.*

The notion of empowered voices, which I believe the *Times* editors to hold sincerely and sometimes against considerable pressure, has made a new and encouraging freedom of expression possible. This freedom is also inherently restrictive. My own experience of not being able to publish my views on needle exchange, safer sex, and AIDS has reminded me of things I should never have forgotten. Most important of them is my reconnection with what "doing something about it" requires. You just have to keep trying, and I hope that the columns in this collection about AIDS will cause some readers to join the heroic and persistent activists who do their work day in and day out and face much greater obstacles than mine. Jane Silver, policy director of the American Foundation for AIDS Research, has been one of those heroes. She has counseled me on the needle exchange and safer-sex columns, making sure that they were accurate and giving me her own keen editorial suggestions. Jane and I are old friends, and I have always been inspired by her work in the world. But on this issue she has reminded me of the necessity of activism and the daunting odds that face people who want to raise issues that do not interest the national media very often.

Finally, I do not share the view of many of my colleagues that journalism is somehow unimportant for the academic, however many dangers it may pose to an academic's vanity and sense of scholarly purpose. I think that scholars' learning to write for the general public is self-serving in the best sense, as well as part of our obligation to the public. Historians need to recognize that our failure to communicate the substance of what has been discovered about the nation's history is one reason the university and public funding for the humanities and the arts are in such straits. If one is concerned that the public does not turn to historians to learn about history, writing about it in publications general readers read makes sense. To a historian, of course, the distinctions between journalist and scholar are not clear. There is no better way of learning to write more clearly than having to earn your readership's attention. I am not giving myself as a successful example of this but am proud of myself for trying.

This should include writing book reviews. I have not reprinted my reviews here, but what I learned from writing them is relevant. I owe my first chance to review books for the *Times* to Art Seidenbaum. I am one of many Art helped. His premature death remains a palpable loss not only to his friends and associates, but to a city he loved and understood in a highly individual way. I have come to think that Art's *Book Review* distilled our fascinating metropolis in a wonderful way. It also infuriated and challenged me because Art did not conform to anyone's parochial view of what mattered to his readers, or should. It was typical of Art that he encouraged me to tell him what I thought about the *Review* (I didn't think much of it) and to be delighted when I held him responsible. Equally characteristic was his response to my . . . shall we say parochial, yet often justified, criticism. He gave me the most unexpected range of books to review, and kept me off balance by giving me the kinds of assignments that he knew would broaden my understanding of what reviewing was about and whom it was for. I shall always treasure his endless joy at fooling with my academic second skin. As so many others do, I miss him and hope the L.A. *Times* Book Prize officials remember that the prize for first fiction is supposed to be awarded in his name for very good reasons.

I owe to Art Seidenbaum one of the most important lessons I have learned. At his request, I substantiated my critique of the *Review* with an analysis of its contents over several weeks. I was especially irritated—all right, threatened—by the irreverent and insouciant reviews contributed by Carolyn See. They really did offend my academic sensibilities, which I needed to take very seriously indeed. Time has shown me that I was defending them against my own inclinations, because I had taken up scholarship to discipline myself to the point of bondage. Art of course shared my views with Carolyn, who was characteristically amused and tolerant when we met.

I realized that there was more going on here than I knew. I decided to read *Rhine Maidens,* one of her novels. The admiration and enjoyment I felt reading her wonderful book made me mistrust my dismissive judgment of her reviews. I wrote to her telling her so, and we began a correspondence that culminated in her appearance at the Claremont Graduate School to read from her manuscript of *Golden Days.* I introduced her by telling my students and colleagues about my misadventure in judgment and, I think, some of the things it was making me rethink. Carolyn's reading was memorable not only because of what she read but because of the emotion that flowed freely, for once, where it should. I think this was a watershed in my work and life, and I am happy to remember Art Seidenbaum's part in my education and to record my debt to Carolyn See.

Sonja Bolle, another memorable editor of the Los Angeles *Times Book Review,* taught me more than any editor has about my own writing and what needed improvement if I wanted readers. She gave me the rare chance to explore the issues that matter in ways that I could not in opinion writing. One thing that links opinion writing to book reviewing is the way in which books encode the very things one writes op-ed essays to dispute. The distortion of what being homosexual means in a subject's life is still commonplace, because the interpretive closet abides. In the fall of 1997, a reviewer for the New York *Times* wrote, with stunning incomprehension: "undoubtedly Whitman's impatience with queries about his homosexuality issued less from circumspection . . . and more from annoyance at such myopic readings." With every passing year, however, it becomes clearer that writers and reviewers who continue to suppress or misrepresent the importance of sexual orientation to the sexual minority are not merely ignorant or in denial. They make mischief, and one must conclude they do it on purpose. This is only one example of why book reviewing for a popular audience is part of a public-spirited scholar's opportunity.

I hope to continue writing in this vein and hope that all of my writing will reflect what I learn in the process. I do think other and younger "voices" may be more important now. I sometimes wonder what good these pieces do. But then I remember some hate mail and nasty phone calls, which proved someone was reading this stuff. Enough people I don't know have written to me so that I know it is important for these opinions to be voiced. Coming out saved my life. I did none of the brave work of liberation that took such heart and courage on the part of my elders and members of my own generation. And the people who made my journey so much easier than I feared never said anything to me but welcome home! I hope these columns honor their example.

# ⚡ The Gay Nineties: Opinion Pieces

THE FOLLOWING COLUMNS are presented within thematic subsections rather than in chronological order. A few were not actually printed, but I have included them anyway to give the reader a sense of what issues I felt were (and still are) important, whether or not the newspaper thought so. The events to which the columns refer are explicitly mentioned within the texts, and all the reader needs to recall is that 1993 was the year in which Bill Clinton was inaugurated, the first president who sought gay and lesbian support, received it, and owed his election in part to the gay vote. Then he proposed to end the ban on gays in the military, and the gay nineties commenced.

# ✂ Gay Rights

## One Percent or Ten Percent—
## The Law Isn't Counting

HOW MANY HOMOSEXUALS there are has no bearing on the validity of their claim to equal standing under the Constitution. The just-released survey of the Alan Guttmacher Institute, which estimates a far lower percentage of homosexuals among American men than was widely believed for forty years, is bound to kick up a fuss. One can already hear the sound bites about "fewer gays" and the "I told you so's" from the antihomosexual activists, followed by defensive positioning from the gay and lesbian spokespeople.

Before we get too deep into such discussion, some clarifications are in order. Issues of gay and lesbian rights have never been based in statistics because, like all Constitution-based claims for equal protection of the laws, gay rights is about the rights of individuals. Classes of individuals who are discriminated against and seek redress as a group are seeking "minority rights." Whether everyone in the group has some things in common is not the key to their claim for equal protection of the laws. A minority group's percentage of the population has nothing to do with the rights of the *individuals* who are being denied equal protection because they happen to be in that minority.

Lesbian and gay Americans have come together in a civil-rights movement as a vast collection of individuals who recognize a common civil disenfranchisement on account of a common minority status—in this case, preferring same-sex partners. As anyone involved in a leadership position in the gay movement will tell you, there is little unanimity. This movement has always been and will remain a movement of highly individualized individuals. Because of what we have to go through to come out in a heterosexual society, lesbians and gays make better leaders than followers. The movement is, above all, a movement of individuals seeking the constitutional protections for individuals that are the hallmark of the American

This piece was originally published in the Los Angeles *Times* on April 16, 1993, just before the 1993 March on Washington for Lesbian and Gay Civil Rights.

system of governance. Next week, when an anticipated one million lesbians and gays converge on Washington for our rights, we will be there en masse as individuals.

For purposes of the Constitution, lesbian and gay Americans just happen to be homosexual and encounter discrimination because of that immutable characteristic. The question of what homosexuals do or do not have in common across gender, race, and cultural lines, and the question of whether there is a gay culture or a lesbian culture are critical and important discussions, but they have nothing to do with equal rights as individually based claims for equal protection of the laws. Our private lives, like everyone's, are our own business and nobody else's.

The systematic denial of equal protection to homosexuals is not and never has been based on our numbers. It is true that the fewer of us there appear to be, the easier it is for our just claims to be ignored. The Guttmacher survey should make no difference in the straight majority's consideration of gay rights, but, before its findings are taken too seriously, it should be remembered that they were established by interviewing American men in their twenties and thirties. When, after World War II, Alfred Kinsey was surveying America's sexual behavior, his questions were asked of a more naïve population, which did not routinely connect sexual acts with sexual orientation or identity. It is hard to imagine in our time young American males answering questions about sex without a consciousness of what it would mean to them to identify as homosexual. Indeed, the whole question of disclosure of one's gayness is so freighted with the American culture's active discouragement of gays from coming out that is hard to imagine an accurate survey.

Societal prejudice and one's concern about these surveys go to the core of the issues raised by gay civil rights. It will be interesting to know someday how many lesbian and gay Americans there really are. We will have that information only when it is no longer necessary for homosexuals to hide their identities, and that will come after the granting of equal protection of the laws. It is the purpose of the movement against gay rights to keep us silent, to pretend that there are fewer of us than there are. Arguments against extending equal protection of the laws to lesbian and gay Americans boil down to an aggressive minority's dislike of homosexuality and a majority's acquiescence in their prejudice.

Gays' rights do not infringe on the rights of others to hold their own religious and personal views. But the same Constitution that guards their freedom to do so also and equally protects the rights of gay men and lesbians to get on with their lives, secure in the enjoyment of basic protections of the law, including property rights, employment rights, protection from violence, and equal access to the benefits of the law.

Civil rights campaigns often confront prejudice and fear, and it is understandable that their organizers summon statistical evidence to persuade their fellow citizens of their rights to an equal share of democracy. One strategy of the gay-rights movement has been to remind our fellow citizens how many of us there are. Kinsey's familiar ten percent was useful shorthand, but statistics cannot substitute for, let alone constitute, fairness. The relevant percentage is not how many young men say they are gay. Pay attention to the percentage that never changes: the hundred percent of Americans who, as individuals, claim equal protection of the laws of the United States.

On April 25, when a million of us gather in Washington, we may be ten percent, we may be ninety percent, or, if the Christian right is to be believed, two hundred percent of all homosexuals. The point is that we will be there, not only for our own individual rights, but because we know what most Americans know, which is that the individual rights of each American depend of the individual rights of every American.

## Clinton Speaks the Haters' Code Word

PRESIDENT CLINTON'S answer to a minister's recent question about gays and lesbians in the military was correctly taken as a retreat from his original stated intention to issue an executive order banning discrimination against homosexual soldiers. The President said that "most Americans believe that the gay lifestyle should not be promoted by the military or anybody else in this country." And, he added, he seeks a compromise that "does not appear to endorse a gay lifestyle."

This phrase, *gay lifestyle,* has become the key code word of antigay activists. For this president to have employed it, especially in a public answer to a question about homosexuals in the military, signals more than a move away from another one of his public positions. It is a changing of sides on a significant civil rights issue.

Central to the antigay position is the notion that sexual orientation is not an immutable characteristic requiring equal protection of the laws, but a matter of choice. It is easier to persist in antihomosexual prejudice if you believe that homosexuality is like adultery, something you choose to do, rather than like heterosexuality, something you *are.*

This piece was originally published in the Los Angeles *Times* on June 15, 1993.

Scientists have only begun to investigate this subject, although recent studies of brain chemistry and of the incidence of lesbian and gay twins suggest that sexual orientation is genetically inherent. Few reputable scientists credit the notion that homosexuals can choose their sexual orientation. Even if sexual orientation results from what some social scientists call "cultural formation," it still presents itself to most lesbian and gay people as a fact rather than a choice.

Talking about a gay "lifestyle" is a rhetorical device by which antigay activists can associate the ordinary lives that gay and lesbian Americans lead with habits and practices that they know will incite other ordinary Americans against us. What homosexual Americans do choose to do, in ever-increasing numbers, is to "come out" and press their claim for equal protection of the laws. This is the real choice that has stirred up controversy.

Early in his election campaign, President Clinton told gay and lesbian groups that they were a part of his encompassing vision and promised executive action to reverse prejudice. When he ran for president against George Bush in 1988, Michael Dukakis refused organized gay money because he knew that if was elected, he could not make good on any promises he might make to the community. Clinton asked for and got our support because he said he believed in our civil rights. And now he is telling the people for whom the promise of gay rights is a threat to their religiously established moral order that nobody is going "to promote the 'gay lifestyle.'"

Maybe one of the various compromises under discussion will end the antigay witch-hunting in the military. Maybe not. But one thing is certain: With or without the president, homosexual Americans are embarked on a civil-rights movement.

Civil-rights movements have historically been necessary because the prejudice that sustains discrimination is widespread and serves powerful interests. Partly for that reason, presidents have generally been followers, not leaders, in civil rights. Even so, the words that President Clinton chose are ominous for Americans who recognize that what is at stake here is not lifestyle but life—as in life, liberty, and the pursuit of happiness.

## First, We Demand Recognition

IMAGINE A SITUATION in which African Americans were routinely required to answer the racism of white supremacists or Jews the anti-Semitism of neo-Nazis or the disabled the claims of radical eugenicists.

This piece was originally published in the Los Angeles *Times* on July 16, 1993.

It is impossible to have a serious conversation with people who do not acknowledge your humanity and your equality before the law. And yet that is what lesbians and gay men are regularly expected to do.

In order to gain a public hearing, homosexuals are commonly expected, when they are allowed access to the media, to "debate" people who regard homosexuality as sin and gay and lesbian people as unnatural perverts. The result is that serious discussion of the situation of homosexual Americans and the discourse of civil rights that might emerge from it is too often over before it has begun. Most discussions about gay rights become demoralizing and unedifying encounters with radical antihomosexual activists whose agenda is our obliteration, however much they decorate their intent with moralistic claims to reasoning about the social good.

Gays and lesbians have still a long way to go to securing equal protection of the laws. The issues of our inclusion in society are complicated and the policy decisions that will ensue equally so. We are a diverse assortment. Being gay is an identity that cuts across all others and does not lead to simple allegiance. What we now require is reasonable space to make our arguments, to identify ourselves and to educate our fellow citizens about who and what we are. The media need to move beyond prejudice and shock value to consider how gays and lesbians will be integrated into the American mix. Most gays and lesbians are eager for this discussion. We have it among ourselves all the time and our views differ as widely as do our lifestyles. We are eager to make the case for our civil rights and to go our contrary American ways after that.

Of course, a significant part of our movement is engaged in trying to respond to the widespread prejudice about and ignorance of homosexuals. The systematic way in which language reflects gender prejudice remains an index of the entrenchment of a patriarchal society. Homophobia, like sexism, has even deeper roots in our inherited culture than do racism and anti-Semitism. It flourishes in significant segments of all of the communities who have been themselves victims of extensive persecution in the United States. The result is that the prejudice against homosexuals is mixed up with the moral and cultural inheritance of most American citizens.

Much of the opposition to the recognition of lesbian and gay Americans comes from self-described religious groups, churches and sects. The argument is sometimes made that their religious and moral opposition to homosexuality is equivalent to the rights of homosexuals to make our case in the public media. Religious events and the views of religious people are prominently covered in the very newspapers that ration gay opinion for "balance." Religious faith is as common among gays as among straights. Many scholars and clergy have shown how little the Bible has to say about homosexuality and how willful is the decision by antihomosexual activists to highlight the prohibition against sodomy as opposed to other equally stressed prohibitions in the Bible. In addition, scholars have shown how much the antihomosexual views of churches have been circumstantial and changing, examples of human rather than divine revelation. Balance means representation of all sides within civil discourse. Even repugnant views require airing, but the issue for gays is the notion that there is an equivalency between views that in effect define us as outside the bounds of civil society or, at best, a tenuously tolerated group within it and our demand for equal protection of the laws.

We do not enjoy exemptions from responsibility in exchange for our pariah status. Indeed, our tax burden tends to be greater for not enjoying the legal rights of heterosexuals to marry. Ditto our health plans. The time has come to include lesbians and gays within the conversation about rights and obligations that define civil society. That is impossible as long as our statements are considered equivalent to the statements of those who do not regard homosexuals as their equals under the law.

Heterosexual Americans may be unused to thinking about the equal rights of their homosexual fellow citizens, but they continue to believe in equal protection of the laws for law-abiding Americans. Democracy must apply to all Americans, or the freedom that a majority enjoys is not freedom but a restrictive privilege. Each of us shares the common right to live free as individuals, and what binds us is our common attachment to individual liberty—not just our own but the other person's. This is why, like it or not, the fate of democracy hinges on the removal of heterosexual privilege as a qualification for full American citizenship.

There needs to be a much fuller conversation about sexual orientation, not only its formation but also its impact on individual lives. Substantial numbers of lesbians and gays indicate that they knew early on that they were drawn to members of the same sex. The alarming rise in suicide among gay teenagers should make us help gay teens adjust rather than persist in the mindless recruitment to heterosexuality routinely practiced by a society that still believes it can make gays straight. It isn't a good idea, it doesn't work, and it serves no public purpose. The role of internalized homophobia, which roughly means how homosexuals learn from society's hatred of gays to hate themselves, needs airing. Family formation, gay marriage, the differences and similarities of gender, race and sexual orientation need to be discussed, as do the ways in which social policy will or will not consider the particular needs of homosexuals.

Reform and civil-rights movements always change the nature of the debate in a democratic society, introducing new participants in civic discourse, raising new concerns and new fears. But the price all of us have to pay for freedom is the uncomfortable accommodation of the apparently different within the circle of people we must regard as equals. Lesbians and gays deserve this respect. We grant it even to our most vociferous opponents. It is time we stopped having to answer those for whom our very existence is an affront.

## Gays and Lesbians Need a Real Movement

THIS YEAR began for gays and lesbians with hope and hype: a new President who accepted our support and returned a solemn pledge to include us within his vision of a just society. He appointed lesbians and gays to government positions and began to make good on his campaign pledge to allow us in the armed forces.

The media responded with a new level of coverage. The march on Washington saw hundreds of thousands of lesbians and gays celebrate and show ourselves proudly to our fellow citizens. It seemed the "Gay Nineties" really had arrived.

Ten months later, it is all too clear how empty was the promise, how premature the celebration. The President had no stomach for the battle that would have accompanied his making a stand on the military ban. It is hard not to be angry with him because he took our money and raised our hopes. But our support for him was always more sincere than his for us. There is even a positive side to the disgusting spectacle of Senator Sam Nunn and the military brass making a media circus out of our right to serve equally in the armed forces. It should now be completely clear that the issue with respect to gay rights, in or out of the military, is prejudice.

In a way, this frees the gay and lesbian movement to rethink its options. We have numbers, we have a cause, we have allies, but we have to do it for ourselves. That probably means scrapping the outmoded organizational style of a movement born in an era when even standing up in public was activism. The work the organizations do is often good, but they do not work well together and they are not prepared to win the battles gays and lesbians are fighting.

The Lambda Legal Defense and Education Fund, for instance, does an excellent job with court cases. But it is free-standing like the NAACP's legal defense fund, but without an NAACP to have given it birth.

We need a national organization, an umbrella like the African American and women's movements have had, with local chapters and demo-

This essay first appeared in the Los Angeles *Times* of October 12, 1993.

cratic processes for leadership and issues choices. There are at least fifteen thousand local gay organizations of all sorts: bowlers, teachers, runners, hackers, square dancers. They could be the gay movement's equivalent of the black churches, which were the galvanizing base of the civil-rights struggle.

Lesbians and gays need to learn how to participate in a long-term freedom struggle. Coming out is the first step, but learning how to regularly contribute time, thought, and money—how to be part of a movement—also is crucial. Joining is particularly hard for homosexuals to do; coming out of the closet means you have stopped heeding the dictates of culture and family. This sometimes feels like a surrender of identity. Lesbians and gay men need to learn how to support their organizations and leaders. What the feminists call horizontal hostility—taking out frustration on a movement's leaders—has also been a feature of gay political and social life. That doesn't excuse leadership failures, of which there have been plenty. But leadership and followership are equal parts of successful movements.

Gays and lesbians need to develop ideas as well as strategies. We need to think individually and together about what our goals are, how to go beyond responding to prejudice. The religious right presents a powerful challenge, but it also presents a false model. To respond to the religious right is to combat prejudice. For instance, the Reverend Mel White argued the Reverend Lou Sheldon to a standstill on *Larry King Live* because White knows the Bible doesn't say the things about homosexuality that the religious right routinely claims.

But that is not enough. We need to develop the information on lesbians and gays that sound, non-homophobic public policy needs. There is no gay RAND, no gay Brookings Institution, no gay Heritage Foundation. There needs to be, for without information our cause is doomed.

There is also a lesson that non-gay Americans should learn from the military ban. One can hear the media's sigh of relief: enough of that, let's get back to the real issues. But precious as health care and prosperity may be, so too is freedom. The ugly truth is that the attempt to lift the ban on gays in the military has resulted in a hardened policy against gays and a temporary victory for the antihomosexual activists who think getting at gays and lesbians is a first step toward restoring the idyllic America of their clouded imaginations. Guess who's next on their agenda?

# The Feds, Civil Rights, and Camp Sister Spirit

FEDS IN MISSISSIPPI, sent there to protect beleaguered citizens from intimidation based on prejudice and an escalating climate of threats and potential violence. Wait—didn't we solve this problem in the 1960s? So what's with Attorney General Janet Reno sending federal mediators to respond to harassment of a local couple?

The Hensons live in Ovett, a hamlet of twelve hundred. They run a women's camp there called Sister Spirit, which they have dedicated to the training of feminists and civil-rights activists. Nobody has accused the Hensons of anything criminal. But they have been subjected to anonymous phone calls, threatening letters, jeers, and random gunfire from their neighbors. A bomb has been exploded in front of their gate and a dead dog left draped over their mailbox. The climate of intimidation has intensified with two meetings led by Baptist ministers to raise money toward forcing the Hensons off their former pig farm.

The clue to what has some of their neighbors so riled up may be that their locked and guarded gate is painted lavender. The Hensons are lesbians, married in their own eyes and presumably in the sight of whatever higher power they cherish, but not in the eyes of the law or their neighbors. Brenda and Wanda Henson have committed no offense, but their neighbors fear that Sister Spirit will become a regional center of gay activism.

Paul Walley, a lawyer advising the groups attempting to purge Ovett of the Hensons, explained that "the area is a conservative religious community that has a standard based on biblical morality. Residents of Camp Sister Spirit reject that standard and have a radical agenda that would seek to change our way of life." Their biblical moral precedent is apparently not the injunction of Jesus of Nazareth to love thy neighbor as thyself.

Enter the Justice Department. Federal mediators commonly respond to threats against racial and ethnic minorities, but this is apparently the first response to a sexual-orientation hate crime. Mediators have met with the two sides in hopes of easing tensions.

Jones County Sheriff Maurice Hooks welcomed the mediators and defended his own record: "We're trying to protect their rights." The difficulty is that lesbians and gay men have no firmly established rights. It is heartening to have the Justice Department send mediators to Mississippi to protect citizens' rights to life, liberty, and the pursuit of happiness. But the case reminds us all of the pressing need for a national gay civil-rights bill.

---

This essay first appeared in the Los Angeles *Times* of February 25, 1994.

## Gays Won't Take Clinton's Betrayal Lightly

THE JUSTICE DEPARTMENT has decided that the government has no interest in the most important gay rights case the Supreme Court will decide, not even to the extent of filing a friend-of-the-court brief. The case before the court involves a ballot initiative passed in Colorado that would deny anti-discrimination protection to homosexuals.

Although not unexpected, the Administration's refusal to stand behind President Clinton's repeated pledges of support for gay rights, and in particular his statement in a public letter that the initiative threatened "the human rights of every individual," is shocking in its opportunism, hypocrisy, and unprincipled cowardice. It must give serious pause to everyone, straight or gay, who values the promise of equality of opportunity, equal protection of the laws, and participation in the political process without discrimination.

It is not hard to figure what led Attorney General Janet Reno to decide that the government has no stake in protecting civil rights when it comes to homosexuals. The Pentagon pressured against the filing of a brief because of the potential for subverting the "don't ask, don't tell" policy for gays in the military. Justice Department lawyers in fact had prepared careful arguments for a brief that avoided subverting that policy.

It is hard to express how disappointing and enraging the Administration's abandonment of principle is. The transparent political cynicism of Reno's decision, made without the President's objection, will send a message to the people who have never supported them and never will, and who will respond as if to the scent of blood. It is not clear what effect a government brief or lack of one will have on the closely divided Supreme Court. But this latest betrayal worsens the situation of lesbians and gay Americans, and any other individuals or groups who thought they could count on Clinton's good will if not his promises.

The election of 1996 is shaping up to be the most problematic in memory. It is truly alarming to envision a Republican President alongside a Republican Congress with the extremist political views now commonly espoused by that party. But the prospect of working for, supporting, and helping to pay for the reelection of President Clinton is not much better. He and his attorney general have shown where they really stand: with the antigay extremists.

I used to think, as Clinton calculated I would, that I would have to vote for him. But now all bets are off for me and many other lesbian and

This essay first appeared in the Los Angeles *Times,* June 11, 1995.

gay voters like me. Gay people should consider alternatives to supporting Clinton. We should devote our money and energy to electing gay and lesbian candidates and those incumbents whose good offices we can count on. We should learn the lesson that other minority groups have had to learn: that all pre-election talk in the world doesn't matter unless you have leverage after election. And leverage is the result of organizing, bargaining, and being willing to make trouble for supposed allies when they betray you.

# ⚡ Clio in the Morning Papers

## Clio in Office?

THE PROSPECT of Newt Gingrich as the driving force of a congressional majority has been worrying me because, not to put too fine a point on it, I fit his description of the abnormal American: gay, liberal, secular, Democratic. The publicity surrounding his accession, however, sounded one hopeful note. Like me, Newt Gingrich is a professionally trained historian (M.A. and Ph.D. in history from Louisiana State University) who makes a point of talking about himself as a history teacher and claims that history is a primary tool for understanding what he calls "the renewal of American civilization." So much of recent political discourse has been carried on in terms of true belief, varieties of what Richard Rorty has recently called the "conversation stopper" of religion, that Gingrich's claim to be resting his arguments on history, especially the lessons American history holds for American civilization, struck me as well worth exploring.

Like the Speaker, I believe in the study of history as one path to good citizenship and more fully realized individuality and to the survival of liberal democracy. To find out what Gingrich's thinking about history added up to, I turned to "Renewing American Civilization," the widely distributed (and controversial) course which Gingrich has said repeatedly is the most important to him of his many projects. I watched the two (two-hour) taped lectures that concern American history and its lessons most directly. I also read the companion reader to the class.

It turns out that the historical content of "Renewing American Civilization" is virtually nil. It is only fair to point out that Gingrich did not do much graduate work in U.S. history; his dissertation concerned educational policies in the then Belgian Congo. Still, for presentations that want to make the case for a certain view of American history and its implications in the present, Gingrich's lectures reveal an alarming ignorance of what at least two generations of historians have been finding out about U.S. history.

---

This essay was first published as "Twisting History" in the Los Angeles *Times Book Review*, January 1, 1995.

For example, Gingrich's classes make a great deal of immigration. Individuals like Arianna Huffington and Arnold Schwarzenegger, and groups such as those gathered at Ellis Island for citizenship ceremonies, stand for the proud claim that America is uniquely a nation of immigrants, who are then assimilated into an American civilization, which *we* (there is much *we* and *they* in these talks) share and which is the envy of the world. Absolutely no attention is given to the hardships and severities of most immigrant experience, to the racism, religious bigotry, and other obstacles immigrants have always encountered, or to the case of forced immigration from Africa.

While historians may differ about some of the comparative experiences of immigration, few would propose the unmediated celebratory model Gingrich advances. From the beginning immigrants were faced with nativist resentments and persecution, as well as opportunity. The significance of this is that the true experiences of immigrants, how universally they found joining American civilization difficult, make much sounder models for public policy than the one-sided myth of celebration. The notion that generation after generation of immigrants "learned" to be American is equally wrongheaded. Indeed, immigrants participated in the constant forming and reforming of that civilization, which has always been dynamic rather than static. Gingrich makes much of Max Lerner's *America as a Civilization,* never pausing to wonder if Lerner, like most other interpreters of American civilization before and since, was inventing as much as discovering a civilization. Much like Gingrich himself.

Gingrich's view of U.S. history owes most of its general plausibility to Daniel Boorstin's three-volume series *The Americans,* which celebrates a kind of American civilization in which the inventive, entrepreneurial spirit energized the progress of a free and ingenious people across a continent and into the world. But Gingrich's reading of Boorstin is superficial: some quotations and some incidents. He ignores Boorstin when that secular historian does not suit his purposes. So the Jeffersonian "Creator" from the Declaration of Independence becomes indistinguishable from Gingrich's "God," although one of the few things historians of the period would agree upon is that Creator and God are not the same. Gingrich uses the encounter between a British officer and a frontiersman from the movie version of *Last of the Mohicans* to illustrate American uniqueness, while elsewhere celebrating the Anglo-Saxon roots of what is distinctive about the United States. In one breathtaking moment, he says in casual wonder, that he supposes American civilization began in 1607 or 1620, at Jamestown and Plymouth, or maybe in the Southwest with the arrival of the Spanish conquistadors, or maybe nineteen thousand years ago with the native Americans. The Speaker-professor appears to have little sense of the truly stupendous differences such dating of American civilization might imply. No more does the racial past of American history interest him, except that he says government has been the evildoer in the three phases of the African American situation: slavery, segregation, and, of course, the welfare state.

The basic claim of American exceptionalism, which Gingrich embraces as a talisman of our distinctiveness, runs contrary to what most U.S. historians would now say. This civilization appears as any civilization—distinct and characteristic, but not the exception to human nature, the laws of history, or other nations that it was once routinely regarded as being. What Gingrich really wants from history are some examples that illustrate his preconceived views. American civilization to him is not a historical movement but an a priori set of "principles" in which "the lessons of American history" can be seen.

The study guide for the lecture on the lessons of American history digests the propositions. Gingrich posits a single (diverse and multiethnic, but single) American civilization. It is in crisis, with the welfare state at fault. The five principles of American civilization are "personal strength, entrepreneurial free enterprise, the spirit of invention and discovery, quality (as described by one Deming, a management guru specially revered by the Japanese), the lessons of American history." The reasons given for studying American history are:

1. History Is a Collective Memory
2. American History is the History of Our Civilization
3. There Is an American Exceptionalism That Our History Illustrates
4. History Is a Resource to Be Learned From and Used
5. There Are Techniques That Can Help You Learn Problem Solving From Historic Experience

It is significant that no attention is devoted to research, how to read the past, and the other techniques of historical work.

An example of how this works is in the taped class discussion of the Gettysburg Address. A short clip from the Ken Burns Civil War documentary is shown which describes how Lincoln spoke for a few minutes and Edward Everett for two hours, how Lincoln was disappointed in himself, and how many people criticized him. Gingrich encourages his students to ask what this teaches them, all before reading the speech or reviewing its content or making any serious attempt to situate the episode. The answers, which are written on large sheets of paper and hung on the walls to facilitate "brainstorming," include don't talk too long, don't listen to critics, past experience can mislead, and things are different in the long term from the short term.

After a while the documentary's account of the speech is shown but not analyzed. In place of analysis, a vaporous discussion of democracy ensues, in which American democracy is contrasted with Stalin's and Hitler's ideologically defended massacres of their own citizens. Not broached are the extermination of native American peoples and the slaughter that was part of the slave trade and slavery, committed respectively in the name of American ideologies of manifest destiny and racial supremacy, and in fulfillment of Gingrich's cherished entrepreneurship. It is hard to imagine a serious student of history for whom these not would pose a significant series of questions, whatever the answers.

Gingrich is not really interested in that kind of historical study. He likes to think of history as the illustration of his otherwise-arrived-at views. His students do not read historians; neither history nor historical sources grace the pages of the companion reader. Rather, Gingrich keeps saying he is a historian and gives an example or two, but many fewer historical than contemporary examples. Gingrich likes biographies (they show you how to lead your life better—although one wonders exactly how), and historical novels (they liven things up), and television like *You Are There,* the old Walter Cronkite series. He recommends Irving Stone and Tom Clancy as equivalent to nonfiction. There's nothing inherently wrong in these recommendations except as guides to history. The whole point of the historian's enterprise is to distinguish historical fact from historical fiction, which is what historians labor to do. To do so, you have to accept a gap between what history teaches and what people need or want to know. And history is almost always ambiguous in its prescriptions.

You need not disagree with Gingrich's politics to find his understanding of history unconvincing and dangerous. Newt Gingrich says we read history to find ourselves back there. He says history is the collective memory, he defining the collective. He says history is "the soap operas of being human." In founding the United States, the leaders of the federal convention and the defenders of the constitution it produced proclaimed themselves students of history. They consulted human experience through the ages to help them decide between institutions and to make choices. It was, for instance, the wars of religion that racked Europe in the Reformation's wake that caused them to make public life a secular preserve. They understood history to show that freedom and flourishing of religion depended on keeping this most individual and least compromisable of human expressions free from the inevitable incursions of the state. They also sought to protect public life from the desire of the religious to spread their private beliefs by public means.

The founders looked for themselves in history and looked for the dangers they needed to avoid in planning a republic. Their method was close study. They wanted their readers to know the same history they did, because they understood the study of history to be a policy study. They disagreed with one another, while making use of the same historical example, because they took history seriously. You do not have to be wary of Gingrich the Speaker to be alarmed by his understanding of history. Plenty of his conservative allies understand—better apparently than he—the dangers of a convenient history as an argument for an expedient public course of action. But it is worth remembering that the history of our country and its abiding lessons are not really decided by elections, even if the present and future sometimes are.

## Seeing the Messiness of America's True History

OUT OF THE CLASSROOM and into the soundbite: Senator Dole wants to make history a campaign issue. Dole blames academic elitist historians, such as those who prepared the voluntary national history standards, for emphasizing "some of our worst moments" as a society to the exclusion of the triumphs of our national history. In his recent speech before the American Legionnaires, Dole asked, "do we embrace ideas that unite us, regardless of our sex or color or religion? . . . Or are we just a crowd of competing groups thrown together by fate between two oceans?" The "false theories" of the "embarrassed-to-be-American crowd" threaten the unity that common language, history and values have enabled the United States to achieve. The problem with Dole's question is that it ignores the actual history of the United States.

Unity has been a sometime thing in American history. It is embarrassing to have to remind a proud Kansan like the Senator that his own state was born out of decades of national disunity that culminated in the nation's costliest and bloodiest war. The issues that gave Kansas its "bloody" reputation were slavery and race, issues that have bedeviled that state until our own day. In case Dole has forgotten, the *Board* in the 1954 *Brown v. Board* decision was the Topeka, Kansas, school board. And then there were the populists who mobilized Kansans against the centralizing power of industrial capitalism in the 1880s; Mary Lease advised farmers to "raise less corn and more Hell." Their critique of American politics and economics resounds to this day. The traditions of his own state, like those of the rest of the country, are not Dole's of concentrating on the good but of democracy in action, trying to make justice apply to everybody "regardless of sex or color or religion."

This essay was originally published in the Los Angeles *Times* on September 24, 1995.

Senator Dole believes that diversity "requires us to bind ourselves to the American idea in every way that we can—by speaking one language, taking pride in our true history and embracing the traditional American values that have guided us from the beginning." This view would have startled James Madison, whose classic argument in Federalist Paper no. 10 was that it was America's very diversity of interests and expanse of territory that would encourage compromise and prevent tyranny. It would also have surprised the generations of Americans who have fought about language, values, and history. It is hard to reconcile with the Bill of Rights, which prefers the risk of debate to the control of imposed unity.

What does Senator Dole mean by "true history"? He means a story that justifies his own hazy and sentimental view of what America has meant to him. But it does not disparage the opportunities many Americans have enjoyed to point out that their advantages were not achieved because of a general equality of opportunity. Any history that tells only about fortunate Americans, like me and the Senator, must ignore the experience of most Americans at any given time. The unity Senator Dole remembers was achieved through systematic restrictions on the freedoms of a substantial number of Americans, identified by race, sex, and religion. It may be that some people would like to return to a time when African Americans, women, native Americans, Asian and Hispanic Americans, lesbians and gay men, and many others were silenced, but that time will not return.

Of course Americans amount to more than a "crowd of competing groups thrown by fate between two oceans." But we are not a chosen people brought by Providence to this continent either. The United States was founded by immigrants who took over the land and systematically eliminated native populations and developed a country with the slave labor of African Americans and the forced labor of immigrant groups and of women. It is a story of complex human motives and actions, some brave, some base, some proud, and others shameful. The whole point of contemporary, diversity-minded U.S. history is to tell how American history happened to everybody and not just a few privileged and notable Americans. If much of it is troubling and even shameful, that should not worry us. The United States has always been a nation that aspired to the free marketplace of ideas that Jefferson imagined. Surely Senator Dole would not have us imitate Japan's apparent incapacity to acknowledge the conduct of its soldiers in World War II.

It is understandable that much of what is being written about has the effect of disorienting those like Senator Dole who have gotten used to being the primary subjects of American history, white male politicians. The narrative of American history Dole advocates is triumphalist and ethnocentric and unfounded. It requires that the contributions, equality, and even the humanity of substantial numbers of Americans be denied. The Senator might have been better advised to make sure there are enough teachers in classes small enough for students to learn about our history. He should try reading the vaunted voluntary standards; like any standards they can be faulted, but they provide an excellent framework for just the kind of history the nation needs and whose absence the Senator laments. He should worry about libraries closing, archives and research projects going unfunded, community histories losing federal support.

## Lott's Wife

SENATE MAJORITY LEADER Trent Lott's revelation that he considers homosexuality a sin and a sickness comes as no surprise. He and his ilk have made no secret of their views on lesbians and gay men. To them our exercise of constitutionally protected rights to life, liberty, and the pursuit of happiness, and our struggle to secure equal protection of the laws, are an opportunity to fuse personal bigotry with political opportunism. I do not happen to believe that their strategy will work in the long run. But in the short term, these comments from a very powerful politician have real consequences. They encourage and legitimate gay bashing. Lott's unwillingness to let James Hormel's nomination as ambassador to Luxembourg come to a vote, because and only because Hormel is gay, is one form. Exploiting the fear of homosexuals to raise money and votes for the ayatollahs of the Christian right is also gay bashing. However much they may try to separate themselves from the hands-on consequences of their campaign of hate, public figures who give bigotry the cover of religious values legitimate the violence done to gays and lesbians.

Lott's comments are worth some attention, however. In his interview, the Senator gives a revealing account of his theological method. He feels "very strongly" about his faith. But his religious certainties are selective, as those who claim biblical authority for living in the modern world inevitably are. Asked about the recent Southern Baptist pronouncement that it is a wife's duty "graciously" to submit to her husband, Lott responds that he would say it differently: a husband and wife "should serve each other." That strikes me as realistic. But it has little to do with the codes of the Bible and nothing to do with the conventual statement of his particular denomination.

---

This essay first appeared in *Newsday,* July 15, 1998.

What it reflects is the mixture of principle and experience of his thirty-four year marriage, and in this instance he emphasizes his own conduct, his determination to be faithful to his vows. By his own lights, Lott appears to be taking responsibility for his own moral conduct. Let him who is without sin cast the first stone might be Lott's view in this.

There are two comments in his interview, however, that indicate that Senator Lott may be kidding himself about what he really thinks. There are all too many people who believe that homosexuality is a sin. Lott, however, is not one of those. He clarifies his views by comparing homosexuality to alcoholism, kleptomania, and sex addiction. He thinks such people should be worked with to help them control their problems. Here, the Senator may still be, as White House Press Secretary Michael McCurry said, "backward." But he has at least moved forward from some biblical past to the late nineteenth century, when "homosexuality" and "heterosexuality" were notions invented to explain sexual difference. In doing so, even the well-intentioned experts who thought they were helping the same-sex-oriented outcast equated homosexuality with mental illness. Being gay was not after all a sin but a deviance, something to be treated not simply punished, hard though it is to tell the difference between the treatment and punishment of homosexuals. This view of being gay has long been discredited.

But Senator Lott, having caught up with nineteenth-century social science, shows that he doesn't know sin from syndrome. Kleptomania is a psychological explanation of an addiction to stealing, alcoholism denotes how some people are addicted to alcohol, sex addiction is about how some people cannnot stop themselves from pursuing sexual encounters. To those who believe in sin, the sin is in the deed. The syndrome seeks by contrast to explain how the individual came to do the deed. Lott's objections to gays exemplify the distortions of true religious conviction that attach to attempts to use religion for political purposes.

Equally revealing is Lott's nostalgia for the Mississippi of his youth, "a good time for America." Well, not for everybody and especially not in Mississippi. When Lott was, like his colleague Thad Cochran, fulfilling the politically important post of Ole Miss head cheerleader, some of his contemporaries (and many others) were cheerleading for a different cause. They were risking life and limb to attain freedom and justice for African Americans. In his youth, Lott probably attended a church that did not admit black people and in which equal relations between Americans of different races were routinely described as sinful. The Mississippi establishment, when not massively resisting court orders, encouraging lynching, and actively spying on and intimidating those who protested conditions, was urging African Americans to submit themselves graciously to the racial order. I am sufficiently past my own youth not to blame people for the circumstances of their upbringings, as well as for the urgings of their sexual orientation. But it strikes me that Lott hasn't learned much from his own history. And when he says that the likes of me are sinful and sick and uses religion to justify it, I am reminded of another truism: people who live in glass houses shouldn't throw stones.

# ✔ The Politics of AIDS, Safer Sex, and Needle Exchange

*The questions raised here are distressingly still open, especially with respect to such issues as distributing clean hypodermic needles and putting the full force of the government behind safe-sex information. More has been accomplished under Clinton than under Reagan and Bush, whose records with respect to AIDS were unspeakable. The situation of AIDS, both its spread and the response to it, has changed dramatically. But we still have a President and too many in Congress who are either willing to exploit this world epidemic for the meanest of reasons or who, knowing the facts, are afraid of the political consequences of decent and responsible action. One wishes they were capable of shame.*

## How About a Policy on AIDS?

WHEN HILLARY RODHAM CLINTON accepts a Commitment to Life award from the AIDS Project Los Angeles in January, it will focus attention on the important work APLA does for people with AIDS and will help APLA raise needed money. It is also an occasion to scrutinize the Clinton record on AIDS.

There are signs of movement. Secretary of Health and Human Services (HHS) Donna Shalala has said that a new AIDS-prevention initiative will be announced soon. The 1994 Clinton budget includes increases for AIDS services and research. And the Clinton health-care plan presents the possibility of more secure coverage for many people with AIDS.

Nevertheless, the Administration's record on AIDS is disappointing. People with AIDS were not represented on the health-care task force, nor have they had much to do with planning the reform. The Administration continues to enforce discriminatory immigration procedures that bar people with HIV from entering the country.

---

This essay first appeared in the Los Angeles *Times,* December 15, 1993.

The Democratic Convention made a point of showcasing people with AIDS—even the Republicans did that—as a signal that it would not continue the callous policies of the Reagan-Bush presidencies regarding the spread of HIV in America and the world. In his campaign, Bill Clinton promised that he would appoint an AIDS czar to direct, coordinate, and energize national AIDS policy. But the Administration's top AIDS appointee, Kristine Gebbie, advises lowered expectations and counsels Realpolitik: if she is the czar, then so is the current Romanov.

To date, the Clinton Administration has failed in the two main areas an effective AIDS policy will require. The nation still has no battle plan, no specific goals, and no coordinated strategy and timetable to reach them. The vaunted Clinton policy focus has not included AIDS and, whatever the press of other business, it is necessary to ask why. One can only hope that the failure to address AIDS at the policy level is not because of who it appears at this point primarily to attack: gay men, African American and Latino populations, drug abusers and their children—all relatively powerless members of the society.

The second indispensable requirement of a government AIDS policy is a sense of urgency, which the Administration has so far failed to inspire. The President brings formidable skills to his bully pulpit. He has already used them to highlight the urgency of women's health-care issues. There is no need to choose between breast cancer and AIDS. Urgency is required in both cases.

The President took advantage of AIDS Awareness Day recently to talk about AIDS at last; time will tell whether this marks the beginning of his leadership in the fight against AIDS. When Mrs. Clinton comes to Los Angeles to accept her award, she will be justly praised for her efforts to reform health care. It is to be hoped that health-care reform will benefit the fight against AIDS, but the Administration's record on AIDS is decidedly mixed. AIDS does not read between the lines. It spreads and it kills.

## Needle Exchange Can Save Lives

IMAGINE IF you were the nation's top public health official and you could save thousands of lives and curb the spread of AIDS with your signature. That is the opportunity facing Secretary of Health and Human

---

This essay first appeared in *Newsday* on March 24, 1998.

Services (HHS) Donna Shalala. On April 1 she can authorize federal support for needle exchange programs for intravenous drug users and thereby significantly reduce the transmission of HIV.

Intravenous drug users habitually share their hypodermic needles, exposing each other as well as their sexual partners and their offspring to the deadly disease. In an exchange program, addicts turn in their used dirty needles for clean ones.

The April 1 date is significant because federal legislation prohibiting federal support of needle exchange expires on March 31. If these programs can be shown to reduce the spread of AIDS without encouraging drug use, then HHS may proceed with the exchange. Needle exchange has been shown to meet these conditions. So what are public health officials waiting for? They must seize this chance to save American lives.

Needle exchange is nobody's ideal solution to the problems of AIDS transmission or intravenous drug use. But there is no doubt that it works. According to studies of five New York City needle-exchange programs, the HIV infection rate was cut by two-thirds. The urgency and effectiveness of needle exchange have been endorsed by the President's own advisory council on AIDS, the American Medical Association, the National Academy of Sciences, the American Public Health Association, the National Commission on AIDS, the U.S. Conference of Mayors, and the American Bar Association, to name a few.

Between 650,000 and 900,000 people in the United States are infected with HIV, and more than 1,000,000 Americans inject illegal drugs. New medical therapies have reduced AIDS deaths significantly, but they have no impact on the rates of new infection. There is a scientific consensus that clean needles and safer sex significantly reduce these rates. But the focus of public response has been on treatment, not prevention, as if these were competitive goals.

The habitual sharing of needles spreads AIDS among users, their sexual partners, and their babies. A large proportion of the estimated six thousand cases of pediatric AIDS can be traced to shared needles. One third of all AIDS cases and more than half of those involving women result from injections of drugs or sexual contact with people who do. Fighting drug use is hard enough. When you add AIDS and its transmission, however, the public health system is overwhelmed.

Needle exchange programs safely dispose of used needles. Most programs refer clients to HIV testing and counseling and drug-treatment programs. A 1997 study published in *The Lancet,* a British medical journal, estimated that needle-exchange programs might have prevented between 4,400 and 9,700 HIV infections in the United States, which would have saved as much as half a billion dollars in health care expenditures. The same study estimated that instituting needle exchange might prevent 11,300 more cases among drug injectors, their sexual partners, and their children.

It isn't hard to figure out why the government is not preparing the public to support needle exchange. Officials seem to have confused saving American lives with saving their own skins. In fact, the political consequences of instituting needle exchange may well be as contentious as the administration apparently fears. But politics as usual will not stop the AIDS plague. Courageous, professional, and mature decisions about public health will. Surely we have learned something from the deadly results of government inaction during the first decade of the AIDS epidemic.

An informed public must make it politically dangerous for the administration not to act on April 1 to save lives. Otherwise a missed opportunity will become a fatal April Fool's joke.

## Clean Needles and Bloody Hands

THE CLINTON ADMINISTRATION has taken another giant step ... in place. HHS Secretary Donna Shalala announced that the Administration has certified the scientific and medical findings that needle exchange significantly reduces AIDS without encouraging intravenous drug use. Having acknowledged that needle exchange works, Secretary Shalala then announced that the federal government will not lift the ban on using federal funds for needles exchanges. *Needle exchange works, but they aren't going to use it!*

What? Needle exchange works but the federal government won't support it? Secretary Shalala said localities should fund needle exchange, knowing full well that they haven't got the money. The real reason for this Orwellian decision is that the President and his political advisers believe needle exchange is controversial and the political risks are real, especially since the President's own sexual conduct is a continuing issue. They are right, of course: needle exchange will never be anybody's idea of an ideal approach to a public health issue. Blustering antidrug politicos will hook up with the ranks of moral authoritarians like William Bennett. They will have no problem is saying that the seven thousand lives needle exchange might have saved in two Clinton administrations cannot be compared to ... well, the consequences of the message that needle exchange would send to youngsters.

---

This essay was written April 2, 1998, and has not been previously published.

What is the message that needle exchange sends? Its message on drugs is that sharing needles is an especially dangerous part of a dangerous addiction. Clean needles help addicts from getting and spreading AIDS. It keeps the health problems separate. Hard as drug addiction is to treat, it is preferable to addiction plus AIDS from the points of view of the person affected, his sexual partners and children, and in terms of the cost to an already overburdened public health system.

Needle exchange also sends a moral message, but it is moral reasoning, not moralistic sloganeering: AIDS is still spreading alarmingly. There is no cure for AIDS, despite the encouraging development of combination drug therapies. Half of new AIDS cases now originate in intravenous drug use or from sex with people who use. AIDS has spread through many American communities, but infection rates have risen markedly among women and their babies and in Latino, African American, and other minority communities, and they are still significant among gay men. It is estimated that nine hundred thousand Americans are infected with HIV. More than a million inject illegal drugs. Needle exchange is routinely tied to addiction recovery services and has the potential for helping addicts. Needle exchange addresses this situation. The moral reasoning is that since we have no other way to stop it, we should use needle exchange to control the spread of AIDS.

To restore human faces to the problem, think of the six thousand children with AIDS, at least a third of whose infections can be traced to parental IV drug use and the sharing of unclean needles. Think about them for a minute, and about so many others who have contracted AIDS, and ask yourself whether you really believe anybody—President, Drug War general, politico, cabinet secretary—who says that the message needle exchange sends is not moral. The truth is that we now have a way to reduce the spread of AIDS without encouraging drug use. This has been certified. What is the morality of not using that method to save real people's real lives?

From the start AIDS has been an epidemic that seemed to challenge people's sense of human community and morality. In the 1980s the federal government made it all too clear that the populations AIDS affected were not among the American people they recognized. We are now seeing another version of this game being played. The failure of the Administration is especially galling: They certified needle exchange, which means they know what is right. But they are scared to do what is right. The pattern is familiar. *Don't ask, don't tell* has become their general policy on controversial matters affecting disadvantaged people. Welfare "reform" showed us the kind of village it takes to raise a child, a Potemkin Village. Now this cowardly and irrational failure to support needle exchange shows us that rhetorical lives matter more to them than real ones.

Americans are fed up with sitting still while the politicians keep talking morals and keep doing dirt. We must not let the President and Congress get away with their latest ritual sacrifice of real people's lives. Make it clear that there are limits to our complicity even in our own prosperity, and that we will not let thousands of people become infected with AIDS at a phenomenal cost in public health funds, just because the issue and the controversy surrounding it threaten political skins. It is not only mortal lives that are at stake here, but moral ones, our own moral lives. Moralizing has not affected the soaring AIDS infection rates. Needle exchange works in reducing those rates. It is moral to think through the alternatives and weigh their goods. On one side, we have thousands of lives that can be saved. On the other. . . .

## Did the President Use a Condom?

THERE IS ONLY ONE THING I want to know about President Clinton's private life, but I am depressingly certain that nobody is going to ask him on August 17 or any other time. Whoever may have done what with what to whom, I want to know whether he wore a condom. At a time when other people's sex lives have become an inescapable and spectacularly unedifying element of the news, the most important and perhaps the only really relevant public concern has been completely ignored. The United States may or may not be in the grip of a significant moral decline, but the United States and the world are in the midst of a terrifying and deadly pandemic of sexually transmitted disease.

The figures speak for themselves. AIDS is the most deadly of the sexually transmitted diseases that plague the world. Although deaths from AIDS have been reduced in the United States, the infection rate has not slowed. Data released this spring by the Centers for Disease Control and Prevention show that the epidemic continues to devastate the African American and gay populations and is dramatically on the rise among Hispanic populations and among women generally. Young people thirteen to twenty-four years old are alarmingly at risk. In certain parts of Africa, one in

---

This essay was written in anticipation of the President's August 17, 1998, news conference acknowledging a sexual relationship with Monica Lewinsky, but wasn't published until November 1998, in *Outspoken: A Six-College Queer Publication,* at the Claremont Colleges, Claremont, California. The Los Angeles *Times* rejected it because "we are a family newspaper."

four adults are infected with HIV. United Nations statistics estimate that 21 million of the 30 million people with HIV are in Africa. The African incidence of HIV now rivals the Black Death that decimated medieval Europe. In parts of Africa over 50 percent of women visiting prenatal clinics are HIV positive. The hopeful news is that in countries that have adopted strong prevention programs, including public education about safer sexual practices, the infection rate has declined; among these countries are Senegal, Tanzania, Thailand, and Uganda.

AIDS is being spread by a fatal combination of intravenous drug use and unsafe sex. Advances in treatment notwithstanding, the plague must be checked where HIV is transmitted. Despite the proven effectiveness of needle exchange, the United States has decided that the thousands of lives needle exchange can save are not as important as the continuing and so-far-ineffective war on drug use. The other way to reduce the spread of HIV everywhere that it occurs is safer sexual practices. Safer sex is not as effective as abstinence. But the promotion of abstinence does not cause the people whose behavior spreads AIDS to stop. There is evidence, however, that the promotion of safer sexual practices does. People can be educated and persuaded to take precautions. Men may not want to use condoms, but if they are the targets of serious public health efforts they can learn to.

Equally important, safer sex is a way that women can begin to protect themselves and their unborn children from infection, but only if they are supported in what remains women's comparatively powerless position in much of the world. Safer sex causes problems to those who believe that contraception or any encouragement of nonprocreative and nonmarital sex is morally unacceptable. But the very populations globally that are most affected by the spread of AIDS are those in which public health efforts have been successfully opposed by religious authority. Perhaps it is time for those who insist that abstinence is the only moral position to explain why they prefer an abstinence that is not working to compromise programs like safer sex that can keep people alive so that they can learn to live right. The fact is, however unpalatable to some people, that the only available methods by which the spread of AIDS and other sexually transmitted diseases have been significantly slowed are safer sex and needle exchange, which are at best unwelcome compromises. The alternative to them, however, is unthinkable. Or should be.

At present the unthinkable is happening because the pragmatic is unsayable. The endless babbling about low sex in high places has not pierced our hypocrisy about sex. It merely extends the life of conflicted prurience. But the stakes are not just the American political crisis of the moment. The stakes of sexually transmitted disease are countless human lives throughout the world. I don't care very much whether the President talks or refuses to talk about his private affairs. Whatever his tactics, he should stand up and say that if he were to have nonmarital sex, he would make sure it was safe and that we should all do the same.

# ∦ The Intolerance Wars

## In Real Life, the Funnies Aren't

IN THE MIDST of the unedifying spectacle of the Senate hearings on gays and lesbians in the military, the right of homosexuals to serve in another cherished American institution is being challenged. Several newspapers have refused to print recent episodes of the "For Better or for Worse" comic strip, in which a gay teenager comes out.

The episodes feature strip protagonist Mike's friend Lawrence, who realizes he is gay. His parents order him out of the house, but subsequently ask him back home and promise to try to accept his homosexuality. This week's strips, published in the View section of the *Times,* show Lawrence coming out to Mike. Having told Mike that he'll never get married, a worried-looking Lawrence explains that he has fallen in love, "but it's not with a girl." Mike—like so many straight people—reacts to a friend's disclosure of his innermost truth by saying, "I don't wanna know what you're telling me, man!" Then Mike attempts to reassure Lawrence by saying, "Look, you're not gay, OK? . . . This guy you've met, it's nothing special, OK? You're just confused!" To the credit of cartoonist Lynn Johnston, Lawrence says what so many of us who are gay wish we had said in such circumstances: "Mike, my mind is crystal clear. Everyone else is confused!"

The newspapers that have refused to run the strips give assorted explanations. The Sedalia, Missouri, *Democrat*'s editor said, "We are a conservative paper in a conservative town. We consider it is a family comic strip and felt our readers would not appreciate this reference to homosexuality being inserted into it." He says what too many people still say to lesbian and gay children and adults: We don't want to know about you, and we will behave as if you did not exist.

In a subsequent panel, Lawrence reaches out to Mike for support and Mike draws back, as if Lawrence's needing his friend is a come-on. "There's a big difference between friends and lovers," Lawrence tells him. "And right now, I really need a friend." With uncanny accuracy, "For Better or for

---

This essay first appeared in the Los Angeles *Times,* April 2, 1993.

Worse" shows how gay invisibility works. Mike thinks Lawrence's homosexuality is about Mike. Lawrence's parents think it's about them. And, apparently, the military brass and the senators and too many millions of Americans think lesbian and gay Americans' sexuality is about them.

The real Lawrence might become one of the one in three recorded teen suicides who turn out to be lesbian or gay. He might become one of the uncounted numbers of victims of gay-bashing. Perhaps he will do what many of us still have to do—deny himself, learn to ignore his human need for intimacy, honesty, connection, and happiness. Maybe he will end up serving his country in the military, where he may be subjected to systematic persecution. Why? What has Lawrence done wrong?

He told the truth about his own nature to a society that doesn't want to know about it. The Las Vegas *Review-Journal*'s editor opined, in rejecting the strips, that the comic was "not offensive at all, but it was condoning homosexuality almost to the point of advocacy." The danger Lawrence poses to the reader is like the one his gay and lesbian brothers and sisters pose to the military self-image: not sex, but visibility. For some reason, this culture does not feel comfortable enough with its majority sexual orientation to tolerate those with a minority sexual orientation. Lawrence is not doing anything, let alone advocating anything. He is just telling the truth about himself.

The secret of homosexuality is no longer one gays and lesbians are willing to keep. We have learned a hard-fought lesson: that our sexual orientation can be the foundation for good and happy lives and that it is society's attitude toward us that is immoral. We have begun to exchange secrecy for privacy; that is the keynote of our civil rights struggle. We understand that democracy requires that we help our fellow citizens see us in the proper light; prejudice and bigotry take time to reverse. But in comic strips and in the military, we are facing the demand that we stay invisible—that we give our country not only the full measure of devotion that patriotic citizenship requires, but that we sacrifice our identities while doing it.

# Holiday Lavender Blue

THE HOLIDAY SEASON always makes me a little queasy, as if I were expecting something that I know I will not get. I think I feel this way because the season is so relentlessly about family and, like so many other gays, I have to cope with the pain and sadness of what it was like for me, and remains for so many like me, to grow up gay in an American family. That experience has left a wound that time, therapy, and even happiness have not healed. I had to grow up knowing that my true self was not welcome in my family. To encounter the bigoted and unsubstantiated views of those who still refuse lesbians and gay men their rightful place in the families and country of their birth is to experience these feelings all over again. A holiday ticket to Hell is what too many families still reserve for their own who happen to be lesbian or gay.

Gays who want the civil right to marry have many motivations, including the right to raise their children within a socially and legally acknowledged relationship. The homophobic activists insist that gay family formation is the danger gay marriage poses. It is worth pointing out that they are simply wrong to think that the history of family confirms the notion that the sexual act that makes a child means that the biological father and mother are best equipped to raise that child. The short history of the two-parent nuclear family is clouded by too many evident failures and widely perceived dysfunctions to make it an exclusive model of effective child rearing. The "pro family" rhetoric apparently ignores that the American family does not conform to their model, if indeed it ever really has, and stubbornly ignores the real history of successful parenting.

The Hawaii gay marriage decision, for example, cited the clear social scientific evidence that lesbians and gay men make good parents. We always have, of course, and there is no reason to think coming out and making same-sex unions will affect that, except to make us better because more honest and happier parents. The claim that it is selfish for lesbians and gays to want to have and raise children makes neither biological nor common sense. The notion that it takes a father to complete a daughter's sexuality will unsettle students of the Greek tragedians or of the domestic violence or incest statistics. It is dangerous nonsense to take the father's love for a daughter and a mother's for a son as a rule for who can and should be parents. The biological bond is only one way in which family is achieved. Too many of us have been well raised by people other than our two biological parents, and badly raised by our biological parents,

---

This essay first appeared in the Los Angeles *Times* of December 26, 1996.

to believe that making a baby creates parents in anything but biological fact.

The sanctimonious profession of love for gay relatives and close friends, and the simultaneous dismissal of their ordinary aspiration to have their relationships honored, by family and law, and to be welcome in their family—all this is familiar if painful. We learned homophobia at home, after all, and continue to expect it. But let's not pretend that this attitude causes anything but pain and distance. The unconscionably high incidence of suicide among lesbian and gay teens is evidence enough for the failure of too many families to protect the children in their care.

What can lesbians and gays teach American families? First, coming out is a process of self-parenting that enriches family life even as it gives gays and lesbians back our own lives. Sharing your true self and your real life with your family frequently inspires your family to be more honest and caring; it isn't just gays who have to disguise themselves from their families, and ours is not the only authentic self unwelcome at home.

Second, gays and lesbians are good at family. Having lived on the margins of our own families, we have found ways to function within them, suppressed our own lives in order to be devoted parents, uncles and aunts, siblings, and children. Most of us have formed our own families, bound by shared experience, values, and love. The families we have created are there when we return from stressful times with the families that raised us, or when we are not welcome at home; too often they have been the ones to care for our sick and dying. It is becoming more common for lesbians and gays and their same-sex partners to form families to raise children. We know that gay parents in gay relationships can make good families, for gays and lesbians have had to discover on our own how to make family a choice, not a habit.

Third, gays know that family is always a choice, however automatic or involuntary it may feel. You don't choose your relatives, but you can choose to make a real family out of the one you have. The proof of family values is how the family treats its own. How you treat your lesbian and gay family members—and most people have them—is one good test of your family's values. Perhaps this very holiday season, American families might choose to welcome their lesbian and gay family members home. In time, we will gain our equality as citizens and our rights as human beings. But for now, being welcomed at last into our families as we really are is no more than we deserve and something important American families can do for themselves.

## Gays Saw Between the Lines of *Ellen*

LIKE MOST of the lesbians and gay men I know, I welcome the coming out of the Ellens, both the character Ellen and Ellen DeGeneres, the actress who plays her. *Ellen* might just turn out to be as historic, indeed unprecedented, an event in our popular culture as the inescapable hype claims. That will depend, of course, on what Ellen does about being a lesbian. I hope she dates, mates, and generally has the good life lesbians can enjoy in places like Los Angeles.

I hope she finds a circle of lesbian and gay friends and gets involved with women's athletics. And I hope she doesn't move in too fast with her first girlfriend—*don't rent a u-haul after the first date, honey*—that she doesn't experience bed death, and that she waits to have kids until she finishes parenting herself. I hope she starts reading the lesbian press; I'll be glad to give her a subscription to the *Harvard Gay and Lesbian Review of Books*. Since she works in a bookstore, she ought to stock (and read) lesbian writers including Gertrude Stein, Willa Cather, Adrienne Rich, Audre Lord, Leslie Feinberg, Katherine Forrest, and L.A.'s own Bia Lowe. If she does decide to be a tad dressier—although I hope she doesn't—she should consult one of her gay friends for fashion tips; make that *all* of her gay friends. And I hope that she experiences an intense and even hostile lesbian-separatist phase. I think Ellen will find her life a lot easier now, but to make sure, she ought to go to the Lesbian Gay Community Services Center, the largest agency of its kind in the world, to get some counseling, support, lots of health and legal and social information.

If they follow Ellen's bliss, the production team should have no trouble making a terrific and funny show. The public doesn't know how much fun lesbians have and give—not just the particular pleasure lesbian sex apparently gives to a vast public of straight men. Let's all hope that the

---

This is the uncut version of a piece on the coming out of Ellen. The edited version was printed in the L.A. *Times* on April 18, 1997. I was prompted to write it, despite all the media already devoted to it, because the gay party line seemed to be that nobody wanted a "lesbian dating show" and I did. I also wanted to mark the passing of Ellen's closet, because I do think it was a unique moment in popular culture, the way this television character was available to a lesbian and gay audience in ways that ended up with life and art not imitating each other but merging. I know I had nothing to do with it, but I am happy to say that the show did what I thought was right. The second "Ellen" piece responded to the network's censorship of the show in spite, or likely because, of the fact that it scored such a success. They got away with it, and the show is over. Damn.

network/advertisers/production company et al. make the choice to do well by doing good.

Just as gratifying is Ms. DeGeneres's own coming out. Lesbians and gay men know the difference between life in and out of the closet. It's better out—not perfect, but better. Scary as it is for most of us to come out to our families and friends, it must be specially challenging to have to come out to the world in the glare of publicity. One difference between Ms. DeGeneres and most of the rest of us is that her coming out in the workplace is not the same kind of risk; she needs ratings, not civil protection. But however the ratings chips fall (or, I hope, rise), Ellen DeGeneres has already made a positive difference in the lives of countless lesbians and gay men and their families and friends by coming out.

Part of me, I must confess, will miss the old television Ellen. There's little question that it was time she came out. My friends and I always recognized her as in the closet. The way she dressed and responded, her hilarious ineptitude in trying to meet conventional expectations for a single young woman, read gay and closet to us. The experience of watching the show was uncanny, knowing what any gay person knew inside out about her character. Millions of our fellow viewers seemed not to know or only dimly to sense what made Ellen so endearing and so funny, and also so angry and self-subverting. The secret story, funny and real, was of a woman whose secret, from herself as well as from the world, was the linchpin of her character and the barrier to her success.

Full citizenship and equal protection of the laws for gays and the fight against homophobia are worth much more than the odd pleasures of recognizing anybody's closet. But I hope people take a moment to think about what Ellen has been sharing with her audience and about why so many people appear not to have known what, I believe, most lesbians and gays knew all along. Ellen made wonderful comedy from the closet and now joins the battle to eliminate it from our lives. But the culture and the government still enforce the closet, which still kills and stunts people for no good reason, and remains a part of most gay people's histories. I am happy for *Ellen*'s new lease on life—and franchise on ABC. But I will also remember the unprecedented experience of seeing the closet on TV. I'll put this nostalgia on hold for the duration of the battle for equality, but some part of me will miss Ellen's closet, although I bet she won't.

# TV-H: Hazardous to Your Hypocrisy

THE ONE SURPRISE about ABC's obscene plan to pin a false and misleading label on their hit comedy *Ellen* is the possibility, against all evidence, that the network poobahs have imagination. It takes imagination to preface this season's episodes of Ellen DeGeneres's Emmy-winning show with a warning: "Due to adult content, parental discretion is advised." In a world where words were still used to mean what they mean, of course, this would be correct, because its adult content is what distinguishes *Ellen*—if "adult" means original, human, funny, heartwarming, professional, innovative, and real. But, of course, that isn't what "adult" means on TV. If only they would put the same fantastic energy into creating shows that they have into sabotaging this one, they might really surprise us.

Of course, everybody knows what's up. Last season Ellen Morgan "came out" as a lesbian. And this season's shows have made affecting and brilliant comedy of the consequences. The concerns that last season's hoopla would result in a preachy, unfunny show have vanished. Millions are laughing along with Ellen and her friends, because her own truth has made her funnier and connected her to shared experiences. *Ellen* is a situation comedy, like *Mary Tyler Moore, Taxi, Cheers,* and *Roseanne,* which sharpens the interactions of real people in plausible situations into comedy. We are learning along with the unpredictable Ellen about what it means to be a lesbian and what a funny, bewildering experience that can be. What is so marvelous—oops! I almost said "fabulous"—about Ellen is how she keeps having to confront her own internalized versions of the society's narrow-mindedness. You don't have to be a lesbian to identify with her, although you may risk having to transcend being scared or intolerant of a different sexual orientation.

What is so offensive about the transparent attempt to censor Ms. DeGeneres is not only its hypocrisy and craven submission to imagined threats to the profits of the network's owners. It isn't even its version of the still-pervasive prejudice. What really stinks is what the network is advising parents. Do we really want kids to be on familiar terms with fantasies of violence, insult, crude stereotypes, to revel in unproductive and unhealthy behavior? Is it really a good idea for children (or anybody) to believe that being different in the way that lesbians and gays are different makes them Other? ABC is censoring the rare show that is sexually reticent and tender. The shows that appear without cautions are routinely lewd, vulgar, blatantly and exploitatively sexual, as well as pointless. Do

---

This essay first appeared in the Los Angeles *Times* of October 19, 1997.

you want your children to learn about their desires and about love by watching babes and dudes? Shouldn't we be worrying about what it does to people to be told one thing in church or at home about morality and responsibility, while their bodies and fantasies are being manipulated by for-profit sexual pandering and merchandizing?

Unlike even the most agreeable gay characters on the tube, Ellen is not reducible to her sexuality. Lesbians and gay men are not the only outsider group to be sexualized in order to be controlled. Women, Jews, African Americans, and too many others have been defined as sexual threats because that made them seem less than fully human. But sexualizing gays is especially treacherous because our sexuality is the key marker of our difference. Part of what makes Ellen so good is that the show has not tried to make her a lesbian who doesn't want love and sex, but created a character who replaces an oppressive stereotype by being, like all great comedians, an extraordinary ordinary human being.

The ABCensors apparently don't watch their own shows. *All My Children* has been featuring a story line about a young man who has to deal with being gay and encounters the hostility of his family and the kinds of quacks who still claim they can "cure" homosexuality. Last time I tuned in, he had found some support from his would-be girlfriend and some sympathetic adults. As I was watching, however, I was terrified that he would end up being another one of those statistics: gay kids who still kill and hurt themselves because the desires that are natural to them interfere with some people's expectations. Such is the kind of universal truth that kills. *Ellen*'s is the kind that heals.

On second thought, maybe ABC *should* warn parents: "Caution, don't let your kids watch this show. It might prove hazardous to your hypocrisy."

## Life, Liberty, Pursuit of Happiness— Gay or Straight

THIS SUNDAY MORNING the twenty-eighth annual Gay and Lesbian Pride Parade will take fabulous flight along Santa Monica Boulevard between Crescent Heights and San Vicente. The weekend's events commemorate the 1969 Stonewall Uprising in New York City, when patrons

---

This essay first appeared in the Los Angeles *Times* of June 26, 1998.

at a Greenwich Village gay bar fought back against routine police harassment and sparked a mass gay liberation movement. Los Angeles's parade has always seemed special to me, not just because I live here but because this city hosted the beginnings of the modern gay movement and has a rich gay and lesbian history. Founded here around 1950, the Mattachine Society, the Daughters of Bilitis, and *One* magazine pioneered what Stonewall ignited into a mass movement. The L.A. Gay and Lesbian Social Services Center is the largest such center in the world. Such Los Angeles–based writers as Christopher Isherwood, Joseph Hansen, and Patricia Nell Warren were models for a burgeoning gay literature. These are but part of the story of gay Los Angeles.

For lesbians and gay men and their friends and families, Pride parades are an annual holiday to be celebrated (or avoided), like any other group's holiday. But most of our neighbors and fellow citizens may not understand. They may reasonably wonder what lesbians and gay men have to be proud of. This is especially true in a nation that still refuses its homosexual citizens equal protection of the laws and where gays are among the victims of choice for hate crimes. Here, then, are some of the grounds for gay pride.

We take pride in our history. Gays and lesbians, and the large number of people who love both men and women, form a disproportionate number of the creators of human civilizations. Socrates and Wittgenstein, Leonardo and Michelangelo (*pace* Mr. Heston), Sappho and Whitman, Proust, Cather, Gide, Stein, Cavafy, Mann, Auden and Mishima, Horatio Alger, M. Carey Thomas, Thornton Wilder, James Beard and Jane Addams, Bayard Rustin and Allard Lowenstein, Tchaikovsky and Samuel Barber, Lorenz Hart, Noel Coward, George Cukor, Travis Banton, and James Baldwin are but a sampling of the historically memorable people who were lesbian, gay, or bisexual. We can take pride in the unique universality of this cultural tradition. For we come in every race, religion, ethnicity, and origin, and the pride we take in our history by definition crosses the borders of xenophobia.

We take pride in our sexuality. Gays are routinely criticized for flaunting private things in public. But American culture is not about our sex lives but about the relentless imposition, selling, instruction of heterosexuals in what is supposed to be their natural inclination. Gays make a public point of our sexuality because secrecy is not a substitute for constitutionally protected privacy, which we do not yet have. Bitter experience has taught us how important it is for people who are branded with shame for no other reason than prejudice to learn to be proud of who they are. Gays cannot be reduced to a figment of their sexuality, but neither dare we forget what happens when you are afraid or ashamed to express your desires and love.

We take pride in our survival. Born into families that do not welcome us, into communities, religions, ethnic groups that disdain us, faced with a culture that still has little place for us, we must make our own ways. We should and do take pride in having survived, each year, the thousand petty harassments and reminders of a special status we neither seek nor merit. We are proud of the organizations we have built to take care of our own.

The parade is important too because it is a time when we can take pride not only in ourselves but in one another. Especially since we share no common religion, race, class, region, lifestyle, personal qualities, or aspiration, beyond a stigmatized minority sexual orientation, we have always to learn how to see ourselves in one another. Being gay cannot erase the things that divide human beings from one another, but it does offer a bridge across many commonplace divisions. When we watch the parade we can often take time out from the enmities, barriers, prejudices, and fears of ordinary life, and take pride in what others do that we do not. It isn't just the straights and the media who complain about the drag queens or the dykes on bikes. Lots of us worry about our public image and project our own sense of the appropriate onto people we would rather not be associated with. Personally, I would not want to see a parade without those tough women and lovely men. They remind me of parts of myself I have tried to stifle, and they give me joy and heart. Too, I remember that it was those girls and boys who could not hide their sexuality who made it possible for people like me, who thought they could, to exchange secrecy for pride.

If all this doesn't make sense, perhaps one last thing will. We take pride because in parading who we are, from the inside out, gays and lesbians are celebrating everyone's freedom. In a time when the world is beset by a craving for orthodoxies and conventions imposed on individuals from the outside, we are proud to represent the possibility of individuality. Taking pride in being gay is another way of taking pride in a nation dedicated to life, liberty, and the pursuit of happiness. Indeed, one of the best ways to get ready for the Fourth of July might just be to join us at a gay pride celebration in Los Angeles, or wherever you happen to be. You won't come away gay, after all, but you might go home freer.

# Notes

## PREFACE

1. Professional organizations like the American Historical Association, it must be said, have never forsaken the profession's obligation to the public, especially the public schools. Increasingly, graduates from the best universities are also doing significant teaching in schools and community colleges. The separation of a popular audience from the schools is another false divide. We can best acknowledge the efforts of Gary Nash (and his colleagues) to develop comprehensive U.S. standards by emulating them. See "Seeing the Messiness of America's True History."

2. My colleague and friend Helena Wall read the collection and identified these themes for me. This account of them borrows liberally from her characteristically lucid thinking and prose. I am much obliged to Professor Wall for this, and for our many years of conversation and fellow feeling about United States history.

3 These are the subjects of *The Genteel Tradition and the Sacred Rage* (University of North Carolina Press, 1992) and a future project titled *White Liberalism: Is There Any Other Kind?*

4. The joke about them, which dates me but which is a significant and timely reminder of how happily such things as the women's movement serve us all, was that if there were a Cornell freshman woman who was still a virgin, the statues would meet and shake hands, and each fall, pranksters would paint their footsteps in white.

## HISTORY . . . BUT

1. J. H. Hexter, "The Historian and His Day," *Political Science Quarterly* 69, no. 2 (June 1954): 219–33.

2. Quoting the lyrics of American popular songs is a case in point. Without the music they sound like doggerel. I gave a talk at a university in which the lyrics to Rodgers and Hammerstein's "Cockeyed Optimist" from *South Pacific* figured, and I'd neglected to bring a tape. Because I was urging that Hammerstein's words deserved serious attention, I did not want to reduce them by reciting them. So I told the story of Mrs. Oscar Hammerstein's answer to Mrs. Jerome Kern as to whose husband had written "Ol' Man River": "Your husband wrote 'dum, dum, dee dum,' my husband wrote 'Ol' Man River.'" Then I sang the song. The result was nothing to make Old Blue Eyes stir from his rest, but it was the thing I was talking about, the song, not its lyrical half.

3. I do not mean to include in this general statement the remarkable accomplishments of certain music writers in connection with reissue projects. The writing included in Mosaic jazz reissues and Miles Kreuger's notes for the complete

*Show Boat* can stand for the many serious and pleasure-enhancing instances of expert music writers working on serious reissue projects.

4. Hayden White, "The Burden of History," *History and Theory* 5, no. 2 (1966):111–34; *Metahistory: The Historical Imagination in Nineteenth-Century Europe* (Baltimore: Johns Hopkins University Press, 1973).

5. See "Some of Those Days," below.

6. This bias is what cultural studies frequently aims to correct, I suppose, but characteristically (to my way of thinking) by substituting the cultural student's willful principles of selection for the comprehensive and comprehensible historical evidentiary basis for comparison. Too, cultural studies seems fatally drawn to expression that mimes popular lingo and parodies scholarly language.

7. Perry Miller's two-volume study of *The New England Mind, The Seventeenth Century* (New York: Macmillan, 1939) and *From Colony to Province* (Cambridge, Mass.: Harvard University Press, 1953), is notoriously "difficult," but the chapters on the "Augustinian Strain of Piety" at the least merit attention along with the essays in *Errand into the Wilderness* (Cambridge, Mass.: Harvard University Press, 1956). Joseph Haroutinian's *Piety Versus Moralism: The Passing of the New England Theology* (New York: Henry Holt, 1932) remains helpful, as especially does Williston Walker, *Creeds and Platforms of the Congregationalists* (New York: Scribner's, 1893), which supplies the Puritan texts without which generations of students have understandably floundered.

8. Edmund S. Morgan, *The Puritan Dilemma* (Boston: Little, Brown, 1958).

9. See "In My Father's House Are Many Closets" below.

## THE JEFFERSONIAN OPTION

1. On the Puritans and especially the eighteenth-century Arminian giveaway that escalated the importance of the individual conscience, see Perry Miller, "The Halfway Covenant," *New England Quarterly* 6 (1933); "From Covenant to the Revival," in Perry Miller, *Nature's Nation* (Cambridge, Mass.: Harvard University Press, 1967); "The New England Conscience," in *The Responsibility of Mind in a Civilization of Machines,* ed. Jon Crowell and Stanford J. Searl, Jr. (Amherst: University of Massachusetts Press, 1979); and Joseph Haroutinian, *Piety vs. Moralism: The Passing of the New England Theology* (New York: Henry Holt, 1932).

2. See, for instance, Robert Lawson, *Ben and Me: A New and Astonishing Life of Ben Franklin, as Written by His Good Mouse, Amos, Lately Discovered* (Boston: Little, Brown, 1951). More detail of this particular interpretation of Franklin can be found in my "Franklin and Jefferson: Before the Democratic Fact."

3. *The Autobiography of Benjamin Franklin,* in *The Writings of Benjamin Franklin* (New York: Library of America, 1987). See the end of *The Great Gatsby,* when Mr. Gatz shows Nick Carraway his son's self-improvement system. F. Scott Fitzgerald, *The Great Gatsby* (New York: Scribner's Classic Edition, 1980), 174.

4. Billie Holiday with William Dufty, *Lady Sings the Blues* (Garden City, N.Y.: Doubleday, 1956), 167; Franklin, *Autobiography,* 1397.

5. There is a William Hamilton *New Yorker* cartoon picturing formally clad parents at the dinner table with their T-shirted offspring. The caption reads, "But, darling, many very successful young revolutionaries—our own Thomas Jefferson among them—dressed for dinner." The Adams-Jefferson exchange on natural aristocracy can be found in volume 2 of Lester Cappon, ed., *The Adams-Jefferson Correspondence* (Chapel Hill: University of North Carolina Press, 1959).

6. My use of "hypocrisy" even in quotation marks is something I regret. I do not believe after all that it is useful to think about so complex and abiding a dilemma as Jefferson's in terms so limiting and easily assimilated. I let it stand here because I need to remember how easily I have fallen into the traps laid by contemporary politicizing. If "hypocrisy "is indeed the issue, I need to look in the mirror, not at Jefferson.

7. See "In My Father's House Are Many Closets," page 84, and Robert Dawidoff, *The Genteel Tradition and the Sacred Rage: High Culture vs. Democracy in Adams, James, and Santayana* (Chapel Hill: University of North Carolina Press, 1992), esp. chapter 4; and Eve Kosofsky Sedgwick, *Epistemology of the Closet* (Berkeley: University of California Press, 1990). In the years since this essay was written, there have been many contributions to the "was he or wasn't he" debate. Gary Schmidgall has written persuasively about how the attempts to un-gay Whitman are implausible in his *Walt Whitman: A Gay Life* (New York: Dutton, 1998). One may not accept all that he writes, but on this central point, he is clear, convincing, and to the point. *The Glass Closet* (forthcoming from W. W. Norton in 2001) will consider Whitman's closet in more detail.

8. Joseph P. Lash recounts Eleanor Roosevelt's visit to Rock Creek Cemetery in *Eleanor and Franklin: The Story of Their Relationship* (New York: Norton, 1971), 358. Ernest Samuels details the story of the Saint-Gaudens statue in *Henry Adams: The Middle Years* and *Henry Adams: The Major Phase* (Cambridge, Mass.: Harvard University Press, 1958, 1964). Adams's observations occur in Book 21 of Henry Adams, *The Education of Henry Adams* (New York: Library of America, 1983), 715–1181, 1020–22.

9. "Off the Record" from *I'd Rather Be Right* (1937), in *The Complete Lyrics of Lorenz Hart*, ed. Dorothy Hart and Robert Kimball (New York: Alfred A. Knopf, 1986), 237; "Anything Goes" from *Anything Goes* (1934), in *The Complete Lyrics of Cole Porter*, ed. Robert Kimball (New York: Alfred A. Knopf. 1983), 121, Leonard W. Levy told me the story about Eleanor Roosevelt's visit to Brandeis.

10. See Lash, *Eleanor and Franklin;* Blanche Weisen Cook, *Eleanor Roosevelt: Volume One, 1884–1933* (New York: Viking, 1992); Susan Ware, *Partner and I: Molly Dewson, Feminism and New Deal Politics* (New Haven: Yale University Press, 1987).

11. Eleanor Roosevelt, *You Learn by Living* (Philadelphia: Westminister Press, 1960). It is worth noting that Eleanor Roosevelt composed this book with a coauthor. This reflects her lack of literary vanity, although not any lack of pride in her work. Her practical, even casual view of writing makes a significant contrast with Henry Adams, one that goes to the heart of what democratic stewardship might mean to each.

12. Ibid., xi.

13. Ibid., xii. Here, she echoes Lambert Strether, the protagonist of *The Ambassadors* by Henry James; see Dawidoff, *The Genteel Tradition and the Sacred Rage,* chap. 2.

14. Roosevelt, *You Learn by Living,* 14.

15. Ibid., 129.

16. Ibid., 194.

17. *Lyrics by Oscar Hammerstein II* (Milwaukee: Hal Leonard Books, 1985), 208; Margaret Landon, *Anna and the King of Siam* (New York: John Day, 1944). There is also the curious story of how John Huston directed Katharine Hepburn in *The African Queen* by telling her to smile like Mrs. Roosevelt. Hepburn, *The Making of "The African Queen,"* (New York: Alfred A. Knopf, 1987), 82.

## FRANKLIN AND JEFFERSON: BEFORE "THE DEMOCRATIC FACT"

1. Recent scholarship has usefully begun to explore such issues as "whiteness" in a color-coded American history. See, for instance, Alexander Saxton, *The Rise and Fall of the White Republic: Class Politics and Mass Culture in Nineteenth-Century America* (London and New York: Verso, 1990).

2. See Robert Dawidoff, *The Genteel Tradition and the Sacred Rage: High Culture versus Democracy in Adams, James, and Santayana* (Chapel Hill: University of North Carolina Press, 1992).

3. Gordon Wood, *The Radicalism of the American Revolution* (New York: Knopf, 1992), 367.

4. Merrill D. Peterson, *The Jefferson Image in the American Mind* (New York: Oxford University Press, 1992). It is interesting to note that we appear to be on the cusp on a Hamilton revival. See, for instance, Michael Lind's July 4, 1998, *New York Times* opinion piece "Restore Hamilton to His Pedestal."

5. On Jefferson's republican vision see Ralph Lerner, *The Thinking Revolutionary* (Ithaca: Cornell University Press, 1987); Michael P. Zuckert, *The Natural Rights Republic: Studies in the Foundation of the American Political Tradition* (Notre Dame: University of Notre Dame Press, 1996); and James Morton Smith, ed., *The Republic of Letters: The Correspondence between Jefferson and Madison,* 3 vols. (New York: W. W. Norton, 1995).

6. Dawidoff, *The Genteel Tradition and the Sacred Rage,* chapter 1 and conclusion. Thomas Bender discusses the Tocqueville-Jefferson distinction as a theme in contemporary intellectual history in "Intellectual and Cultural History," in *The New American History,* ed. Eric Foner (Philadelphia: Temple University Press, 1997), 185. See also Michael G. Kammen, "Alexis de Tocqueville and Democracy in America" (Washington, D.C.: Library of Congress, 1998) for a learned, lively, and differently poised view of Tocqueville.

7. Lester J. Cappon, ed., *The Adams-Jefferson Letters,* 2 vols. (Chapel Hill: University of North Carolina Press, 1959). See especially vol. 2, section 10, 341–413.

8. Albert Jay Nock, *Memoirs of a Superfluous Man* (New York: 1943), chapter 14 especially.

9. Clark Kerr, *The Uses of the University* (Cambridge, Mass.: Harvard University Press, 1963); James Perkins, *The University in Transition* (Princeton: Princeton University Press, 1966). Richard Hofstadter, *Anti-Intellectualism in American Life* (New York: Knopf, 1963).

10. See my essay on "Jefferson's Political Visions" in *The Politics of Nature: Rights and Republicanism in the Thought of Thomas Jefferson,* ed. Thomas Engeman, forthcoming from the University of Notre Dame Press.

11. For Franklin, Carl Van Doren's splendid biography (New York: Viking, 1938) remains the best place to start, best read with Van Doren's selection of *Benjamin Franklin's Autobiographical Writings* (New York: Viking Press for the History Book Club, 1948) at hand. The Library of America's Franklin volume, Benjamin Franklin, *Writings* (New York: Library of America, 1987), compiled by J. A. Leo Lemay, is characteristically good; I have used it as the source for Franklin quotations.

12. Robert Lawson, *Ben and Me ...* (Boston: Little Brown, 1951). Adam Smith, *The Powers of Mind* (New York: Random House, 1975), 71; David Parker kindly and acutely brought the Smith passage to my attention. Larry Gonick, *The Cartoon History of the United States* (New York: W. W. Norton, 1991).

13. Benjamin Franklin, *Writings,* 1138.

14. Ibid., 1139.

15. Ibid., 1308.

## "TAILS IN THE AIR": HENRY ADAMS AND THE AMERICAN HISTORY OF THE EUROPEAN MIDDLE AGES

1. This account of Adams and the *chanson* is taken from Harold Dean Cater's biographical introduction to *Henry Adams and His Friends: A Collection of His Unpublished Letters* (New York: Octagon Books, 1970), xcvii–c.

2. Even when this paper was first given, this was a hope in decline. Nowadays....

## WILLIE'S AND HARRY'S EXCELLENT ADVENTURE

1. John J. McDermott, ed., *The Writings of William James* (New York: Random House, 1967), xxxvi–xxxvii.

2. *Pragmatism* (Cambridge, Mass.: Harvard University Press, 1975), 123.

3. William James to Sarah Wyman Whitman, 22 August 1903, Houghton Library, Harvard University.

4. William James to Alice James, 6 July 1891, Houghton Library, Harvard University.

5. Alice James to William James, 30 July 1891, Houghton Library, Harvard University.

6. Fred Kaplan, *Henry James: The Imagination of Genius* (New York: William Morrow, 1992). Sheldon Novick's *The Young Master: Henry James* (New York: Random House, 1996) makes claims about Henry James's sexual life that run counter to these, claims that his "evidence" simply does not support.

7. Gay Wilson Allen, *William James: A Biography* (New York: Viking Press, 1967), 490–92.

8. Leon Edel, ed., *Henry James: Selected Letters* (Cambridge, Mass.: Belknap Press of Harvard University Press, 1987), 388.

## FISH OUT OF WATER: GEORGE SANTAYANA

1. John McCormick, *George Santayana: A Biography* (New York: Scribner's, 1987), 97.

2. Douglas Wilson's collection of Santayana's invaluable essays on the Genteel Tradition in America, long out of print, is now available in a Bison Books paperback edition: *George Santayana, The Genteel Tradition: Nine Essays* (Lincoln: University of Nebraska Press, 1998), with my introduction.

3. McCormick, *George Santayana*, 52.

4. Did Thornton Wilder owe this perception, which shadows *Our Town*, to Santayana? Or was theirs a coincidental situational insight? See below, "In My Father's House Are Many Closets."

5. It is only fair to add that since writing this, I have been reading Santayana's philosophy, especially his aesthetics, with the kinds of responses this essay slights.

## IN MY FATHER'S HOUSE ARE MANY CLOSETS

1. I have let stand this white liberal's rather awkward reach for "political correctness" because at the time I wrote this, I had not learned enough about the role of gays in the American populations that my education had not included and that my research and self-education had only begun to address. I have learned much since then, and hope my forthcoming *The Glass Closet* will reflect that. But it seems important to emphasize my early understanding on this point, because I am glad that I had the sense to state candidly both my ignorance and intention to remedy it. Surely this is a case of why a certain earnestness in matters of diversity is a good thing. This is but one instance of how I have profited from the advice, work, and encouragement of the scholars and activists who made my belated learning possible.

2. Quoted in John McCormick, *George Santayana: A Biography* (New York: Scribner's, 1987), 97. See also Dawidoff, *The Genteel Tradition and the Sacred Rage: High Culture versus Democracy in Adams, James, and Santayana* (Chapel Hill: University of North Carolina Press, 1992), chapter 4; and my "Fish out of Water," above.

3. William McBrien's new biography *Cole Porter* (New York: Knopf, 1998) is a welcome and reparative study of the songwriter. Porter's lyrics are collected in *The Complete Lyrics of Cole Porter*, ed. Robert Kimball (New York: Knopf, 1983). Ethan Mordden's essay on Porter in *The New Yorker* (October 28, 1991) is characteristically and variously illuminating.

4. Frederick Nolan's biography *Lorenz Hart: A Poet on Broadway* (New York: Oxford University Press, 1994) is useful, but not on the subject of Hart's homosexuality, which Nolan adds to the causes of Hart's dissolution. See my

review in the Los Angeles *Times Book Review* (Sunday, April 23, 1995). For Hart's songs see Dorothy Hart and Robert Kimball, eds., *The Complete Lyrics of Lorenz Hart* (New York: Knopf, 1986).

5. For Matthiessen see: William E. Cain, F. O. *Matthiessen and the Politics of Criticism* (Madison: University of Wisconsin Press, 1988) and Louis Hyde, ed., *Rat and the Devil: Journal Letters of F. O. Matthiessen and Russell Cheney* (Hamden, Conn.: Archon, 1978). Newton Arvin's relationship with Truman Capote is detailed in Gerald Clarke, *Capote: A Biography* (New York: Simon and Schuster, 1988), esp. 104–21, 184–87.

6. Richard Goldstone, *Thornton Wilder: An Intimate Portrait* (New York: Saturday Review / E. P. Dutton, 1975) and Gilbert Harrison, *The Enthusiast: A Life of Thornton Wilder* (New York: Ticknor and Fields, 1983) are useful accounts of Wilder's life, especially read along with Donald Gallup, ed., *The Journals of Thornton Wilder 1939–1961* (New Haven: Yale University Press, 1985).

7. Michael Gold, "Wilder: Prophet of the Genteel Christ," *New Republic,* October 22, 1930, 266–67.

8. All quotations come from *Our Town* (1938) in *Thornton Wilder, 3 Plays* (New York: Harper Perennial, 1985).

9. Steward's account is in Winston Leyland, ed., *Gay Sunshine Interviews,* vol. 2 (San Francisco: Gay Sunshine Press, 1982).

10. Wilder, *Journals,* 70–71.

11. Ibid., 71.

## CRITICISM AND AMERICAN CULTURAL REPAIR

1. Nina Baym, "Early Histories of American Literature: A Chapter in the Institution of New England," *American Literary History* 1, no. 3 (Fall 1989): 479–80.

2. Casey Blake emphasizes (and disputes) the historiographical irony that the "Young Intellectuals" are seen to have influenced a middlebrow genre of capitalist-friendly pleasing, when they meant to inspire a generation of individuals in the opposite vein. Casey Blake, "The Young Intellectuals and the Culture of Personality," *American Literary History* 1, no. 3 (Fall 1989), 510–34.

3. See Paul Longmore's remarkable essay about Bourne, "The Life of Randolph Bourne and the Need for a History of Disabled People," in *Reviews in American History* 13, no. 4 (December 1985): 581–87.

## THE KIND OF PERSON YOU HAVE TO SOUND LIKE TO SING "ALEXANDER'S RAGTIME BAND"

1. Darius Milhaud, "L'évolution du jazz-band des negres d'Amérique du Nord." Cited in Mathew Jordan's comprehensive survey of French attitudes toward American jazz in his dissertation, "Jazz Changes: A History of French Discourse on Jazz from Ragtime to Be-bop," Claremont Graduate University, 1998, 117–18.

2. This general point does not mean that there are not extraordinary moments when a particular performer—like Robeson singing "Ol' Man River" in James Whale's movie of *Show Boat* (Universal, 1935)—receives, because his talent demands, more than the customary detachable crawl space. Another instance is John Stahl's version of *Imitation of Life* (Paramount, 1934). But these were exceptions to a racist rule.

3. See Nelson George, *The Death of Rhythm and Blues* (New York: Pantheon Books, 1988), especially 3–14.

4. John Ford and Dudley Nichols's 1939 movie *Stagecoach* presents the alliance of Union and Confederate partisans to fight the Indians, whose defense of their lands is presented as an aggressive attack. Indeed, it is always startling to see the racial antics of cartoon African Americans translated to the West in movies. See George Frederickson, *The Inner Civil War* (New York: Harper and Row, 1965), for a discussion of how sectional differences were buried in such adventuring.

5. My account of Irving Berlin is based on Laurence Bergreen's *As Thousands Cheer: The Life of Irving Berlin* (New York: Viking Press, 1990). It is an invaluable source for Berlin's career. Ian Whitcomb's *Irving Berlin and Ragtime America* (New York: Limelight, 1988) offers a personal and suggestive account of Berlin's accomplishments and context, well worth reading. Alec Wilder's chapter on Berlin in *American Popular Song: The Great Innovators: 1900–1950*, ed. James T. Maher (New York: Oxford University Press, 1972), 91–120, gives a wonderful account of Berlin's genius and accomplishments. Wilder makes two comments that should preface any consideration of Berlin:

> I am convinced that were Irving Berlin ever to read these pages, he would be more puzzled than pleased. I think he would be pleased at the evidence that a painstaking examination has been made of his songs, but puzzled as to why it was made.... I'm sure he is as eager for praise as anyone, but I believe the kind of praise given his work in a study like this would appear to him to be a waste of time. If, on the other hand, I were making an attempt to determine the precise elements needed to make a hit song, he would probably be interested. For I think that to Berlin, as well as to many other song writers, a good song and a *hit* song are synonymous. (pp. 91–92)

> Berlin has most clearly been one of the great contributors to this medium of music and, unlike many of the great song writers, has never deviated in his purpose of writing songs which stem from the music of the people, whether it be ragtime, swing music, country music or the work of his contemporaries. He was obviously a persistent listener. Anything which he liked he absorbed and re-created in his own uniquely singing fashion.... Let it be said that he is the best all-around, over-all song writer America has ever had. In this area or that, I will say, and have said, that I believe so-and-so to be the master. But I can speak of only one composer as the master of the entire range of popular song—Irving Berlin. (pp. 119–20)

For the history of the American popular song, see Charles Hamm, *Yesterdays: Popular Song in America* (New York: W. W. Norton, 1979). At the time I wrote this essay, I did not have the benefit of Hamm's study of Berlin: *Irving Berlin: Songs from the Melting Pot: The Formative Years, 1907–1914* (New York: Oxford University Press, 1997), but now we all do. His discussions of "Alexander" are characteristically enlightening.

6. While on the subject of Russian Jewish immigrants and anglophilia, England boasted its own I. Berlin, the late historian of philosophy Sir Isaiah Berlin. Among the people who mixed them up was Winston Churchill, who conducted a conversation with Irving Berlin in 1944 thinking he was talking with the author of the dispatches from wartime Washington that Churchill so admired. The prime minister asked Irving Berlin what he thought was the most important piece he had done "for us." The puzzled songwriter replied "White Christmas." In another example, Britain's chief rabbi congratulated Irving Berlin in 1932 on his election to a fellowship at All Souls (Antony Gottlieb, "The Man Who Did Not Write Christmas," London *Sunday Times*, 24 February 1997). Elazar Barkan brought this to my attention.

The two Berlins are worth comparing. I think Irving was a foxy hedgehog, and several of his songs make his views of higher learning clear: "Folks like us, would never fuss with schools and books and learning / Still we're happy as can be / doin' a what comes naturally" ("Annie Get Your Gun"). Or what about the professor in "He Ain't Got Rhythm" from *On the Avenue*: "He excited some attention / when he found the fourth dimension / but he ain't got rhythm / so no one's with him / the loneliest man in town."

7. Quoted in Bergreen, *As Thousands Cheer*, 58.

8. See my "Franklin and Jefferson: Before 'the Democratic Fact,'" above.

9. Quoted in Bergreen, *As Thousands Cheer*, 46. On Foster see William W. Austin, *"Susanna," "Jeanie," and "The Old Folks at Home": The Songs of Stephen C. Foster from His Time to Ours* (Urbana: University of Illinois Press, 1989). I had originally identified Foster and his outsider status as gay, following Martin Greif, *The Gay Book of Days* (Secaucus, N.J.: Lyle Stuart, 1982), 117. On the basis of my own research, I would prefer something less modern to describe Foster's status as sexual outsider. He will figure in my book about gay men in the formation of American culture. But Foster was an outsider to the sentimental pictures his most beloved songs painted. And the complications of his feelings for men formed a part of this distance. Barry Weller alerted me to my unwise taking of the identification of Foster as "gay" for granted.

10. Bergreen, *As Thousands Cheer*, 45–46. Joan Morris and William Bolcolm perform "That Mesmerizing Mendelssohn Tune" on *Blue Skies: Songs by Irving Berlin* (Nonesuch Records 79120-4).

11. Rudy Blesh and Harriet Janis, *They All Played Ragtime* (New York: Knopf, 1958) is the standard book about ragtime; see also Gunther Schuller, *Early Jazz: Its Roots and Musical Development* (New York: Oxford University Press, 1968).

12. See Bergreen, *As Thousands Cheer*, 49–61; see also my chapter "Some of Those Days."

13. Bergreen, *As Thousands Cheer*, 57.

14. Ibid., 57–58.

15. There is a growing literature on this crucial subject. Eric Lott, *Love and Theft: Blackface Minstrelsy and the American Working Class* (New York: Oxford University Press, 1993) is especially good. See also Nelson George, *The Death of Rhythm and Blues* (New York: Pantheon, 1988) for a clear account of the dynamics at later period; also see my essay "Some of Those Days."

16. In 1924 Kern wrote to Alexander Woollcott regarding the biography of Berlin that Woollcott was preparing. He concluded, "In short, what I really want to say, my dear Woollcott, is that Irving Berlin has *no* place in American music. HE IS AMERICAN MUSIC." Quoted in Bergreen, *As Thousands Cheer*, 223.

17. Miles Kreuger, *Show Boat: The Story of a Classic American Musical* (New York: Oxford University Press, 1977).

18. In an essay on Roy Lichtenstein, Adam Gopnik distinguishes the ironist from the faux naif: "The ironist believes in his own knowingness: the faux naif believes in someone else's innocence" (Gopnik, "The Modest Modernist," *The New Yorker*, October 13, 1997, 72). I think this is the distinction between the modernist and the primitive other, and that it bears on the appropriation of the African American in popular music. But I am not ready to call Irving Berlin any kind of naif.

19. It will not do to underestimate anti-immigrant, anti-Jewish feeling in the United States. George M. Cohan once introduced Berlin as "a Jew boy that had named himself after an English actor and a German city. Irvy writes a great song. He writes a song with a good lyric, a lyric that rhymes, good music, music you don't have to dress up to listen to, but it's good music. He is a wonderful little fellow, wonderful in lots of ways. He has become famous and wealthy, without wearing a lot of jewelry and falling for funny clothes. He is uptown, but he is there with the old downtown hard sell." Quoted in Charles Hamm, *Yesterdays*, 332.

20. Bergreen, *As Thousands Cheer*, 65–70. The 1938 Twentieth Century Fox movie *Alexander's Ragtime Band* gives a fantastic version of the song's creation, apparently not Berlin's own fantasy as represented in a script he vetted. But the movie, which has a lot of good singing—especially by Alice Faye, who ranks with Fred Astaire and Ethel Merman as one of the best performers of Berlin's music— is an unintentional template of the confusions and coverings up that attended attempts to tell the story of how whites invented a music they appropriated. See Bergreen, *As Thousands Cheer*, 358–62, and see the movie. The recyclings of "Alexander" by Berlin would make the subject for another essay.

21. Gilbert Vivian Seldes, *The Seven Lively Arts* (1924; repr. New York: Sagamore Press, 1957), 71. Michael Kammen's welcome book about Seldes (*The Lively Arts: Gilbert Seldes and the Transformation of Cultural Criticism in the United States* [New York: Oxford University Press, 1996]) discusses Seldes's view of and relationship to Berlin and is wonderfully informative on the state of cultural thinking in the United States during this period.

22. Carl Van Vechten, *Nigger Heaven* (New York: Knopf, 1926); Blair Niles, *Strange Brother* (New York: H. Liveright, 1931).

23. Bergreen, *As Thousands Cheer*, 69.

24. Ibid., 68.

25. Barry Singer, *Black and Blue: The Life and Lyrics of Andy Razaf* (New York: Schirmer Books, 1992), 334–37. This illuminating study of Andy Razaf is indispensable to the study of the subject of this essay. Razaf was clear-eyed and militant about the situation of the black songwriter in the era of appropriation Berlin apotheosized.

26. I intend no disrespect to Miss Lee. Indeed, I'm crazy about her and respect the distinctive and original stamp she put on the songs she sang. But borrow she did, and part of her accomplishment was the taste with which she borrowed and what she made of what she borrowed. Here I only meant to note the irony that some borrowings can be litigated and others would take a time machine or a social transformation to sort out.

27. See below "Fred Astaire."

28. Nicholas Jenkins, ed., *By With To and From: A Lincoln Kirstein Reader* (New York: Farrar, Straus and Giroux, 1991), 32.

29. The political and hierarchical implications of this number are worth thinking about. It is also instructive as an example of Astaire's dancing with men.

## SOME OF THOSE DAYS

1. Jean Paul Sartre, *Nausea,* trans. Lloyd Alexander (New York: New Directions, 1964), 21–23.

2. In this essay, I am working, as cultures do, with stereotypes. *White, black, Jew, American,* as I use them here, were real enough categories, demonstrably so, but they do not describe the complex and varied historical realities of region, class, family, individual, and so on. They do describe how the culture expressed, in generalizing and pointed terms, situations at once oppressive, exploitative, and creative.

3. Shelton Brooks, "Some of These Days" (1910).

4. *Nausea,* xii.

5. Sartre's version makes something philosophically interesting that the real thing would not have done. Reversing the creative positions made his an emblematic story of highfalutin, existential discontent, and an experience significantly removed from the ordinary distractions available to the Babbitts and bromides also out on the town in Jazz Age Paris.

6. James R. Morris, "The Selections," in "Six Decades of Songwriters and Singers," accompanying text to *American Popular Song,* Smithsonian Collection of Recordings (Washington, D.C.: Smithsonian Institution Press, 1984), 31–32. Sophie Tucker's *Some of These Days: The Autobiography of Sophie Tucker* (Garden City, N.Y.: Garden City Publishing, 1946) is the best place to start finding out about Sophie Tucker. Three CDs collect various Sophie Tucker recordings, with only some overlap: *Sophie Tucker: Jazz Age Hot Mamma* (Take Two TT404); *Some of These Days: Sophie Tucker* (Flapper: Past CD 7807) and *The Legendary Sophie Tucker: I'm The Last of the Red Hot Mammas* (Parade 2031). *Broadway Melody of 1938* (MGM) includes a wistful older Sophie singing her anthem. It is available on video cassette.

7. *Some of These Days,* 260.

8. Ibid., pp. 257–60.

9. Billy Rose, Willie Raskin, and Fred Fisher, "Fifty Million Frenchmen Can't Be Wrong" (recorded in 1927).

10. See Eric Lott, *Love and Theft: The Blackface Minstrelsy and the American Working Class* (New York: Oxford University Press, 1993) and Michael Rogin, *Blackface, White Noise: Jewish Immigrants in the Hollywood Melting Pot* (Berkeley: University of California Press, 1996).

11. *Some of These Days,* 33.

12. Ibid., 35.

13. Ibid., 40–41.

14. Ibid., 60.

15. Thomas "Fats" Waller and Andy Razaf, "What Did I Do To Be So Black and Blue."

16. *Some of These Days,* 63.

17. Recording of "Some of These Days" from *The Original Sound of the Twenties,* Columbia C3L 35.

18. *Some of These Days,* 70–87, 76. The chapter in which she tells about Mollie Elkins is called "Mollie & Co."

19. Fannie Hurst, *Imitation of Life* (New York: 1933). There are two movies based on this remarkable book. The 1934 version, directed by John Stahl, with Claudette Colbert, Louise Beavers, and Fredi Washington as Peola, is the one to see in terms of the issues raised here. The later version with Lana Turner has its own ineffable merits, especially as the luxe studio fifties tried to cope with such issues as race and career and a woman's lot.

20. Whitney Balliett, *American Singers* (New York: Oxford University Press, 1979), 29.

21. Columbia has issued the complete recordings of Bessie Smith (C2K 47091; 47471; 47474; 52838; 57546). Volume 3 includes "After You've Gone," which Tucker recorded.

22. *Some of These Days,* 114.

23. Ibid., 275.

24. See "For Sidney Bechet," *Collected Poems of Philip Larkin* (New York: Farrar, Straus and Giroux, 1989), 83.

25. Irving Townsend liner notes from *Mildred Bailey, Her Greatest Performances* (Columbia Records, JC 3L-22).

## FRED ASTAIRE

1. On an early seventies Oscar show, Frank Sinatra introduced Astaire to present an award. Sinatra wanted Astaire to dance a step or so. Fred demurred. Frank insisted, forced him really, and an embarrassed Astaire acquiesced. Then he seemed to stumble—oh, no, please don't let Fred disgrace himself—but, of course, it was a gag, and he stumbled into his customary grace. For a memorable evocation of how Astaire influenced his audience, see Patrick Dennis's novel *Auntie Mame,* where Patrick and his college chums try to live up to their hero.

## FROM OHIO TO THE BIG ROCK CANDY MOUNTAIN: LOS ANGELES AS THE TERMINUS OF AMERICAN DEMOCRATIC CULTURE

1. Anita Loos, *A Girl Like I* (New York: Viking, 1966) 45; Gavin Lambert, *Running Time* (New York: Macmillan, 1983), 134, 209.

2. I am indebted to my colleague Vicki Ruiz for alerting me to Michael Gonzalez's work on California republicanism in his dissertation, "Searching for the Feathered Serpent: Exploring the Origins of Mexican Culture in Los Angeles, 1830–1850," University of California at Berkeley, 1993.

3. My favorite L.A. intersection is the corner of Jefferson and Beethoven in west L.A.

4. I am grateful to Judson Emerick of the Pomona College Department of Art for teaching me about this connection and for our memorable visit to the cathedral.

5. The beginnings of a continuous gay liberation movement in Los Angeles—Chicago's 1924 organization, for example, had no such continuity—is lucidly discussed by John D'Emilio in *Sexual Politics, Sexual Communities: The Making of a Homosexual Minority in the United States 1940–1970* (Chicago: University of Chicago Press, 1983) (see especially 57–122). See also: Joseph Hansen's *A Few Doors West of Hope: The Life and Times of Dauntless Don Slater* (Universal City, Calif.: Homosexual Information Center, 1998); Stuart Timmons, *The Trouble With Harry Hay* (Boston: Alyson Publications, 1990); Eric Marcus, *Making History: The Struggle for Gay and Lesbian Equal Rights: An Oral History* (New York: Harper Collins, 1992), esp. 5–92.